DOYLE

The Greatest Hurling Story Ever Told

John Harrington

IRISH SPORTS PUBLISHING

Published by Irish Sports Publishing (ISP)
Unit 11, Woodview Court
Tandy's Lane
Lucan, Co Dublin
Ireland
www.irishbooksandauthors.com

First published 2011

A CIP record for this book is available from the British Library

ISBN 978-0-9563598-5-8

Printed in Ireland with Print Procedure Ltd
Typesetting, Cover Design: Jessica Maile
Photographs and Back cover images: The Doyle family personal collection and
Mid-Tipperary GAA 1884-2007 A Photographic History
Front cover image: Kennelly Archive

CONTENTS

DEDICATION

This book is dedicated to the memory of
John Doyle and Paddy Leahy

ACKNOWLEDGMENTS

First and foremost, I'd like to thank the Doyle family for granting me their blessing to write this book, and then giving me their full co-operation thereafter.

Anne Doyle, especially, has been a huge help and an invaluable source. Her contribution to the finished product has been immense, and our conversations were always hugely enjoyable.

If you ever want to prove the maxim that 'behind every great man is a great woman', then Anne Doyle should be your first port of call.

John Doyle was fortunate to have a strong and supportive woman in his life, and so am I. Writing this book monopolised my time for a good many months, but my wife, Siobhán, was always hugely patient, supportive and helpful.

She believed in me and encouraged me throughout, and I'd like to thank my parents, PJ and Mary, for doing the same.

This book wouldn't have seen the light of day without Irish Sports Publishing. Liam Hayes put a lot of faith in a first-time author and, along the way, provided encouragement and sound advice when it was needed most. Thank you, Liam.

Many of the photographs in this book are courtesy of Martin Bourke and Aoife Percy, who put together the marvellous *Mid Tipperary GAA 1884-2007 – A Photographic History*. Their contribution is hugely appreciated.

I consulted a number of books while writing this one. The most helpful were *Tipperary's GAA Story – 1935-1984*, by Seamus J. King; *Gaelic Games in Holycross-Ballycahill – 1884-1990*, by Bob Stakelum; *A Lifetime of Hurling*, by Tommy Doyle; and *Hurling's Top 20*, by Colm Keane.

I'll forever be indebted to the many former team-mates and opponents of John Doyle who graciously gave me their time and insights. It was a privilege to have walked down Memory Lane with them.

Finally, thanks to the man himself, the legend that was John Doyle, for providing the inspiration for this book. I hope I've done him justice.

AUTHOR'S NOTE

My introduction to John Doyle was like that of so many others of my generation. A Munster Championship match in Thurles, and my father bending low beside me and pointing through the crowd.

"That's John Doyle."

Who Doyle was had already been long-established in my young mind, by countless tales of Tipperary hurling's golden era.

Seeing the man with my eyes for the first time didn't diminish his legend in any way. He was in his late-50s by now, but the years had done little to rob him of the power or presence that had made him such a force of nature on the hurling field.

He was striding towards Semple Stadium along a street choked with hundreds of Tipperary and Cork fans, but he somehow towered above everyone else and the path seemed to magically clear before him.

As he passed on his way, everyone took notice. Tipperary and Cork fans alike shouted out his name and one or two more adventurous souls diverted their path to clap him on the back.

Doyle responded with a crooked grin and an occasional wave that only drew even greater roars of encouragement. The impression that was left on my adolescent mind was a lasting one.

We have always needed heroes. Men who inspire by the greatness of their deeds and, in doing so, somehow make us feel greater ourselves.

For Tipperary people, John Doyle was such a man. Fearless, flamboyant and utterly unique; in an age of hurling giants none stood taller.

He won eight All-Ireland titles, 10 Munster Championships, and 11 National League medals between 1949 and 1967, but it was the way he won that made him such a hero for Tipperary people.

In an era when hurling was a far more physical sport than it is now, Doyle never missed a match through injury and finished every one he started.

He was indestructible, uncompromising and the first-ever defender to become a superstar of the game. He was far more than just a Tipperary hurler, he was the county itself made flesh.

His good friend, Tommy Barrett, summed this up eloquently when he delivered the graveside oration at Doyle's funeral, on December 31, 2010.

"John Doyle was a veritable Matt the Thresher, in whom Kickham's Knocknagow took immense pride," said an emotional Barrett.

"His deeds on the field brought much enjoyment to his county men – the memories of an indestructible colossus, not standing on ceremony, ignoring personal safety, can stir deep emotions within us to this day.

"We gloried in his performances, which were fearless and full-blooded. We relished the hip-to-hip duels, the shoulder-to-shoulder tackles and the body check against opponents.

"We have lasting memories of John bringing the ball out of defence, leaving opponents sprawling in his wake and making a mighty clearance to lift the crowd and inspire his team.

"John epitomised Tipperary – immovable like Slievenamon, displaying power and raw courage."

With Doyle's passing, another link to a very different Ireland, and a very special era for hurling, perished.

This isn't meant to be the ultimate book of record of Doyle's life, but it will, hopefully, give the reader a sense of the time, place and sport that shaped him into the very distinctive hurler and character he was.

Ireland of the 1950s is often painted as drab, grey and uninspiring, but, as far as hurling goes, it was the most colourful and controversial decade of them all.

Stadiums were packed with tens of thousands of often over-enthusiastic fans, hours before throw-in, and the men they came to watch played a brand of hurling that was ferociously tough and often reckless.

It's an era that's becoming more and more shrouded by the mists of time with every passing year, but it deserves to be remembered, and so does John Doyle.

This is his story.

"If you beat me once, you'd find it very difficult to beat me the second time. I didn't like being beaten, even if it was only for a box of matches we were hurling."

Doyle in conversation with Eamon O'Dwyer, Tipp FM.

PROLOGUE

1967 All-Ireland Senior Hurling Final – Tipperary Dressing Room

The bile rose from Doyle's guts and tasted sour in the back of his throat. It was the same before every big match but it always reassured him. If he didn't feel tense, he didn't feel ready.

It was getting worse with every year, though. Most people thought the weight of countless medals won must anchor any butterflies in his stomach, but the opposite was true.

Nineteen years of Championship hurling, 8 All-Ireland titles, 10 Munster crowns, 11 National Leagues and God knows how many matches won, had only served to raise the stakes every time he pulled on the beloved blue and gold.

He was the great John Doyle, the pride of Tipperary hurling, and the fear of falling from the throne he'd created through countless acts of heroism twisted his insides into knots.

And the knots had never before been so tightly wound as they were right now. But then, the stakes had never been higher.

Outside the dressing room door, destiny awaited at the end of a long, dark corridor that opened into a glaring, braying cauldron of light and noise.

His last match for Tipperary and an opportunity to go out on the most glorious high possible by winning his ninth All-Ireland medal and moving above his old friend and enemy, Christy Ring, at the top of the honours list.

That meant more to others than it did to him but, still, it would be a sweet final chapter.

None better to do it against than Kilkenny, too. But no worse a crowd to lose to, either.

Jesus, the waiting was killing him. It always did. Stand up to swing the arms and roll the shoulders but then nothing to do, only sit back down again. Up and down. Up and down.

No room to stretch the legs with that gaggle of selectors, priests and God knows how many other hangers-on cluttering up the place. Caged. Up and down. Up and down.

Tony Wall sat beside him looking anything but, giving a few quiet words to the lads that needed them most, and generally being his usual, unflustered self. How the hell did he do it?

"Hey, Wall."

Tony moved closer and cocked an ear.

"Tell them we won't go out on the field unless they give us a tenner a head."

Wall cocked his eye now. Was he serious or looking for a rise? You could never be sure with him.

It didn't matter, the answer was the same. Short, to the point and agricultural. The sort of language Doyle appreciated best.

Team trainer, Ossie Bennett, was moving along the line now, the distinctive smell of wintergreen announcing his arrival as he administered last-minute rub-downs with those shovel-like hands of his, whether they were requested or not.

Bennett was usually worth a playful dig for an easy laugh, but Doyle couldn't summon one now.

As the minutes slid by with painful sloth, his feet tapped more quickly and his knuckles whitened and coloured again with every squeeze of the hurley.

Getting closer at last, because here come the speeches. None worth listening to, though, now that Leahy isn't around any more. God rest his soul. He wouldn't be sitting here if it wasn't for Leahy. Wouldn't have won all he had won. The ninth is for Leahy.

At last, the call. With a volley of shouts, the players rise to their feet like dominos in reverse, and none is quicker to spring from the bench than Doyle.

He knows it's at times like this that the others look to him. Today more than ever. Not just because it's his last game and the ninth is on the line, but because there are seeds of doubt sprinkled all over this dressing room.

And when Doyle puts those shoulders back, darkens his brow and sets that jaw, it has a way of convincing you that what's outside that dressing room door should be more afraid of you than you of it. They draw strength from him, and he can only see the same in them.

Kieran Carey's ruthlessness, Tony Wall's assurance, Theo English's brawn, Jimmy Doyle's class, Donie Nealon's energy, Liam Devaney's guile and Sean McLoughlin's opportunism. Men he's campaigned with for ten years or more. The spine of the greatest hurling team there has ever been.

All the wrong side of 30 now, though, and down the corridor a room full of Kilkenny men in their prime, driven by a mixture of ambition and hatred to finish Doyle and his fellow veterans once and for all, and create their own legacy.

Let them try.

For weeks, Doyle had his own doubts, but they were gone now. They'd put manners on Kilkenny before, and they would do it again. Kilkenny could do the running and Tipp would do the hurling.

He gripped his hurley hard, and roared.

The dressing room door flew open.

CHAPTER 1

Shortly after John Doyle was born on February 12, 1930, fate dealt him the unkindest hand possible. His mother, Margaret, died from purpureal fever, a form of blood-poisoning that can affect women after childbirth. Today, it would be simply and effectively treated with an antibiotic but, in the 1930s, it was a killer. Most women it afflicted died within a week, but Margaret Doyle clung stubbornly to life for forty-six days until her strength finally subsided, and she passed away on March 30.

Before he ever had a chance to know her, John Doyle had lost his mother. Little over a year after marrying her, his father, Tim, had lost his wife. They'd walked down the aisle together in Moycarkey Church only a year and a day before John was born, their happy-ever-after all too brief.

With the loss of his mother, Doyle was destined to grow up in an environment that would always lack a vital element. In his adult years, he rarely spoke about his mother, and wasn't a man who felt comfortable betraying his emotions. But, once or twice, that mask slipped. On one such occasion, in conversation with a close friend, he expressed the opinion that a child can, in time, recover from the death of a father, but never from the death of a mother.

Her premature passing didn't just deny him the loving attention of a mother, it also denied him the constant presence of a father in his early years.

Forty-two years of age by the time John was born, Tim Doyle had lived most of his life as a bachelor farmer. He was ill-prepared to raise a child on his own, especially with a family holding of around one hundred acres to farm single-handedly.

The Doyle house was typical of the time, in that it had no running water or electricity, so nursing a new-born baby was no easy task. For the first year of John's life, Tim somehow got by, thanks to the help of both his and his wife's families and neighbours, but eventually, it all proved too much. Tim decided he had no option but to entrust John's care to his younger sister, Mary.

Her life, too, had been touched by tragedy. Her husband had recently passed away, leaving her four children to raise. But with her brother offering financial support, she didn't flinch from the prospect of taking on a fifth mouth to feed. And so, before he'd even reached his first birthday, John Doyle moved from the family home in Glenbane, Holycross, to live with his aunt in the Waterford coastal town of Dungarvan.

Every summer, she would return to Holycross for a few weeks, bringing John and her four children with her. But, for the rest of the year, the only life he really knew was the one he lived in Number 13, St Thomas's Terrace in Dungarvan.

As childhoods go, John's was a pretty idyllic one. His first cousins – Sonny, Paddy, Masie and Birdie – provided a ready-made family, and Doyle was doted on by his two maiden grand-aunts, Lena and Mamie, who lived a few doors down. He had no shortage of friends, either. In those days, the traditional large Irish family was very much a feature of life on St Thomas's Terrace. The Veale family had 11 children, the Bourkes had seven and the Kellys five, so the sound of children playing echoed up and down the street from dawn until dusk.

The young John also had partners-in-play in Joe Harrington at Number 15, and the Looby brothers, Eddie and Liam. From very early on, hurling was the game that consumed them most.

Even before the other boys on the street regarded him as old enough to join them in their impromptu matches, John was keen to get in on the action. He'd watch from a safe distance before suddenly tearing into the thick of the action like an over-exuberant Jack Russell terrier, even though he didn't have a hurley to help him in his endeavors. Occasionally, his persistence earned him the brief loan of a stick that was more often than not as big as he was but, even if he could barely drag it behind him, he'd charge into the fray, undaunted.

This exuberance caught the eye of his neighbour, Nicholas Kelly. One day, he dropped by to Number 13 with a freshly-made hurley he'd carved especially for John. Now that the tow-headed three-year-old was accessorised with his very first caman, it was a rare game of street-hurling that would pass without the enthusiastic participation of wee John.

When he wasn't belting a ball around the place, Dungarvan was the sort of town that offered plenty of other exciting adventures for impressionable young minds. Standing on tip-toes, John could look out the upstairs front-window of Number 13 and see the River Colligan sweep down to Davitt's Quay, where the steam-boat, Lady Belle, unloaded her daily cargo at Moloney's hardware store before puffing back out to sea.

A trip down to the quays through the bustling town centre was always a treat, with the first port of call being the shop at the end of St Thomas's Terrace, where the owner kept a litter of pigs in her front garden. From there, it was only a short stroll down to Moloney's Grocers and Bakery on Main Street, where John's aunt, Mary, worked. The aroma of freshly-baked bread whispered a promise of the batch she'd bring home for tea that evening.

He wanted for nothing in this happy, contented little world of his, but then, one day, he was plucked from it and returned back from where he'd come.

Tim Doyle was missing his son. The summer holidays John would spend in Holycross with his aunt and four cousins were no longer enough to fill the void his long absences left. So the boy was summoned home, and the wrench of leaving Waterford was made all the worse by what awaited him back in Tipperary.

He was still too young for National School, and Tim couldn't watch over him during the day while he worked the farm, so John was enrolled in the Sacred Heart College for Little Boys in Thurles. Run by the Presentation Order of nuns, it was a boarding school that catered for young boys, many of whom, like John, had lost their mothers.

In reality, it was more of an orphanage than a boarding school, even if it was a relatively upmarket one by the standards of the day, with the boys quartered two to a room, rather than huddled in dormitories. It might have been a step-up on most orphanages in 1930s Ireland, but it was still a far remove from John's carefree life in Dungarvan, and he found the transition a traumatic one.

As an adult, he preferred to gloss over that period of his childhood by glibly joking that the nuns, "gave me my touch of class". The reality is that it was an unhappy time for him.

When he was occasionally allowed home to Holycross at weekends, he always put up a fight on the Monday morning when he was due back at the Sacred Heart. Tim would have to drag him all the way onto the bus into Thurles, and his son's protests would continue until he was dispatched beyond the wrought-iron gates of the College.

He stayed there for just over a year until he was finally of an age to attend National School. Four years after he'd first departed, John Doyle finally came home for good.

CHAPTER 2

The bread-van driver whistled a breezy tune as he negotiated the twisting ribbon of tarmac out of Holycross village that would eventually take you to Cashel, if you had a mind to go that far.

The road straightened out as it approached the Doyle Farm and, after the driver shifted down through the gears and rolled to a halt, he gave the usual couple of blasts on the horn to hail Tim.

The pair had a well-worn routine by now. He came by this way at the same time every week, and both men looked forward to their regular chin-wags.

Sure enough, Tim wasn't long appearing from the house with his usual friendly wave and smile, his pipe and tobacco pouch already in hand to fragrance the conversation.

Unknown to the two men, Tim's son was also familiar with the schedule of their regular pow-wows, and was laying in wait with his less-willing accomplice and best friend, Michael Maher.

With a reckless grin, Doyle broke from cover and slowly crept his way to the back of the van where he liberated the first loaf he could grasp.

Booty in hand, he tore back the way he had come with a yelp of excitement, and made for the hay-barn to enjoy his ill-gotten gains. The thrill of the theft was the only jam he needed.

• • • ● • • •

Even when he was in short trousers, John Doyle had a strong and distinctive personality.

His father, Tim, was renowned in the area for being a quiet and genial man with a famously sunny disposition, but the sapling wasn't cut from the same tree. A head-strong and stubborn child, when he didn't get things his own way, John's brow would crease and his eyes would darken. He was the sort of boy who could never sit still and always had to be in the thick of some sort of action or misadventure.

Hurling was the constructive outlet that most satisfied his boundless energy, and it quickly became John's obsession. Some say that hurlers are born rather than made, while others insist they're conditioned by their upbringing and surroundings. In John's case, it was immaterial which side of that coin carried the most weight, because he benefited from both good genetics and the best environment possible.

His size, strength and natural athleticism probably came more from his mother's side of the family than his father's. Tim was a handy-sized man who hadn't played too much hurling in his youth, but John's uncle on his mother's side, Pake Spillane, was a hurler of some renown, having won Munster championship medals with Tipperary in 1922 and 1924.

John came from good stock, but the love for hurling which first took seed in Dungarvan couldn't have found more fertile soil than it did in Glenbane, Holycross.

As a boy, John's hurley rarely left his hand, and he found plenty of occasion to use it. Right across the road from his house was Maher's top field, and it was here that his natural talent was hot-housed from an early age.

Every day after he returned from school, he'd quickly gulp down whatever dinner his father had left in a pot on the stove for him, grab his hurley and ball, and dash across the road and over the stile. Before too long, John would be joined by the Maher brothers – Francis, Philip, Kevin and Michael – and a ball would ping between them until dusk fell or they were called home.

It hadn't taken very long at all for John and Michael Maher to become fast-friends after he'd returned home to Glenbane. There was just a difference of two weeks in age between them, and they shared a common love for hurling.

"We were like brothers. We were best friends. And hurling together only strengthened that bond," recalls Michael.

"Every evening after tea and after the cows had been milked, we'd assemble there as a meeting place and as a hurling place. The hurling posts were just a pair of coats on the ground.

"There wasn't much else to do back then; only hurl or, if the weather was good, go for a swim in the River Suir. There was a nice bathing spot near us and it was very simple and easy. There'd be no bathing togs or anything like that. In you'd go and out you'd come."

As boys, it was a rare day that went by without them pucking a ball between one another. As men, John and Michael would win five All-Ireland titles together and form two-thirds of the infamous Hell's Kitchen full-back line.

"If you didn't know him you might be put off by his manner, but once you did get to know him, you didn't mind him," says Michael with a chuckle.

"He was completely different to his father, Tim. His father would be gay and pleasant; John would be dour and telling people to 'fuck off'. He had good points too, but that's the sort of character he was. He wouldn't be palsy-walsy at all. I was used to his form, though, and wouldn't give any heed if he gave a bark."

The Mahers quickly became the only-child's surrogate family, and most days, he took advantage of Mrs Maher's culinary generosity or roused the Maher boys for a game of hurling or some mischief-making.

"He used to be down around the house a good lot as a young lad, alright," says Francis Maher. "He was always full of energy and anxious to be getting going and doing something. There was an old staircase in the house back then, and he used to go up the steps, climb out over the edge of it and drop down to the kitchen floor.

"He was interested in the hurling the whole bloomin' time, too. He always had an edge for it and would be constantly watching his hurling elders and peers to see what they would be doing."

Even at the age of five or six, John wasn't just hurling for the pure fun of it. It always had to have a competitive element. Every puck-around in that top field with the Maher brothers would end up with a couple of jumpers being thrown on the ground for goal-posts, and two would stand between them while the others took pot-shots.

He might have been giving five years to the likes of Francis Maher, but if John couldn't score more goals than his neighbour, that familiar scowl would darken his face. He wasn't inclined to return home unless he could claim some sort of victory, be it a great shot or save he could hang his evening's efforts on.

"He was competitive at everything, from hurling to skittles," says Francis. "Anything that he was involved in, he had to be top-dog.

"I remember when Roscommon played Kerry in the 1944 All-Ireland Final, he bet sixpence with me that Kerry would win. There was a big, strong, tough lad playing for Kerry at the time by the name of Bill Casey. He was a real tough brute of a lad altogether, who used to elbow his way out of all sorts of corners at the expense of his opponents. That's the sort of lad John liked. I can't remember if I got that sixpence. He would have given it grudgingly if he did. He didn't like losing at anything. He always had to be on the winning side."

That naked desire to win became very apparent when Maher's field hosted a casual match of hurling every Sunday. After the boys and young men of the area had their souls and bellies replenished by Mass and dinner, they'd troop in their twos and threes to the field for a match that could last for four hours or more.

While others came and went over the course of the meandering game, John would be in the thick of it from the moment the ball was thrown in until there was no one left to play with. Known locally as the Sunday League match, if John happened to be on the losing team, he'd argue long and loud that the ball be thrown back in and a Sunday Championship match be commenced.

The games were as much a social occasion for non-combatants as they were for the players themselves. A bench sat on the side of the road that ran alongside the field and, before too long, it would be occupied by spectators whose own playing days were fading, but still cherished, memories. Pipe and cigarette smoke would hang like a cloudy canopy above these hurlers on the ditch, as the merits and weaknesses of the next generation were debated and discussed in between proclamations on the weather.

Some opinions carried more weight than others, but none were as valued as those of Paddy Leahy, who had won All-Ireland medals with Tipperary in 1916 and 1925, playing alongside his brother, Johnny. Two other brothers in the Leahy family were also All-Ireland medal holders – Tommy won one with Tipperary in 1930, while Mick won his medal in the red and white of

Cork in 1928.

As hurling families go, the Leahys were Tipperary royalty, and when the famously shrewd Paddy held forth on the merits of a hurler, his audience tended to crane a neck and cock an ear. So when he proclaimed one day while watching one of those regular Sunday tear-ups that Tim Doyle's son was, "a good 'un", the young Doyle's potential had been officially franked for the first time.

●●●●●●●

Hurling wasn't just a pastime for the evenings or weekend for John. His trusted hurley also accompanied him to school every day.

Rather than walk the two miles along the main road to Holycross National School to further his education, John instead joined the Maher brothers in Gaile National School, in the neighbouring parish of Moycarkey. Getting there entailed a safer cross-country route through five fields but, at a good mile in length, it was still a fair old trek for a five-year-old to make, especially in wet weather. On those days, the school-teacher, Timmy Maher, would be obliging enough to seat the Glenbane gang beside the fire and allow them to shed their shoes and dry out their socks.

When it was wet or cold, the mission was to make it to the school house as quickly as possible but, on fine days when there was no incentive to rush, there was always a chance of some sort of horseplay along the route.

One day, the lure of a turnip patch in Flanagan's field proved too strong, and a dozen or so vegetables were dug up and kicked around like footballs or smashed into smithereens with hurleys, with Doyle leading the charge.

By the time they made their way home that afternoon, the morning escapade had been long forgotten. The sight of a none-too-impressed Mr Flanagan surveying the damage with his hands on his hips must have quietened the merry troupe. An inquisition was held and confessions swiftly followed but, to the boys' relief, the ultimate punishment of having their crimes relayed home was avoided.

Mr Flanagan instead requested that the young students produce their pencils and jotters, write a solemn declaration that they would never pull turnips again, and legally bind it with their signatures. Everyone was a winner. The boys went home without fear of further censure, and it surely took some time before the smile completely faded from Flanagan's face.

In Doyle's first couple of years at Gaile, there wasn't much space to hurl in, and any contests amounted to little more than clustered skirmishes in the playground. But after the school purchased a neighbouring field, there were daily matches at lunchtime where the Holycross 'invaders' would compete against the Moycarkey boys.

This new tribal dimension appealed to John's competitive instincts, so when it was announced one day that Gaile would take on the neighbouring Ballytarsna school in a match, the eight-year-old John immediately demanded to be part of the team. Although he was strong for his age, and good enough to more than hold his own in the lunchtime contests, the older boys deemed him too young to play.

Undaunted, John still turned up for the match that Sunday in Gaile with his hurley in hand but, despite arguing his case long and loud, he was once again told he was surplus to requirements. Used to getting his own way, he didn't take the rejection well. As far as he was concerned, the snub amounted to nothing less than a betrayal.

So the following Monday morning, instead of joining the Mahers on the walk through the fields to Gaile as usual, the defiant boy set off alone and marched the two miles down the main road to Holycross National School instead. He wasn't turned away when he got there. The headmaster, Willie Tuohy, was a hurling fanatic, and the caman that Doyle clutched in his hand ensured a quick enrolment.

The one-boy protest didn't last all that long, though. By Tuesday, he was back in Gaile as if nothing had happened. That ability to move on quickly from defeats would also stand him in good stead in later years.

•••●•••

As hurling was always more of a priority than school books, it was only natural that John should seek to further his education in the most renowned finishing school for the game in Tipperary – Kitty's Field in Tubberadora.

The epicentre of the 'Golden Square Mile' that had produced 89 All-Ireland winning medals, it was a short bicycle ride along the Cashel Road for Doyle who would have been reared on stories of the legendary Tubberadora team that sprang from that fertile Field.

At a time when counties were represented in the All-Ireland Championship by their club champions, rather than an all-county team, Tubberadora were crowned All-Ireland champions in 1895, 1896 and 1898. In those three years, they were unbeaten over the course of 14 matches, with a total of 71 goals and 108 points scored, and just 17 goals and 46 points conceded.

They didn't compete in 1897 because one of their players seriously injured another during a training match in Kitty's Field. The man who struck the blow was so remorseful he refused to hurl again, and the team decided to withdraw from the Championship entirely.

Had they competed in 1897, Tipperary might have completed an epic six in a row as they also went on to win the 1899 and 1900 All-Ireland titles, under the banners of the Horse and Jockey (1899) and Two Mile Borris clubs (1900); who both featured former Tubberadora players after their club disbanded again following their 1898 triumph.

Tubberdora's most famous player was Michael Maher, an uncle of the Maher brothers from Glenbane. Six foot three inches tall, and cut from oak, he was the first real superstar of Tipperary hurling, a status that gushing newspaper reports like this one illustrated vividly:

"Mikey Maher, the Tubberadora captain, was the most dangerous man on the forty yards mark that a back was ever up against, and many of his shots sent terror into a goalkeeper's heart.

"A big score against his team never made him quake. When things looked black for Tipp, Maher would suddenly rise, tear up the field, sweep down all opposition and shoot. That score would change the whole aspect of the play.

"Those Tipperary men's blood would boil; their virility would assert itself; they would drive into their men reckless of life and limb and actually walk over the stretched bodies of their opponents to victory."

Tubberadora disbanded after their 1898 All-Ireland, but the area remained a hurling nursery, and supplied many of the men that made Boherlahan the dominant club in the county in the 1920s, including the Leahy brothers.

By the time John Doyle and the Mahers arrived on the scene, Kitty's Field was still very much a hurling hub and, on most summer evenings, there would be casual puck-abouts and impromptu matches involving up to twenty people or more.

One man they were guaranteed to meet whenever they dropped by was little Jimmy Maher, at the time the Tipperary county team goalkeeper. Jimmy was no more than five foot five, and went by the nickname of Small Lemonade – but not to his face. The fact that he liked to wear an outsized flat cap when he played only served to make him appear even more diminutive.

Jimmy compensated for his small stature with a fiery temperament. You had little business being a goalkeeper in those days if you weren't able to fight your corner.

For most forwards of the time, flattening the opposition goalkeeper came a close second on a list of priorities to scoring a goal or two, but if you had designs on giving Small Lemonade a belt, it was always advisable to have a quick exit strategy.

In a match against Cork in the late-'40s, Small Lemonade ended up in the back of his own net with his cap pulled down over his face after a goal-mouth ruck. When he released himself from the rigging and cleared his eyes, he spotted Cork forward and recently-elected TD, Jack Lynch, trotting back up the field. Jimmy tore after him, lashed him across the backside with his hurley and roared: "Fuck you, Lynch. If you fuckin' try that again, there'll be an early fuckin' by-election in Cork."

When he hurled in Kitty's Field, Jimmy wasn't the type to suffer men or boys who weren't good enough to keep the ball pucked into him while he honed his reflexes between the goal-posts evening after evening.

Doyle and Michael Maher were only nine or so when they started joining in games at Kitty's Field, but Jimmy didn't make any allowances, and lashed the ball at them as hard as he did anyone else. You were either up to it, or you had no business being there. John Doyle wasn't long in proving he was plenty good enough.

CHAPTER 3

Mick Looby, the cattle-dealer, arrived home caked in dust and sweat after a long journey from Limerick. It was the sort of hot, sticky August day that made you feel like a lump of melting butter, so he set off for the nearby River Suir to take a restorative plunge.

As he walked down through the meadow that led to the local swimming spot, the sound of echoing laughter and furious splashing gave warning that his swim and sunbathing wouldn't be of the peaceful variety. The Maher boys, Tim Doyle's young fella and a few other tearaways from the area were dunking, diving, whooping and hollering to their heart's content.

Looby exchanged a few wise-cracks, washed the day away and then lay down on the sand-bar that stretched out on the bank to soak up some rays. Strongly built, hairy-chested and with a deep-brown tan a Greek would have been proud of, he was the sort of man who didn't require an invitation to shed his shirt and show off these attributes. He had a feeling, though, he wouldn't be given much of a grace to quietly enjoy the hot sun beating down on him and, sure enough, his prime suspect wasn't long sidling his way over.

"Hey, Mick."

Looby squinted his eyes and looked up at the bould-headed Doyle, silhouetted against the sun and blocking out its precious heat.

"What do you want, young Doyle?" he replied with a wary sigh.

"If you keep watering and sunning that chest of yours it'll soon be ready for harvest," said Doyle with his usual lop-sided grin.

Encouraged by the response from his audience of peers, Doyle kept up his attack with a series of jibes about the body-beautiful Looby, who soaked it up quietly and waited patiently for his moment. When Doyle stepped a yard too close, Looby stretched out his arms slowly as if to yawn and then suddenly moved, quick as a cobra, to grab the youngster's ankle before he could jump out of range.

With Doyle's ankle trapped in his meaty hand, Looby stood up, yanked him off his feet and swung him around with the ease of an Olympic hammer-thrower. Releasing him with perfect timing, Doyle flew through the air into the middle of the river, where he landed with a great splaying splash.

Satisfied with his work, Looby dusted his hands off for dramatic effect and stretched himself back out beneath the sun.

The good was soon taken from his victory though as an unrepentant Doyle began firing handfuls of water his way from the relative safety of the river. Rather than give his torturer any satisfaction, Looby grimly sustained the liquid assault for as long as he could until, eventually, his resolve was broken. With a loud oath, he grabbed his shirt and made for home.

A man familiar with stubborn bullocks, Looby knew the sort of hoor who wouldn't give in too easily when he saw one.

••• ● •••

With every passing year, John's talent for being at the heart of some sort of harmless trouble grew more pronounced. He was the caffler at the crossroads, who was happiest when he was getting a rise out of you or stirring some sort of devilment.

The one thing he was always deadly serious about, though, was hurling. While most youngsters idly dream about maybe someday playing for their county, from a very young age, John was resolutely focused on realising that ambition. In those hurling matches in the field across from his house, he'd always insist on being John Maher, the Tipperary centre-back, and made no secret of his desire to follow in his hero's footsteps.

His hurling education took its next step forward when his father decided to take him out of Gaile National School when he was 11, and have him finish his primary education in Thurles CBS instead. The school was, and remains, the greatest hurling nursery in the county, and John's uncommon physical strength and natural talent quickly brought him to the attention of the hurling-mad Christian Brothers.

He was so good that, rather than hurl for the CBS Primary School, he was instead drafted into the secondary school's Under-15 Croke Cup team in 1942.

Though John was only 12, he was already bigger and stronger than many of his older team-mates. Among them were Pat Stakelum, Paddy Kenny and Seamus Bannon, boys who would later earn hurling glory alongside him as grown men. With John hurling at wing-forward, they won the competition easily. Among their victims was a Holycross team, who Thurles hammered by a resounding 8-5 to 0-1.

Much of his adult career would be consumed by the challenge of beating Thurles Sarsfields, so there is no little irony in the fact that he won his very first medal in the town's blue colours, beating his beloved Holycross along the way.

His hurling and academic education in Thurles, however, was cut short when his father, Tim, fell ill and John had to leave school and return home to work the farm when he was just 14. He was already built like a man, and now he had little option but to become one. Tim was no longer able to do much of the heavy physical labour, so his son had to take up the slack, and did so with zeal. There was no shortage of help offered from neighbouring farmers, but the teenager only accepted it when he had no other option. He was as driven by the same desire to be a winner at farming as he was at hurling.

Up until this time, John and Michael Maher had done all their hurling in nearby Tubberadora, but once the Holycross club established a juvenile team, they were brought in from the fringes of the parish, and their days in Kitty's Field were over.

It wasn't long, either, before they'd won their first medal in the green of Holycross, when they beat a Moycarkey team, that included some of their old lunchtime opponents from Gaile, in the Mid-Tipperary Juvenile Final by 4-1 to 4-0, courtesy of a last-minute goal.

Doyle stood out in every way possible. The 14-year-old was already touching six feet tall and blessed with uncommon strength for someone his age. Allied with that farm-hardened physique was the timing and balance of a natural-born hurler. While other boys did well to hit the heavy sliotar out of their way, John was driving it 60 yards or more with a great, sweeping stroke that made the Holycross mentors look at one another and smile.

He wasn't inclined to wait for the ball to come his way, either. Like a fire-fighter on commission, he always had a desire to be where the action was hottest. His long-legged stride hungrily ate up the ground, and he'd tear into rucks for the ball with no regard for his opponent's health, or his own. His only focus was on winning the ball, and he'd use his knees, elbows or whatever else it took to knock an opposing player out of the of the way. And once John claimed the ball, standing in his way was more foolhardy than brave.

By now, he was already a recognised name both locally and further afield, and he embellished his growing reputation further in an Under-15 match against a neighbouring parish. Playing at centre-back, Doyle dominated the first half so completely that the opposition felt obliged to resort to desperate measures for the second.

Considering his size and the impressive growth of hair on his upper-lip, the substitute they summoned was either remarkably mature for his age or wouldn't see 20 again, never mind 15. But Doyle's cough remained un-softened. The substitute was left in a heap on the ground after the first ball they contested and came out on the wrong side of every other tussle, too, as John hurled better than ever in the second half. By the time the final whistle was blown, the opposition's enforcer was a sorry sight as he hobbled off the pitch, looking older than ever.

The upward trajectory of the young Holycross star was being watched closely by one man in particular – his neighbour, Paddy Leahy. Ever since first watching him rampage around Maher's field all those years ago, he'd taken a personal interest, and John couldn't have asked for a more valuable patron. Leahy's brother, Johnny, was County Board secretary at the time and, on Paddy's recommendation, posted out a letter to John in May 1946, requesting his presence at trials in Thurles for the Tipperary minor team.

Doyle was only 15, but the opportunity didn't faze him, and, the following day, he readied his bicycle for the journey. He wedged his hurley between his gear-wheel and front-bar. After stuffing his shorts into one pocket and his socks into the other, he tied his boots securely to his handle-bar. With Michael Maher at his side for moral support, he set off on the seven-mile journey to meet his destiny, his legs pumping almost as fast as his heart.

Not for the last time, John would justify Leahy's faith in him, because although he was one of the youngest boys who attended the trials, he managed to nail down a place in the team at right corner-back.

"He was already a big, strong, well-built young lad," recalls John O'Grady, who also hurled his first year at minor level with Tipperary in 1946. "He was always burly. That was his trademark. He'd be tearing in there and taking the ball away, shouldering others out of the way.

"You couldn't say he had fierce finesse at that stage. But he was a great tackler and had great courage. He was never hanging back, and had a great knack for the coursing the ball out of a bunch of players. He was never a man for fancy sidestepping. He would horse them out of his way and then lash it down the field."

The two stars of the team were Borris-Ileigh's Paddy Kenny, Doyle's former Croke Cup colleague, and the exotically-named Wilhelm Steiglitz, a native of Czechoslovakia who had moved to the town when his father was hired as an engineer in the sugar factory.

With John performing solidly in defence, Tipp cuffed aside Limerick, Cork and Galway on the way to an All-Ireland Final showdown against Dublin. In the previous year's showpiece, Dublin had beaten what was regarded as the greatest every minor team to come out of Tipperary, so the 1946 Final was billed as a revenge mission.

••• • •••

September 1946
All-Ireland Minor Hurling Final

With the lancing rain stinging his eyes, Doyle couldn't see whether Paddy Kenny had managed to put the free over the bar, but then the rumbling roar that rolled around the ground like low thunder gave him the answer.

The score-board at the Hill 16 end now read Tipperary 0-7, Dublin 0-6, and the clock beside it told him that time was up.

It had been a ferocious slog in the rain and muck, but they were nearly over the line now. The Dubs had been better than he expected, but Tipp had slowly ground them down, and now only had to hold on for one more minute.

He knew they would. Himself, Nolan and Sheehy hadn't given an inch all day in the full-back line and, by Jesus, they weren't going to now.

Doyle's confidence soured into fear when the Dublin puck-out went straight to their danger-man, Donnelly. Too far out to score with a heavy, wet sliotar, Doyle knew a dropper was on its way. The high delivery came scudding through the air, hard to spot against the lead-grey sky and driving rain.

The Dublin forwards chased its flight and Doyle could see by the murder in their eyes that the sliotar itself was only a secondary consideration. Billy O'Brien was the main target.

Doyle moved in from his corner to stand between them and his goalkeeper, but by the time he arrived the square was already a battle-zone and Tipp were outnumbered by the pale-blue horde. The sliotar landed amidst a thicket of straining legs and flashing hurleys, no-one winning it cleanly.

O'Brien made to burrow his way towards it, but was flattened in the melée. Just as Doyle went to flake on the ball, he was met by a meaty shoulder square in the chest, and ended up in a tangled heap in the goal's rigging, where he was swiftly joined by the sliotar itself.

The Dublin players wheeled away in celebration, leaping over the prone body of O'Brien, where he still lay broken on the ground.

It was only now the referee arrived on the scene with doubt etched all over his face. For a full four minutes he consulted with his umpire until the order was given to raise the green flag. With it, Doyle's heart sank.

CHAPTER 4

Seamus Leahy pumped his legs like pistons to build up speed then weaved his bicycle in and out through a cluster of potholes with the practised ease of a downhill skier.

Alongside him raced a panting Jack Russell terrier, occasionally drawn into hedgerows by the lure of a strong summer scent but never leaving his master's side for long.

The ten-year old was on his way to his Uncle Paddy's house in the permanent rush of an adolescent, but, as he approached the Doyle farm, he stood on his pedals and free-wheeled slowly.

John Doyle was a county minor hurler now, and in Seamus' mind that status elevated him above other mere mortals into a category populated exclusively by superhumans who wore the blue and gold.

His hero was in a field piloting a plough behind a broad-chested draught-horse and, when he spotted Leahy cruising by, he hailed the youngster to a halt.

Doyle wasn't usually the kind to pause from work once he'd begun but, as a nephew of Paddy Leahy, young Seamus was worth more of his time than most.

After he'd strode his way over to where Seamus stood outside the gate, the wide-eyed youngster had only one question to ask him.

"John, why aren't you wearing any boots?"

Doyle looked down at his feet, which were caked in the dark soil he'd churned from the meadow.

"It makes the ankles stronger for the hurling," he replied with shrug, as if ploughing a field in your bare feet was the most natural thing in the world.

•••●•••

Even before the GAA was founded, in 1884, there had been a long tradition of hurling in Holycross.

Cross-country matches against the neighbouring parish of Moycarkey were regular events but they bore little similarity to the codified game of hurling we have today.

The teams would meet in Paddy Maher's field, which straddled the border between the two parishes, and the purpose of the match was to get the sliotar to a predetermined spot on your side of the divide, often a mile or more from the starting point in Maher's field.

There were little or no rules to be observed, and the matches were probably more faction fights than they were sporting contests.

After the GAA was formed, Holycross quickly earned a reputation for being one of the finest club teams in the country, winning a series of tournaments in the late-1880s and beating renowed teams such as St Finbarr's from Cork and Commercials from Dublin.

Despite those early glory years, hurling declined in Holycross after 1889 when the parish was badly sundered by the bitter rivalries between Parnellites and anti-Parnellites and struggled to recover thereafter.

County Junior titles were won in 1922 and 1941, but these were pallid triumphs compared to glories neighbouring clubs Boherlahan-Dualla, Moycarkey-Borris and Thurles Sarsfields were achieving at senior level.

After that Junior success in '41 the club was promoted to the senior grade, but struggled to make any real impact.

So, by the time Doyle was drafted into the senior team for the first time as a 17-year-old in 1947, there was little expectation of the glorious chapter of the club's history his arrival would herald.

It wasn't just Doyle's coming of age that propelled the Holycross team towards greatness. He was only one of a clutch of talented young players in the parish who arrived on the scene around the same time.

Pat Stakelum and Michael Maher would also go on to become Tipperary legends, and others, such as Liam Skelly, Bob Stakelum, Jim Ryan and Gerry 'Bowler' Doyle, John's cousin, would also don the blue and gold with distinction.

Allied to the youthful vigour of the new generation, Holycross also had a core of older, more experienced players to complement them.

Dinny O'Gorman had won an All-Ireland title with Tipperary in 1937, and, though now in his early-30s, the ferociously tough centre-back was still a formidable force.

His younger brother, Ned, was a hugely effective barrelling, bustling full-forward, while Doyle's friend and neighbour, Francis Maher, was the team captain and inspirational midfielder.

The first sign that all these elements would suddenly alchemise base lead into gold came in the first round of the 1947 Mid-Tipperary Championship when Doyle made his senior team debut and Holycross trounced Moycarkey by 7-5 to 1-4.

In those days there were far fewer senior clubs in the county than there are now, and that one victory qualified Holycross for a Mid-Tipperary final show-down with Thurles Sarsfields.

It would be another three months before the match would be played though and, by the time it came around, Doyle had already won his very first All-Ireland hurling medal.

A solid and steady performer for the county Minors in 1946, a year later Doyle announced himself as a star in the making.

Now 17, three years of full-time hard labour on the family farm had turned him to fire-hardened steel and it was a rare minor who could match him physically.

Victories over Limerick and Waterford earned Doyle his second Munster medal and, in both matches, his uncompromising defending and sweeping clearances from corner-back earned rave reviews in the local press.

Few heroics were required in the All-Ireland final though, as Tipp mended the heartbreak of the previous year's defeat to Dublin by crushing Galway 9-5 to 1-5.

Doyle had finally won the All-Ireland he'd coveted as a kid in Maher's Field and, just a week later, came another red-letter day as Holycross played Thurles Sarsfields in the Mid-Tipperary final.

Few people gave Holycross much hope. Certainly not the Tipperary Star newspaper's main correspondent who, assuming a Sarsfields' victory was inevitable, went to watch the South-Tipperary final that day instead.

His presumption was understandable. Sarsfields had been County

Champions for the previous three years running and had defeated the famed clubs Glen Rovers, of Cork, and Ahane, of Limerick, in high-profile tournament matches.

Almost all of their players had hurled for Tipperary at some stage and they boasted one of the outstanding forwards in the county at the time in Tommy Ryan.

It was an era when most forwards were powerfully-built men who traded more on raw strength than skill.

Third-man tackles and frontal charges weren't just within the rules, they were the primary tools of the defender, so a forward had to be capable of taking plenty of punishment and not averse to dishing it out himself.

Scoring returns in matches were pretty miserable compared to the winning totals posted at inter-county level today, but that's because the dice was loaded against the forward in other ways too.

The sliotar used in the '40s, '50s and '60s was much heavier than its modern equivalent and, on a wet day, most players would do well to hit it more than forty yards.

Hurleys of the day didn't help in that regard either. The width of the average bas was less than half of those used today, which is one of the reasons why ground hurling was still the main method for moving the ball from A to B.

That's why the prototype half-forward of the day was broad-shouldered and hard-pulling, but Tommy Ryan was something totally different altogether. He wasn't all that big or all that strong but was quick, hugely skilful and a lethal finisher.

Unlike other forwards who would stand shoulder to shoulder with you for 70 minutes and duke it out, Ryan was always on the move, flitting here and there elusively and causing mayhem wherever he went with his quick wrists and clean striking.

He was a nightmare to mark, but that's the task that faced the 17-year-old Doyle in just his second ever game of senior club hurling.

$$\bullet \bullet \bullet \bullet \bullet \bullet \bullet$$

September 14, 1947.
Mid-Tipp Final v Thurles Sarsfields.

Doyle's lungs burned and his heart hammered to a bodhran's beat. Ryan had already escaped him for one point and scored two more from frees. Though they had the wind at their backs, Holycross were in retreat.

Doubt was spreading like a virus through his team-mates and Doyle knew if they didn't get a toe-hold in this match soon they'd fall away altogether.

A rare foray into Sarsfields' territory yielded a 70, and the 17-year-old strode forward and demanded the task of taking it.

But, as soon as referee Willie O'Donnell handed him the ball, his bravery started to feel a little like foolishness. A steady rain was falling and the already swollen and sodden sliotar felt as heavy as a cannon-shot.

He set it down, hunkered, lifted it and struck. The satisfying hum that ran quickly from his wrists to his shoulders told him he'd met it on the meat.

The umpire raised his flag and Holycross spirits lifted with it. Now every man in a green jersey was hurling like a dervish, none more than Doyle.

Time and again, he blew Ryan aside in a battle for possession, and launched the ball down the field with a mighty stroke.

Wherever Ryan went, Doyle stuck to him like tar. Ryan was fast but, like so many other players would later discover, Doyle was remarkably light on his feet and quick across the ground for such a big man.

Holycross were hurling with renewed self-belief, but Sarsfields were unflinching and the exchanges grew fiercer and fiercer as men on both sides threw flesh in the way of ash.

For 20 minutes neither managed another score but then, in a chaotic few minutes before half-time, Holycross plundered 2-1 and Sarsfields managed two points in reply.

The no-hopers were leading by 2-2 to 0-5 at half time, and the dressing room that awaited them was no less intense than the field of battle they'd left behind.

Team trainer Rody Dwan was a man who always became consumed with the fervour of an Old Testament zealot whenever Holycross were in action, but now his eyes burned like never before.

He'd toiled through the bad days when Holycross struggled to win a match at Junior level, and now that they were just a half of hurling away from their first ever Mid-Senior title he was ready to do his part.

By the time the Holycross players came back out onto the field for the second half, Dwan's words had left their ears ringing and their chests fit to burst. There was going to be no lying down to the townies today.

No one was resisting more than Doyle, who flung himself into every ruck ferociously, his thick mop of hair flying this way and that with every shoulder charge and swing of the ash.

After one almighty collision his hurley was splintered in two: "Hey, Rody," roared Doyle at the sideline as he waved the smashed stick above his head. "Hurley."

Good hurleys were a scarce commodity, and what Dwan threw into him was closer to a pick-axe handle. Doyle grimaced when he felt the weight and saw the shape of it. He'd be hitting no more 70-yard frees.

It was a handy weapon, though, in any ruck or clash, and Doyle swung it for all he was worth as he kept a by-now totally chastened Tommy Ryan in check while Holycross hung on grimly.

Two second-half goals for Sarsfields were replied in kind and, for the final five minutes, Holycross desperately defended a slender one-point advantage – 4-2 to 2-7 – as Sarsfields swarmed all over them like angry bees.

When the final whistle came it was followed by a second of perfect, stunned silence, and then the Thurles Sportsground erupted with a great roar as hundreds of Holycross fans flooded the field to carry their heroes away, shoulder-high.

Doyle's back was slapped raw as he surfed a sea of shoulders and smiles. In just his second match for Holycross he'd played a huge part in winning the club's first ever Mid-Title. The boy was now most definitely a man.

•••●•••

CHAPTER **FOUR**

September 28, 1947.
Tipperary County Semi-Final v Carrick Swans.

Holycross was eerily quiet. Houses lay empty and wary-eyed dogs lay on doorsteps with their ears flattened and their tails between their legs, unnerved by the absence of their masters.

Ten miles down the road, Cashel was a chaotic canvas of colour and sound as the town hosted the biggest crowd anyone had ever seen at a County Semi-final.

Over 8,000 souls, most clad in the green and white of Holycross, shoehorned themselves into the town's humble hurling field.

The sideline gates of the ground were locked a couple of hours before the game with every seat already full, so streams of people scaled gates and walls and forced their way onto the sidelines.

With the pitch surrounded by a tightly-packed swaying wall of people, those who'd queued early for seats had no option but to stand on them while hundreds of others perched themselves on outer walls and barbed-wire fences like over-sized crows.

The entire parish had emptied to witness the club's first ever County Semi-final, and the atmosphere in the ground was one of frenzied expectation.

The screaming Holycross fans might have had the best of intentions, but the super-charged atmosphere infected their young team with a panicked rashness.

They dominated possession and territory and created chance after chance, but shot wildly time and again.

Had they been content to go for points they would have won comfortably but, instead, they were overcome with a desperate urge to continually go for goals.

They scored five of them, but the Carrick Swans goalkeeper, Paddy Fleming, was still named Man of the Match as the South Tipperary team won by 5-7 to 5-3.

The Holycross convoy headed for home in considerably lower spirits than those they'd set out in, but they'd soon have reason to cheer again.

CHAPTER 5

1948

The semi-circle of Holycross players listened with focused intent while Paddy Leahy spoke. He wasn't the sort of man to waste a word, so you made sure to register every one.

Brought in as a team advisor at the start of the year, his considered voice of reason had been the perfect foil to Rody Dwan's fire and brimstone.

With a quiet word of encouragement here, and an understated guiding hand there, he had a knack of making you a better hurler, or at least of convincing you that you were better than you were.

They were hanging on his word tonight more than ever. The County Final against Lorrha was on Sunday, and this was their last get-together before the match in Nenagh.

No better man to tell them how to win the club's first ever County Final. Leahy himself had won nine as a player with Boherlahan.

After going through a lengthy list of do's and don'ts for the days before the big match he ended with a well-worn piece of advice he and many others of his generation were always fond of giving.

"And lads, whatever ye do, don't be lying down in wet grass after training. Ye'll catch a cold, or, worse again, a dose of the TB."

As Leahy strode off the field Francis Maher called his players together and the loose crescent became a tight circle around him.

"Right, lads, there's not much more to say, I think Leahy has told us everything we need to know," said Maher.

"Bejayus," piped up someone from the back of the huddle, "he told us nothing about women."

"You mustn't have been listening at all," fired back Bob Stakelum. "Didn't the man say not to be lying down in wet grass?"

●●●●●●●

A year after falling short against Carrick Swans, Doyle and Holycross had made it to their first County Final, but their journey there had been anything but smooth and straightforward.

Thurles Sarsfields were beaten again in the first round of the Mid-Championship after another ferocious struggle, but even tougher was to come in the Semi-Final against Moycarkey.

Still bitterly remembered by Moycarkey fans of a certain vintage as the 'game of the long-count', Holycross benefited from a period of extra-time in the second half that stretched into double digits.

They needed every additional minute, too, only securing their passage to the Mid-Final thanks to a goal in the dying embers of the match.

Boherlahan were narrowly beaten in the Mid-Final after another hard-hitting match, but the contest didn't end after the final whistle had been blown.

It was an era when teams had no qualms whatsoever about seeking to have a result overturned if they could prove that even the most trivial technical rule had been broken by their victorious opponents.

The act of winning a match by crooked means rather than fairly on the field of play was almost seen as a badge of honour and, in a very Irish way, the source of a dark, but deep satisfaction.

Over the years so many clubs had victories taken away from them by successful objections to the Tipperary County Board that the room where the Board met in Thurles Confraternity Hall became commonly know as the 'Chamber of Horrors'.

Even by the standards of the day though, Boherlahan's objection in '48 was deliciously imaginative and underhand.

They'd heard a rumour that the Holycross goalkeeper, Mikie Ferncombe, was actually living outside of the parish in neighbouring Drombane and not as a lodger with a Holycross farmer by the name of Pake Fogarty as the club insisted, so was therefore illegal.

So two Boherlahan club members posing as National Health Insurance inspectors called to the house one day where they spoke to Mrs Fogarty.

After warning her that if Ferncombe was living there without a properly stamped insurance card there could be severe consequences, Mrs Fogarty signed a letter stating that Ferncombe had never lived there and only worked there for two months.

This letter was produced with a great flourish by the Boherlahan delegate at the Mid-Tipperary Board meeting held to adjudicate on the objection, but, ultimately, all their considerable efforts were in vain.

Sometimes it pays to have friends in high places, and it surely did Holycross no harm that Mrs Fogarty's brother-in-law was the Very Reverend Canon Fogarty, Chairman of the Tipperary County Board.

••• • •••

While the Holycross club fought their corner in the boardroom, Doyle continued to enhance his reputation on the hurling field in the blue and gold of Tipperary.

In his third year as a County Minor he was named team captain, and even made his debut for the County Senior team in a League victory over Kilkenny in February.

It was only a cameo appearance though. When some of Tipp's front-line players returned, Doyle was released from the panel.

He was very much the senior figure on the County Minor team, though. Now playing at centre-back, he had the reassuring presence of his best friend, Michael Maher, playing in the full-back position behind him.

Limerick were hammered 8-5 to 1-6 in the first round of the Munster Championship and Cork beaten just as easily 7-9 to 1-2.

Such impressive victories ensured Tipp were hot favourites going into the Munster Final against Waterford, but the reigning champions were hurled off the pitch as Waterford triumphed by 3-6 to 0-3.

It was the first time Doyle discovered that Waterford teams are never to be underestimated, a painful lesson that would be repeated in the years to come.

• • • ● • • •

With Boherlahan's boardroom shenanigans successfully overcome, Holycross set their eyes on the County Semi-Final where, once again, Carrick Swans awaited.

Rather than suffer again on the tight, uneven Cashel pitch, Holycross decided to travel to enemy territory in South Tipperary where the match would be played in the broader, lusher expanses of Clonmel's hurling field.

The parish emptied again even though the journey to Clonmel was considerably more challenging than a trip to Cashel.

Very few people would have owned cars, so all sorts of buses were hired and hundreds more walked the train tracks to Thurles Station from where the CIE had laid on a special train for the match.

This time the faith of the travelling hordes was rewarded as Holycross persevered by 3-9 to 3-2 with Doyle, Pat Stakelum and Francis Maher their leading lights.

So excited were the Holycross fans at the prospect of a first ever County Final appearance that, after the match, an impromptu conga line strung itself behind a band that paraded all the way from the field to the centre of Clonmel town.

When they reached Gladstone Street the parade's leader was hoisted shoulder-high with unforeseen consequences. His trousers split and the unfortunate man had chosen the same day not to wear any underwear.

The merriment continued on the train home after a few cases of beer had been purchased to shorten the journey but, unfortunately for the revellers, the carriages lacked toilet facilities.

So when the train stopped at Farnaleen, Fethard and the Horse and Jockey on the way back to Thurles, men emptied from one side of the carriage and women from the other to give the track-side vegetation an unexpected watering.

• • • ● • • •

One man wasn't best pleased by the air of giddy excitement that suffused the parish in the three-week build-up to the County Final against Lorrha.

Rody Dwan was a stern-faced taskmaster at the best of times, but the thought that his young charges might have their heads turned before the biggest match of their lives sent him into over-drive.

It was threshing season in Holycross, a time when the farming community would come together as one and spend long hours piking sheaves, clearing chaff spat from the threshing machine and filling sacks with the separated grain.

It was dry, thirsty work, but the great attraction of the communal labour was that a barrel of porter would be set up in the field from which the men could regularly refresh themselves.

Not only did Dwan ban his hurlers from dipping their mugs in the porter barrel, he even went as far as insisting that no threshing dances were to be allowed.

This was an extreme measure because the threshing season was the highlight of the social calendar.

While the men worked in the field the wives would compete with one another to provide the 'best feed', and in the evening there would often be an impromptu threshing dance where the younger men and women of the area could become better acquainted.

As far as Dwan was concerned though, drink and women were evils that could only serve to sap the strength of his hurlers in the weeks before the biggest match of their lives, so both had to be strictly censored.

The players also found that another measure of Dwan's also served well to limit their hopes of a romantic dalliance.

In the weeks before the County Final the services of the masseur, Tim Crowe, were employed and, for the first time, the players were introduced to a substance called wintergreen.

An ointment designed to warm the muscles and prevent injury, it had a powerfully pungent odour and, once it seeped into your clothing, people were likely to smell you coming before they saw you.

There were no showers to be had after training or hurling matches in those days, and the fairer sex were already accustomed to carrying a perfumed hankie to make the close companionship of a young hurler more bearable.

The cologne hadn't been invented though that could cope with the sensory assault of a man liberally covered in wintergreen, so even the Holycross players with a mind to have their strength sapped would have struggled to find a maiden willing to oblige them.

• • • ● • • •

October 3, 1948, Nenagh.
County SH Final v Lorrha.

The air in the function room of Cadell's Hotel crackled with coiled energy and nervous anticipation as the Holycross players hurriedly pull on their togs, shorts and jerseys.

The din of players, mentors and supporters shouting above one another echoed loudly off the four walls and only subsided when Leahy stood to speak.

But even his words were barely listened to and it was a blessing for the agitated players when the call to arms was finally given and they marched out of the hotel and onto Kenyon street.

Their route to the pitch was choked with hundreds of fans happy to sacrifice a prime seat for a chance to form a cheering, shouting guard of honour.

The crush of bodies was so tight at the gate to the grounds that the players could only squeeze through one by one until they were propelled onto the pitch as if spat out by a pea-shooter.

Every green-shirt was greeted with an almighty roar as the record crowd of 12,000 made the ground shake.

Lorrha were already out on the field, and Doyle and the rest of the Holycross players immediately scanned their ranks for the man everyone was talking about – Tony Reddin, the goalkeeper they said could stop hayseed and puck the ball a country mile.

By the end of the match Reddin had proven his reputation wasn't all that fanciful but, despite his heroics, Holycross weren't to be denied.

Doyle hurled up his customary storm at wing-back, the midfield axis of Francis Maher and Pat Stakelum were supreme again and Philip Maher at centre-forward had the game of his life.

Ahead by 2-7 to 2-3 at half time, Holycross took total charge in the second half with the wind at their backs and cruised to a 4-10 to 2-4 victory.

As soon as the final whistle blew the pitch was thronged by the delirious Holycross masses who lifted their heroes shoulder-high.

After Francis Maher was presented with the Dan Breen Cup, he and his team-mates were chaired by a cheering river of humanity all the way back to Cadell's Hotel where the atmosphere was now much different to what it had been a couple of hours previously.

The victorious players were made freemen of the bar, but as thirteen of them, including the 18-year-old Doyle, were non-drinkers, the Hotel's generosity wasn't financial suicide.

There was no shortage of Holycross fans keen to pick up the slack, and it was some time before all the buses could round up their passengers before journeying back to the village.

Many of those who'd made the 40km journey by bicycle weaved their way unsteadily home, their inner compasses knocked awry by one stiff drink too many.

They all made it home safely in the end though, the final leg illuminated by the orange glow of bonfires licking the night sky above Holycross.

The pubs of the parish did a roaring trade that night and for many more after it. For so long the serfs of Mid-Tipperary hurling, the celebrations to mark their coronation as kings of the whole county were fittingly royal.

CHAPTER 6

Holycross May 8, 2011

Dark clouds bloated with rain gathered threateningly on the horizon and a rising gale snatched away GAA President Christy Cooney's words as he declared the John Doyle Centre open.

It wasn't the sort of weather that Holycross GAA club would have hoped for on their big day, but perhaps the conditions were apt considering the man they were honouring.

John Doyle, too, was a force of nature, and never a man inclined to make things easy on others, either on or off the pitch.

Whatever else he was, though, he was a Holycross man first and foremost. He might have earned his fame in the blue and gold of Tipperary, but the green of Holycross was closest to his heart.

The day they told him they were naming the new state-of-the-art clubhouse in his honour his shoulders pinned back and his chest puffed out.

Even though by then his body was wearing the toll of two strokes, he informed his family that he'd be walking from his house to the Holycross club grounds in Glenreigh on the day of the grand opening.

In the end he didn't live long enough to make the journey. The Grim Reaper was always going to be the only man who could keep John Doyle away from Holycross hurling field.

"For me the club in Holycross was always first," Doyle once said. "No matter how often I played for Tipperary, I never once missed a night's training with Holycross.

"Not once. I can say that without fear of contradiction. If you don't look after your own club then you're going nowhere."

None were as committed as he, but he never thought they had a good excuse not to be. In the 22 years he hurled for the Holycross hurling team he gave everything of himself and he demanded his team-mates did too.

If he felt they weren't as committed as they could be, he wasn't the type to gently cajole them along. Instead of patting them on the back he preferred to aim a few inches lower and deliver an almighty kick in the back-side.

His old captain, Francis Maher, is 87 years old now, but the thought of Doyle in full-flow still makes his eyes twinkle like a boy's.

"He wouldn't have been afraid to give out to lads at all. He was always more of a Gadaffi than a diplomat," says Maher with a laugh.

"He'd always be very determined that everyone would pull their weight properly and that they wouldn't be ducking out of anything because he just hated losing."

No sort of defeat sat easily with Doyle, but losing to a neighbouring club was the bitterest blow of all.

It was the tribal nature of hurling that appealed to him most. As a boy in Gaile Primary School there was great pleasure to be had from beating the Moycarkey lads at lunchtime, and little changed in his psyche as an adult.

"He'd viewed the whole thing as beating people rather than winning," says his oldest friend, Michael Maher. "That was his motivation. To beat Sarsfields, to beat Moycarkey, to beat Boherlahan.

"It wouldn't be as important to beat a team like Nenagh. He really fed off the local rivalries. Very much so."

Tournament matches, where there was some prize at stake, were also guaranteed to get his competitive juices flowing.

Teams would sometimes play for a set of gabardine coats or hand-watches, but most regularly a set of suit lengths would be sponsored for every member of the winning side.

The players would then have to take the material to a tailor so it could be properly fitted to best fit their size and shape.

According to Doyle's neighbour and close friend, Mikey Ryan, it was such a prize that memorably animated Doyle before one particularly infamous tournament match.

"We arrived below in Carrick-On-Suir to play this match and there were twenty-one suit lengths for the winners," recalls Ryan.

"This was back in the early-1950s. It was a hard time to get a suit, of course, things were bad.

"We togged out in the bus anyway. The selectors said their words in the bus but, just as we were ready to go to the bus, himself stood up and said: 'Hold it there lads for a minute I want a word. Lads, we're playing for 21 suit lengths here tonight. Now, I've never been as badly stuck for a bloody suit. I could do with one, and so could everyone of ye. I'm just going to say this once. Woe be to the man that lets us down this evening. I'll guarantee ye one thing, he won't come back on this bloody bus with the rest of us.'

"We won by two points, thank God."

The extent to which the Holycross players were determined not to let Doyle down still brings a smile to the face of another of his friends and former team-mates, Liam Quinn.

"Oh, stop, that was some game altogether," chuckles Quinn. "Playing for a set of suit-lengths was a serious business and I remember after the match there were eight of us who needed to be stitched up.

"It was tough going, but Gerry 'The Bowler' Doyle probably got the worst belt of all. This woman ran in off the sideline and hit him down on the head with her handbag. Well everything went flying out if it, her purse, her cigarettes, the whole lot. I've never seen anything like it."

The following Monday morning at the creamery, Gerry's misfortune was the source of much mirth. As per usual it was his cousin, John, who led the charge.

"The craic would be mighty with him at the creamery every morning," says Quinn. "All he'd want to do would be to talk about hurling and get a rise out of a few lads.

"He was a real hurling fanatic, really. It was his life, simple as that. He just loved it, and the example he set for everyone else in terms of dedication to the club was something else.

"Himself and Pat Stakelum had nothing to prove but they used to tear into one another at every training session like it was the All-Ireland Final they were playing. You'd be doing your best to stay well clear of them.

"John was the first man at training every night and if he didn't think you were putting in enough of an effort he'd give you a belt of a hurley across the arse.

"Although the worst belt I got off him was for something I did right rather than something I did wrong. It was above in Gaile field. A ball went past our goalkeeper, Rodgie Dwan, but I came running across the goal-line and collected it before it went into the back of the net.

"After I cleared it he hit me an almighty clatter across the back with his hurley and shouted, 'Good man Quinn!' Shur, he didn't know his own strength at all – he nearly broke me in two. It was meant to be a friendly tap, but it didn't feel like one."

Doyle was demanding of his team-mates, but he earned that right because no one gave more to this cause than he did. Ploughing in his bare feet to strengthen his ankles wasn't the only extra length to which he was prepared to go.

In winter time, he'd also regularly recruit Francis Maher to go running with him through the fields at night time with just the watery light of a couple of battery-powered torches to show the way.

"We did that a fair bit alright in the top field where we used to do all that hurling," says Maher, smiling at the madness of it all.

"It was divided into a couple of old ditches and gaps and we'd go out through one gap and into the next field and around in a sort of a circle.

"One particular occasion he met my brother, Philip, somewhere and told Philip to tell me to come up to him in the evening. Philip was quizzing him then what he wanted me up for, but he wouldn't tell him. 'Ah, he knows himself. He knows himself,' says Doyle. He wouldn't tell Philip what we were up to. He didn't want people to know he was doing the extra training."

Doyle might have won eight All-Ireland, 10 Munster and 11 National League medals with Tipperary, but he didn't cherish them nearly as much as he did the three county medals he won with Holycross.

He might have been John Doyle the famous Tipperary hurler to most of the country, but in his own mind he was John Doyle the Holycross man.

"The club always came first with him," says Mikey Ryan. "He'd always say the most important thing he ever won were the County Finals with Holycross. He thought an awful lot of the club and the parish, and we thought an awful lot of him.

"In all the years I saw him play for Holycross I doubt if he ever had a bad match. He was the man who led the charge from centre-back. He'd take the long-range frees, which he was very good at, and if you needed someone to produce a moment of inspiration, Doyle was the man we'd turn to and he'd always come up trumps.

"His consistency was remarkable, even to the day he finished with Holycross, his last match. You could never say he was beaten.

"I don't think we'll ever see his likes again."

CHAPTER 7

The door swung open and Paddy Leahy bowled into the room with his usual bristling purpose.

His eyes glinted like cut-glass beneath the jaunty brim of his fedora, reflecting a glow from the Woodbine clamped by the crooked grin that creased his weather-worn face.

"Well, how's the patient?" he demanded as he playfully tousled his nephew Seamus's hair.

The youngster had been feeling sorry for himself. Bad enough to be sick, but the penance of missing Holycross beat Lorrha in the County Final only added insult to injury.

A smile quickly came unbidden though, cajoled by his uncle's knack of lifting your mood and drawing the best from others.

Animated on an average day, Holycross's victory had Leahy buzzing with an infectious energy that ran through the room like a current.

He'd brought two able conductors with him – Jimmy Maher, the Tipperary goalkeeper, and Dinny Byrne from Thurles, father of Tipperary defender, Mickey Byrne, and a champion melodeon player.

The room soon hummed to talk of the day's deeds and the occasional foot-tapper from Byrne, the enjoyment of both for Leahy aided by his favourite tipple of whiskey and milk.

Seamus slipped away and returned with an autograph book he presented to Maher, who would only write 'Tipperary Goalkeeper' beside his name after repeated urgings from Leahy.

"I'm not the Tipperary goalkeeper any more," said Maher with a sad shake of his head. "Not after Reddin's performance today."

Time would prove Maher right, and the passage that Leahy wrote in his nephew's *little book was no less prophetic.*

"Sensation. Holycross win first County Championship 1948. We'll win the 1949 All-Ireland Final. Paddy Leahy."

••• ● •••

The 1948 County Final win wasn't just a red-letter day for John Doyle, it marked a watershed in Paddy Leahy's life, too.

The honour of picking the Tipperary team selection committee for 1949 now fell to Holycross, and they nominated Leahy as Chairman of the selectors.

In those days there were no team managers as we know them today, and, instead, the teams were prepared and selected by a committee of men who had equal voting rights.

Until Holycross' success in 1948 it was customary for the County Champions to supply four of a seven-man committee, so the Tipperary team was often heavily populated with players from their own club at the expense of picking the very best team in the county.

Holycross had the maturity though to make a far-reaching decision by only putting forward two of their own – Phil Purcell and Tom Dwan – along with three others, Leahy, John Joe Callanan, from Thurles Sarsfields, and County Board Secretary, Phil Purcell.

It was the model every other club adopted thereafter, and Leahy would retain his position as Chairman of the Selectors for the next seventeen years.

In theory his fellow selectors had as much power as he had, but, in practice, Leahy was the boss who called all the shots. He was the team manager before that title ever became a staple of the GAA.

Holycross have earned renown as the club who supplied two of the greatest hurlers to ever grace the game – Doyle and Pat Stakelum – but the club's decision to nominate Leahy after their '48 County Final success is arguably an even greater legacy.

He presided over the greatest era the county has ever known, and those who campaigned for him are in no doubt Tipperary wouldn't have achieved all they did in those seventeen years without Leahy's guiding hand.

Managing the Tipperary team was the job he was born to do. Hurling was his obsession, and he had a native cunning and instinct for the sport that bordered on the genius.

"He was full of psychology," remarked Doyle once. "He was a very unusual guy with a very unusual manner. I've never met a man like him before or since. I couldn't explain it to you, but one story sums him up.

"We were playing a match in Croke Park one day and I was playing at centre-back and having a reasonably good game. There was a fella beside me at wing-back who was having a poor match.

"Leahy walks in from the sideline with his hat down low as usual and says to the fella who wasn't going too well to switch with me because I was playing poorly.

"Leahy winks at me and walks over to the far sideline. The lad who went in centre-back played a blinder after that. There's not too many men who could be smart enough to pull a stroke like that.

"He had that something special, I don't know what it was. But he was wonderful. A once-off."

Living less than a mile from each other, Leahy and Doyle already had a warm relationship before 1949, but campaigning together with Tipperary was the glue that forged a special bond between the two.

Every morning they'd drink tea together at Holycross Creamery, and, over the course of the day, Doyle would always find another excuse to drop into Leahy's for a chin-wag.

If they weren't discussing hurling or farming, they were talking politics. Leahy had fought in the War of Independence and went on the run during the Civil War, which only endeared him further to Doyle who had very strong Republican convictions himself.

"They were very close in every way, politically and hurling-wise," says Francis Maher. "When Pat Stakelum would be passing Leahy's house he'd call in there too and the three of them would have sessions of their own.

"Oh, they'd be sorting everything out. Hurling, politics, local issues and further afield."

Leahy's stewardship of Tipperary would be hugely influential in Doyle's development as a hurler, but even before his mentor took charge of the team

Doyle had already made his first big breakthrough at senior inter-county level.

He came on as a sub in the delayed 1948 League Final against Cork – played four weeks after Holycross were crowned County Champions – but it wasn't a happy experience.

Thrown in at midfield with fifteen minutes left to play, he struggled to cope, both with the demands of the unfamiliar position and the fleet-footed Bernie Murphy, as Tipperary were well beaten by 3-3 to 1-2.

Despite the defeat, even reaching the League Final was viewed as progress because Tipperary's hurling stock was at a pretty miserable low by the time 1948 came to a close.

Since winning the 1945 All-Ireland Final they'd been heavily beaten in the first round of the Championship three years in a row by a Limerick team that itself was viewed as past its best.

Little was expected of the team in 1949, but, like all revolutions, Tipperary's would be sudden and spectacular.

Such a confluence of events conspired to transform them from no-hopers to National League and All-Ireland Champions in 1949 that it's easy to believe that destiny's hand weighed heavily on the team.

Two comets like Doyle and Leahy appearing in the sky together at the same time was portentous enough, but you didn't have to look far to find other shooting stars.

Tipperary legends like Tony Reddin, Mickey 'The Rattler' Byrne, Pat Stakelum, Paddy Kenny and Sean Kenny also blazed forth in '49, but perhaps the cases of Tommy Doyle and Jimmy Kennedy best sum up how serendipitous a year it was for Tipperary.

••• ● •••

April, 1949

Tommy Doyle walked slowly. He was in no rush to get to his destination.

When he marched in Tipperary teams before championship matches he made a point of sticking his chest out, pinning his shoulders back and swinging his arms forcefully like a solider on parade, but there was no such snap to his stride now.

In his hand was an envelope and in the envelope was the happiest chapter of his life, about to be posted into the past forever.

He paused by the letterbox for a whole minute, before finally depositing the envelope with a deep sigh. He was no longer a Tipperary county hurler.

He'd just made the hardest decision of his life, and now that it was finally done he felt no better about it. Still, better to jump yourself than be pushed, and he'd felt a hand leaning more and more heavily on his back.

The new Tipperary management had used him sparingly during the League and he hadn't featured at all in the League Final victory over Cork.

He was 34 and had won All-Irelands in '37 and '45 so he'd had a good innings, but confidence in his own ability was something Doyle never lacked and he was convinced he still had a lot more to give.

Known as 'The Rubber Man' for his ability to bounce back from punishment, fitness certainly wasn't an issue for the Thurles native.

He was an avid boxer as well as a hurler, and had built a homemade boxing gym where the walls were adorned by posters of his heroes, Joe Louis and Sugar Ray Robinson.

He'd train rigorously there every day, never drank or smoked and was in bed before 10pm every night. There might have been a good few miles on the clock, but the engine and bodywork were still in mint condition.

There was a touch of class to everything Tommy did on a hurling field. He was a stylish, swashbuckling player, and made sure to look the part by wearing his socks pulled up high and sporting a pair of shorts that were always brilliantly white.

The style was complemented by steel. Tommy was a born winner and a ferocious competitor on the hurling field, but now he'd never don the blue and gold again.

Dark thoughts of regret were still swirling through his mind when he was awoken from his sad reverie by a tap on the shoulder.

It was John Joe Callanan, the Tipperary selector, and possibly the last man Tommy was in the humour to talk to.

"Tommy, the very man," said Callanan with a broad smile. "How are you fixed for the first round of the Championship against Cork?"

"Actually, John Joe," replied Doyle, "I'm just after posting a letter of resignation to Phil Purcell. Shur ye hardly need me anyway at this stage?"

"By God we do. Tommy Purcell is sick and won't be able to play and we think you're the best man in the county to hold Christy Ring."

For a couple of seconds Doyle was struck dumb, then that familiar smile split his face and he stuck out his right hand to shake Callanan's.

Maybe because of his love for boxing, testing himself against the best, mano a mano, had always appealed to Tommy. For him, hurling was as much a duel between individuals as it was a team sport.

Few had ever bested the great Christy Ring in an individual battle, but 'The Rubber Man' would earn his place in hurling folklore by doing just that in spectacular fashion in '49.

•••●•••

When Jimmy Kennedy pushed open the front door of his digs on Leinster Road, in Rathmines, his eye was immediately caught by the brown manila envelope lying on the floor.

Inside was a letter from the Tipperary County Board Secretary, Phil Purcell, requesting that he fill out and return the enclosed inter-county transfer form and declare for his native Tipperary.

Kennedy read and re-read the letter a couple of times while he sipped a cup of tea at the kitchen table. When his cup was drained dry, he tore up the transfer forms and binned them.

As far as he was concerned his allegiances now lay with his adopted county, Dublin. He'd won two County Championships with UCD since arriving in '47, and had played in the '48 All-Ireland Final for Dublin.

Tipperary, it seemed, had only cottoned onto the fact that they were letting a special talent slip through their fingers when the man from Puckane captained Leinster in the '49 Railway Cup Final.

A tall and willowy forward, Kennedy wasn't the most physical player in the world, but he was a gifted sticksman who had a knack for being in the right place at the right time and the predatory instinct to make the most of almost every opportunity that came his way.

He was fastidious in his approach to the game. Most hurlers at the time were happy to take whatever stick was thrown to them from the sideline if they broke their hurley, but not Kennedy.

He would only play with a caman made by renowned Kilkenny hurley-maker, Tom Neary, and brought two of them with him to every match he played.

His perfectionist streak was also illustrated by his mechanical, but hugely effective method of free-taking.

He'd approach the ball at a right-angle to the goal-posts, and, when he lifted it, he stood almost directly over it so the handle of the hurley came back between his legs.

The sliotar would be raised above his head but he'd only strike it when it returned to knee height and make sure to follow through fully. The process never deviated and it was rare the result did either.

Specialist free-takers were thin on the ground in those days, and none was as consistently accurate as Kennedy.

Tipperary were in dire need of a high-scoring forward in '49, so even though Kennedy rebuffed their initial advances, neither Paddy Leahy nor Phil Purcell were ready to accept defeat.

The deadline for inter-county transfers was midnight on Easter Saturday, so that day Purcell travelled to Dublin and arranged to meet Kennedy in Barry's Hotel where he locked him in a room and wouldn't let him leave until he'd signed the transfer forms.

Kennedy took a lot of convincing because he wasn't sure he'd be a first choice pick for Tipperary. The deadline had passed by almost two hours before he put ink to paper but Purcell somehow still ensured the transfer was ratified.

Not only would Kennedy nail down a place in the Tipp team in '49, he'd finish the championship campaign with a total of 6-37 from six matches.

••• • •••

Tommy Doyle and Jimmy Kennedy were coaxed back into the fold after the '49 League Final victory over Cork, a match that didn't feature John Doyle either.

He'd seen action in the League up until then, but in a final trial match between a 'probables' and 'possibles' team, his under-par showing for the 'probables' saw him miss out on selection for the final itself.

His grand entrance would have to wait, but other newcomers had already strode onto centre-stage, most notably goalkeeper Tony Reddin.

His dashing style of play in that '49 League Final both won and struck fear into the hearts of Tipperary fans.

Reddin wasn't just a shot-stopper, he was a showman. Rather than take the safety first option of batting a ball clear whenever it came his way, he preferred to kill it dead on his hurley, take it in hand and dash his way clear of the crowded goal-mouth.

Just when it looked like he was going to be bulldozed into the ground by an onrushing opposition forward, he'd produce a side-step of such exquisite timing that even the spectators in the stand would almost slip off their seats.

Reddin's coup de grace was pretty special too. He'd open his broad shoulders and drive the ball such a distance that those who were seeing the feat for the first time would utter an involuntary oath.

He did all this with a hurley that, even by the day's standards, looked more like a medieval instrument of war. It was almost twice as heavy as an average hurley, and its narrow bas was encased in four evil-looking metal hoops.

And, unlike other hurleys, the top of the bas was just as thick as the bottom of it because Reddin didn't want it twisting in his hand when he attempted to save a well-struck shot.

It wasn't just his hurley that Reddin was fastidious about, his training regime was also specifically tailored for the requirements of goalkeeping.

He strengthened his arms and shoulders by cutting turf and stacking it as high as he could, and would then take a 30-yard run at the exposed bank left behind and drive into it, shoulder first.

For a time he'd also pepper the bog walls with punches to harden up his hands, but stopped doing this after spearing his fist one day on a shard of bog-oak.

That wasn't the only unusual training accident he suffered. Cross-country running was also a big part of his regime, but one day he got more than he bargained for when he jumped over a ditch to find that the drop in the other side was considerably steeper than he imagined.

He was just as conscientious about developing his hurling skill as he was his athleticism. He grew up on a farm, and even when the day's labour required him to plough a field the hurley wouldn't leave his hand.

The well-trained horse could be trusted to plough a straight line with little or no direction, so Reddin would walk along behind it, driving a sliotar straight up into the air and killing it dead when it returned from orbit.

His flamboyance on the field wasn't all that intrigued Tipperary fans, the fact that Reddin wasn't one of their own gave him an added air of mystery.

A native of Mullagh, in Galway, he'd hurled for his native county before moving to Lorrha in 1947.

The presence of another great goalkeeper in Sean Duggan was a considerable barrier to him really making his name with Galway, and an innate shyness probably did him no help either.

He had been born almost completely deaf and this, in turn, meant he developed a speech defect, so in his younger years Reddin wasn't inclined to push himself forward.

When he moved to Lorrha though, the local priest, Fr O'Meara, developed a friendship with him and did much to develop his confidence by travelling with him to matches and supporting him in every way he could.

Reddin's cause with Tipperary was helped hugely too by the presence of Tony Brennan at full-back.

Brennan had briefly hurled with Reddin in the Galway colours before returning home to Clonoulty to take over the family farm, so he knew his idiosyncrasies well and immediately forged an instinctive understanding with him on the field of play.

In that '49 League Final both men performed heroically and the name Tony Reddin adorned every match report the following day, though typical of Tipperary's new man of mystery, 'Tony' wasn't even his real name.

He'd been christened Martin but in his youth had always gone by the pet name, Thaudy. When he moved to Lorrha and introduced himself as such the locals presumed he was trying to say Tony but couldn't enunciate the name properly because of his speech defect.

Reddin didn't bother trying to correct them, so Tony he became and Tony he would remain.

Tipp's new goalkeeper had performed with such dash in the League Final that he was retained for the first round of the Championship along with five of the same six defenders, the only change was Tommy Doyle's introduction for the ill Tommy Purcell who had contracted TB and would tragically die a few months later.

Tipperary's victory over Cork in the League Final had heightened interest in their Championship showdown, and the capacity crowd of over 40,000 that flocked to Limerick for the latest instalment weren't disappointed.

A rollicking game of hurling that swung to and fro eventually ended in a 3-10 apiece draw, the impressive work of a Jimmy Kennedy-inspired Tipperary attack undone by some slack defending in the closing minutes.

A lack of ruthlessness and physicality in their full-back line had been exposed by Cork's late equalising goal and point that came after long solo-runs by Jack Lynch and Bernie Murphy, and Paddy Leahy reckoned he knew just the man to supply both qualities for the replay.

John Doyle's hour had come.

CHAPTER 8

June 26, 1949, Limerick.

Munster SH Championship first round replay v Cork.

Rivers had been hushed and the countryside burnt brown by the three-week heatwave that showed no sign of easing its fiery grip.

Limerick City's concrete arteries were choked with a dry dust and tarmac ran like warm treacle where it wasn't shielded by shade.

Even the mighty Shannon seemed cowed by the blazing sun, the stench that rose up from its exposed bed and banks hanging over the city like a sour shawl.

By 11am thousands of tightly-packed Tipperary and Cork fans stood waiting for the Gaelic Grounds to open, their impatient mood salved little by the high-pitched notes of the two blind fiddlers who busked for coppers before the stadium's locked gates.

Three hours before throw-in the ground was already wedged and red-faced stewards struggled manfully, but unsuccessfully, to prevent the banks of swaying masses from bursting out onto the sidelines.

Respite from the sun was sourced however possible. Handkerchiefs were knotted atop ever-reddening heads, and umbrellas more used to rain were opened against the rays.

One canny entrepreneur ahead of his time made a killing with the novel idea of bottling water and selling it, but a rival flogging ice-cream didn't fare so successfully, much of his stock turning to curdled milk before he could off-load it.

The Tipperary was a temporary structure that amounted to little more than a wooden hut, and inside its thin walls Doyle was sweating as much as the hottest supporter on the terrace.

One man dominated his thoughts – Cork corner-forward, Mossie O'Riordan. Six-foot tall and powerfully built, O'Riordan was also uncommonly skilful for such a big man.

He'd be no easy customer to deal with, and as Leahy gave the order to leave the dressing room, Mickey The Rattler Byrne leaned across to offer his tuppence-worth of advice to the 19-year-old.

"Doyle, don't ever tell him you're going to hit him," said The Rattler, with his eyes already narrowed for the battle ahead.

Leaving the dressing room was like running from an oven into a furnace, and, as the teams paraded around the scorched pitch together, dust rose in their wake like talc from beneath the dead grass.

The drawn match had been open and free-flowing but, like many replays, the second encounter was anything but.

There were scores to be settled on both sides, and Christy Ring took less than a minute to ink his.

Tommy Doyle had held him scoreless from play in the drawn match, and, under the first high ball that came down between the pair, Ring let it be known he wouldn't be so easily tamed this time.

Doyle staggered from the exchange with blood gushing freely from a gaping head-wound, but The Rubber Man quickly returned to the fray shrouded by a hastily wrapped bandage that turned red and then brown as the blood dried quickly under the blazing sun.

He was the first casualty, but there were many more to come. It seemed as though the suffocating heat had risen the dander of both teams like mercury, because, all over the pitch, fiery exchanges were breaking out.

●●●●●●●

Three other Tipperary players – Tony Brennan, Sean Kenny and Seamus Bannon – would also finish the match with their heads bound by bloody bandages and, with ever-increasing frequency, the game had to be halted while the over-worked Order of Malta attended to injuries on both sides.

Whenever the referee did call a time-out, players on both sides would fall to the ground, eager to make the most of the temporary reprieve.

The mood on the field of play wasn't long spreading to the crowd. Stewards struggled to hold back fans on the sideline keen to administer justice for the crimes on the pitch, while many supporters on the terraces chose to turn on one another with fists raised.

Amidst all the madness, Doyle's debut didn't get off to the most ideal start as O'Riordan slipped him for the very first point of the match, but with every passing minute he grew with the game.

Cork were dominating play for long stretches, but they were finding out the hard way that the newly-cast Tipperary full-back line of Doyle, Brennan and Byrne was a formidable obstacle.

The Rattler, in particular, was revelling in the lawless mood that gripped the game, displaying an ability to finish something before it had even started that would become his hallmark.

Further out the field the bloodied Tommy Doyle was continuing to stifle Ring, while, in midfield, Pat Stakelum and Sean Kenny were also hurling up a storm.

Kenny was known as 'The Iron Man from Borrisoleigh' and it was an apt moniker. Lean and muscular, he liked to show off these attributes by rolling up his jersey sleeves high past his bulging biceps.

Those guns weren't just for show either – there were few better practised in the art of delivering a sickening shoulder charge than Kenny.

His other talent was for taking the fight to the opposition by driving down the middle of the field on a solo run, a tactic that was rare for the times because its exponents tended to come to unfortunate ends.

That was Kenny's fate on two occasions against Cork, as twice his charge was halted by challenges that left him bleeding from the temple.

After he'd been bandaged up for the second time, he proved his spirit was unquenched by ripping off his boots and socks and casting them aside before tearing back into the fray again.

The Tipp backs and midfield might have been giving as good as they were getting, but everything they hit was being returned with interest because only Jimmy Kennedy was making any impact in the forwards.

Leading by 1-2 to 0-2 at half time, Cork were convinced they'd scored another goal in the second half when O'Riordan briefly escaped from Doyle's clutches and unleashed a pile-driver of a ground-stroke.

The sliotar fizzed through the air and appeared to hit the stanchion supporting the net at the back of the goal before rebounding a full 20 yards back down the field.

The Cork forwards roared "Goal!" as one, but the referee ignored their pleas and waved play on despite getting an earful from an increasingly frustrated Christy Ring who was still failing to escape from the web Tommy Doyle was weaving.

His mood wasn't helped when Tony Reddin made a couple of spectacular second-half saves, and the Cork star unloaded his frustrations by slashing the unfortunate Tipp custodian across the legs in the midst of yet another goal-mouth tear-up that ended without reward for the Rebels.

Cork kept attacking in wave after wave, but the full-back line of Byrne, Brennan and Doyle hurled like men possessed to hold back the tide.

Even their desperate resistance didn't look like it would be enough to save Tipperary though, because, with time almost up, they trailed by 1-5 to 0-5.

Jimmy Kennedy had accounted for all five of Tipp's points, but he wasn't done yet. In the final minute of normal time he lanced through the Cork defence one more time and smashed the ball to the back of the net for a dramatic equalising goal.

A minute later, the final whistle blew and hundreds of relieved Tipperary fans rushed onto the field to celebrate their team's unlikely salvation.

Confusion now reigned as to whether there would be extra time or a second replay. Both sets of exhausted players were in no humour for another 30 minutes action in the broiling conditions, but agreement had to be reached between both team managements.

Leahy strolled towards the middle of the field where he and his captain, Stakelum, met Cork trainer Jim 'Tough' Barry and the Rebels' captain, Jack Lynch, for a parlay.

"Begod lads," said Leahy, "'tis wonderful stuff, we can't be separated. What's going to happen at all?"

"I don't know," replied Lynch, "but I've had enough of it anyway."

"Arragh," said Leahy as he nudged Stakelum in the back, "shur we might as well sort it once and for all and play the extra-time I suppose."

Agreement reached, Leahy strolled over to the rest of his players, who lay scattered and broken on the battlefield, looking like they'd nothing more to give to the cause.

"Right, lads, everyone on their feet and into the dressing room," he ordered. "C'mon now, look lively."

They looked anything but as they limped their way back to the dubious sanctuary of their rickety dressing room, the Cork players choosing to continue resting their weary bones by lying out under the sun.

Almost everyone in the Tipperary dressing room was nursing some sort of war wound, but none was in as much pain as Tony Reddin. The belt he'd suffered from Ring had left one of his knees grotesquely swollen and he could hardly put his weight on it.

"Paddy, I can't play the extra time," said the goalkeeper as he held his leg out in front of him, his face drawn with pain.

Leahy examined the patient through narrowed eyes and delivered his verdict. "Listen to me young lad, you're playing the rest of this match and that's that, do ya hear me? And whatever you do, don't let them see you limping."

Reddin mumbled in doubtful agreement, and, as Leahy looked around the dressing room, all he could see were more sorrowful expressions.

With a hurley in his hand he stepped onto the low table in the middle of the room and hit it an almighty clatter that instantly quieted the room.

"All of ye listen up," said Leahy, his jaw set and his eyes burning. "Anyone who feels he cannot fight on for the blue and gold can go to that corner of the dressing room."

Every gaze followed the direction his outstretched finger pointed to, but none took up the invite.

"Now," said Leahy, his tone more even, "I want all of ye to take off yer shirts and come over here to Mick for a tonic."

Mick Blake, from Coolquill, was the team masseur and the most famous cross-country runner in the county.

As well as his usual bottles of wintergreen and other ointments, he'd also had the foresight to bring a milk churn full of cold water with him to Limerick that day.

One by one the Tipperary players were doused in the blessedly cooling waters by Blake while outside their opponents lay baking under the hot sun.

Blake and his fellow helpers from Coolquill Athletic Club also rubbed new life into aching muscles and fresh bandages were applied to the walking wounded as repeated requests from Munster Council officials for the Tipperary team to return to fray were ignored.

"Let them wait," growled Leahy.

Twenty minutes passed without any sign of the Tipp team emerging from their conclave. Hundreds of fans were camped outside the dressingroom, some occasionally trying to burst their way through to see what was going on.

Someone shouted out that Tipp had thrown in the towel, and the rumour was swiftly relayed around to ground to great cheers from the Cork fans.

It was the Tipperary supporters turn to roar when their team suddenly burst on to the field in a blur of blue and gold, bearing little resemblance to the men who'd wearily hauled themselves away 30 minutes earlier.

Now it was they who were pinning a weary Cork team back into their own half, and a goal from centre-forward Mick Ryan just four minutes after the resumption propelled them to a 2-8 to 1-9 victory.

Cork fought grimly right to the death, but they simply couldn't overcome Tipperary's new effervescence.

Even when Christy Ring flung away his boots and socks to signify a renewed effort, he was unable to inspire his team like he had so often in the past.

"Christy, you can leave them on. You're not going to get any points today," said Tommy Doyle chirpily into the Corkman's ear.

The Rubber Man was true to his word, his famous feat of holding Ring scoreless for 90 minutes over two matches franking his status as a Tipperary great.

The veteran had played his part, but the day really belonged to the new generation. John Doyle, Pat Stakelum, Jimmy Kennedy, Tony Reddin, Mickey Byrne and Sean Kenny had won their first ever Championship match in the blue and gold, and they were only getting started.

A new dawn for Tipperary hurling had broken, on the hottest day of the year.

• • • ● • • •

While Tipperary were slogging their guts out against Cork, Clare were quietly preparing an ambush.

Under the watchful eye of Fr Paddy Solan they'd undergone a rigorous training camp in Lisdoonvarna and came into the Munster semi-final in the shape of their lives.

The Clare footballers had already beaten Kerry in the football Championship and the tens of thousands that travelled for the match against Tipperary testified to belief in the Banner County that they could take another big scalp.

That confidence looked justified when their team led by two points with ten minutes to play, but a Bob Stakelum goal for Tipperary, and an inspirational three-point cameo from substitute Tommy Ryan, eased Tipperary to a 1-15 to 1-7 victory.

Doyle had held his man, PJ Quane, scoreless but his instinct to drive forward saw him caught out of position on a couple of occasions and he was dropped for the team for the Munster Final against Limerick.

Either Leahy had a late change of heart or it was a ploy all along to get the best from his young charge because, in the dressing room before the match, he announced that Doyle would start, wearing No. 17.

Once again Leahy's faith was justified because Doyle produced his best match yet in the blue and gold as Tipperary just about edged to a 1-16 to 2-10 victory, having trailed by 2-8 to 0-10 at half time.

For the first time in four years Tipperary were crowned Munster Champions. It had been a hard, bruising campaign, but the reward for Tipperary's young team was an easy passage to the All-Ireland Final.

Antrim were swatted aside 6-18 to 1-4 in the All-Ireland Semi-Final, which set up a final showdown with an unheralded Laois team who had shocked Kilkenny in the Leinster Final and then beat Galway in the other All-Ireland Semi-Final.

There was a touch of glamour about the mystery men of Laois, particularly captain Paddy 'Rusty' Ruschitzko who had been born in New York to a Polish emigrant father and Irish emigrant mother.

The novel pairing captured the public's imagination more than any other

All-Ireland Final had for years, so much so that 30 'special' trains were laid on to ferry hurling enthusiasts from all over the country to Dublin.

When Tipperary had played in the 1945 All-Ireland Final only one special train left Thurles on the morning of the match for which all seats had been booked beforehand.

Hundreds more tried to board it regardless, and even though its doors were locked to anyone without a ticket, dozens managed to force their way through open windows even as it was pulling out of the station.

Four years later, there was an even bigger buzz in the county in the run-up to the All-Ireland Final, so Paddy Leahy took steps to ensure his young players wouldn't be distracted too much ahead of the biggest match of their lives.

Normally Tipperary would stay in Barry's Hotel in the City Centre on the night before the All-Ireland Final, but Leahy didn't want his players exposed to the hundreds of Tipperary fans who would also be congregating at the landmark hotel that night for the traditional pre-match session.

His brother, Johnny, was friends with the President of Blackrock College in Dublin, so he arranged for the Tipperary team to instead stay there the night before the big match.

The chances of running into a hurling fan in the greatest rugby nursery in the country were slim to none, and the greatest inconvenience the players had to put up with was being quartered together in eight-bed dormitory rooms.

They were all tucked up in bed before 10pm on the Saturday night, and, after breakfast the following morning, a couple of relaxing hours were idled away pucking a ball or two on the Blackrock rugby pitch and watching the steamboats puffing their way from Dun Laoghaire harbour to England.

It was only on the bus journey from Blackrock to Croke Park that the players were exposed to the pageantry of All-Ireland Final day, whereas their Laois opponents had endured a busy morning of meeting and greeting friends, family and assorted supporters in their city centre hotel.

Their contrasting preparations must have played a part in what happened next. Laois failed miserably to rise to the occasion and Tipperary stormed to a hugely anti-climactic 3-11 to 0-3 victory, holding their opponents scoreless for the entire second half.

Doyle, Brennan and Byrne ground the Laois full-forward line into dust, and, further out the field, every other Tipp player won their individual battles too.

Even when centre-back Flor Coffey was forced to go off injured it didn't knock a beat out of Tipp.

Tommy Doyle moved to centre-back and hurled up a storm while Paddy Kenny, Sean's younger brother, came on as a sub and scored the goal that helped Tipperary into a 1-5 to 0-3 half-time lead.

They took total control in the second half as midfielders Sean Kenny and Phil Shanahan swept aside the much-vaunted Laois pairing of Joe Styles and Billy Bohane, while, in attack, Jimmy Kennedy capped off an incredible year with a haul of 2-4.

The celebrations that followed that evening were more austere than ribald. The majority of the panel were pioneers, and there was very little carousing at the reception for the team organised by the Dublin-based Tipperary Association in Clery's Ballroom.

Speeches were given by assorted dignitaries, from Dan Morrissey, the Government's Minister for Industry and Commerce, to Michael Kehoe, the President of the GAA.

The biggest cheer of the evening though was reserved for Laois captain Paddy Rustchizko, who dropped by to congratulate Tipperary on their victory.

Music and dance followed the dinner and speeches, but Doyle and his team-mates were back in their Blackrock College dorms before midnight.

The Tipperary team might have been keeping things low-key, but their fans made sure to pick up the slack.

When the team train pulled into Thurles train station the following Monday night, thousands of cheering supporters from all corners of the county had gathered there to greet them and the night sky was lit up by a huge brazier burning a welcome atop the Abbey Road Railway Bridge.

Firebangers had been laid on the tracks, so as the steaming train slowed to a halt, staccato explosions erupted beneath its steel wheels and fog signals split the air.

Loudest of all though was the roaring that acclaimed Pat Stakelum when he emerged from the train holding the Liam McCarthy Cup aloft and was chaired through the crowd by Phil Purcell and John Maher, the 1945 Tipperary captain.

When the players had eventually squeezed through the throngs on the station platform they climbed onto a couple of open-top lorries that slowly made their way along a packed Friar Street to Liberty Square.

Leading the procession was the Sean McDermott Pipe Band and, alongside the trucks marched boys carrying blazing torches that lit up cheering faces and gave colour to waving flags.

After a lap of Liberty Square the procession halted at the Archbishop Croke Memorial where Pat Stakelum gave a heartily acclaimed speech before the players and officials retired to the Glenmorgan House restaurant for supper.

When the team had eaten their fill, Stakelum re-emerged with the Liam McCarthy Cup and tied it with a piece of string to the handlebars of his bicycle.

Along with Doyle and the rest of the Holycross contingent he headed for home and was aided on his way by the back-slapping crowd that still waited outside the Glenmorgan for another glimpse of their heroes.

At the cross of Killinan the Cup came loose and fell to the ground with a great clatter. Three years would pass before it slipped from Tipperary's grip again.

CHAPTER 9

Tim Doyle and his neighbours Jim Kennedy, Jack Bannon and Tom Pollard sat around the fire, their conversation as warming as the burning wood that crackled and popped in the hearth before them.

Most Saturday evenings they'd congregate at Doyle's where they'd unravel the week's goings on in the parish and further afield.

Any minor scandal was enthusiastically aired and gratefully received, but the conversational staples rarely extended beyond talk of farming and hurling.

"God, my young lad didn't play great at all last Sunday, did he?"said Tim with a grimace and slow shake of the head as he carefully thumbed tobacco into his pipe.

His companions exchanged knowing glances. Tim's routine was well-worn at this stage, but they never tired of humouring him.

"God no," replied Kennedy, "shur didn't he nearly bate them on his own, single-handed, in the second-half."

"Maybe he wasn't too bad at all, I suppose," nodded a pleased Tim as he puffed his pipe to life with practised ease and flicked the dead match into the fire.

"He's a good auld trier anyway."

The front door swung open after a couple of warning knocks and the smiling face of Mikey Ryan peered around it.

"Well, how are the men?" enquired the 15-year-old as he came into the room.

"Ah, young Mikey, not a bother on us at all, and yourself?"

"The solid finest, Tim, thanks," replied the youngster as he made a beeline for the radio quietly playing a ditty in the background and turned it up as loud as he could before joining the men at the fire.

"God Almighty, Mikey, that bloody thing is fierce high altogether," said Kennedy, "would you ever go back and turn it down a bit?"

"Sorry, Jim," said Mikey, who only slowly made his way back to the blaring radio

after first re-tying a shoelace that appeared perfectly knotted to begin with.

A good deal of humming and hawing followed before he finally managed to locate the suddenly elusive volume knob, and it was only after considerable direction from the increasingly frustrated men at the fireplace that he managed to lower the music to a level they were happy with.

All the while John Doyle was waiting patiently behind the wheel of the Morris Eight parked in the haybarn.

As soon as he heard the music blare a few seconds after watching his young undercover agent enter the house he gave the order to Philip Maher: "Now, Philip, push as hard as you can."

With the gearbox in neutral the car moved easily down the lane and silently ghosted its way past the house and out onto the road where Maher pushed it for another 100 yards before Doyle finally gunned the engine.

His breathless accomplice joined in the passenger seat and the pair lit off for the dance in Thurles, eagerly anticipating the impressed looks their carriage would win them from the young ladies there.

"He'll surely know you're after taking it," said Maher.

"That man never notices. He hasn't caught me once," replied Doyle confidently.

The last thing Tim Doyle did every night of the year was stroll up to the cattle shed and make sure everything was as it should be.

When he passed the haybarn he saw his son had stolen off in the car yet again. He paused for a second, allowed himself a warm chuckle, and continued on his way.

••• ● •••

The 20-year-old Doyle was a good-looking young man, and he knew it.

He might have looked rough and ready when working on the farm, but when he ventured forth at night he took care to make the most of what God had given him.

His shock of black hair was carefully moulded into a sleek and glossy mane by a liberal application of Brilliantine, and whenever a lock threatened to fall from place it was quickly tamed by the comb he carried with him.

As catches go, there were few more prized amongst the young women of Mid-Tipperary than the Holycross farmer.

The '49 All-Ireland win had earned him fame throughout the county; he was tall, dark and handsome, and, at a time when cars were a very scarce commodity, the fact that he drove one was another considerable point in his favour.

When Doyle walked into a dance hall everyone reacted to his arrival. Men near him would square their shoulders and stand a little straighter, and women would glance his way and whisper to one another behind their hands.

The hottest night-spot in Tipperary was Kenny's Dance Hall in Borris-Ileigh. It was run by Doyle's Tipperary team-mate, Sean Kenny, and attracted the best musicians in the country.

Big Bands, such as The Clipper Carlton drew massive crowds. Dressed in tuxedos, they'd play seated on a raised stage while men lined one side of the hall with women on the other.

If a young woman caught your fancy you had to pluck up the courage to cross the divide and pray she accepted your invitation to dance. There was no lonelier walk than having to return to your grinning friends on the other side of the hall if your advances had been spurned.

The dance floor would remain empty for the first song or two as the men chain-smoked nervously while the women waited patiently in perfumed anticipation. Eventually one brave soul would run the gauntlet and others quickly followed.

Doyle would never have been one of the first men to cross the dance floor. He'd have been fairly certain of a good reception if he did, but in his late teens and early twenties the confidence and self-assuredness he displayed on the hurling field weren't qualities that came easily to him off it.

In social settings in general he just wasn't the type to push himself forward or demand the audience of others, preferring to stay in the background and stick close to those he knew best.

As he grew older he became better at masking any shyness and insecurities he had, but, as a young man, he was more likely to be seen rather than heard.

That was his form in the Tipperary dressing room too, where he deferred to the older men and more exuberant personalities and quietly went about doing all he could to make himself a better hurler.

The successful 1949 campaign had reinforced both his and the entire team's self-belief, and, by the following year, it was clear they had matured into an even more potent force.

The full-back line of Doyle, Brennan and Byrne were now set in stone, and had developed an instinctive relationship with their goalkeeper, Reddin.

Brennan was the key figure of the foursome. A former solider who'd returned home to take over the family farm, he never lost the air of assurance and authority the army code had instilled in him.

He was a natural leader of men and fiercely protective of Reddin, who probably would never have made his name with Tipperary were it not for Brennan.

The two had played together with Galway when Brennan had been stationed there, so he wasn't at all put off by Reddin's deafness and speech defect in the way others were.

Brennan had total trust in his team-mate's ability, so much so that when a high ball was delivered towards the goal, he'd never try to catch it himself.

Instead he'd use his ferocious strength to keep the full-forward away from its flight-path and let it straight through to Reddin who could always be counted on to claim it safely.

Once Reddin had won the ball, Brennan and Doyle would use their considerable bulk to hold back or flatten any forward who tried to run in on him, while Byrne could always be relied upon to clear a path out of the goal-mouth schemozzle for the goalkeeper.

He weighed less than 11 stone so he wasn't a big man like Brennan and Doyle, but what Byrne lacked in size he made up for with utter ruthlessness.

Off the field you couldn't meet a more good-humoured or likable fellow, but the Thurles man became a different animal when he crossed the white-wash.

His nickname – The Rattler – was an apt one considering his no-holds-barred style of play, but he didn't earn it because of his exploits on the hurling field.

When he was a youngster a cowboy serial was showing in Delahunty's Cinema in Thurles every week and the baddie of the piece was know as the 'The Rattler'.

When he'd appear on the screen all of the other young boys in the cinema would boo except for Byrne, who would leap from his seat and roar, 'Come on The Rattler!'

His moral compass could be dubious on a hurling field too, and, over time, he earned a well-deserved reputation as the Tipperary team's most enthusiastic and effective enforcer.

The Rattler's favourite tactic when a corner-forward attempted to intercept Reddin was to meet him in the gullet with the length of his hurley and send him flying into the middle of the straining melee between Doyle and Brennan and their men.

With his path cleared, Reddin would sidestep to the right and have the time to deliver one of his trademark lengthy clearances.

Doyle, Brennan and Byrne weren't just very effective bouncers, they were also the most skilful hurling full-back line of the era.

Brennan had started his career as a full-forward so was well able to hurl, while Doyle and Byrne were both confident enough in their ability to play their man from the front rather than stay goal-side and hope to spoil him.

Doyle had one of the lengthiest clearances in the game, while Byrne was a sure enough sticksman to seek out his half-backs with short, wristy passes.

Reddin and his full-back line further gilded their growing reputations when Tipperary beat Kilkenny by 3-8 to 1-10 in the 1950 National League Final.

It was a highly charged and frequently ill-tempered match, as both sets of players fought desperately for the prize of a trip to New York for the winners.

Their League trophy retained, Tipperary started the defence of the Liam McCarthy Cup in impressive fashion as Limerick were beaten by 4-8 to 0-8, Jimmy Kennedy doing most of the damage with a personal haul of 3-6.

A three-point victory over Clare in the Semi-Final was much less convincing, but quickly forgotten as another battle with Cork loomed large.

The previous year's drama only served to heighten the anticipation for the latest instalment.

For many months after their defeat in '49 Cork had complained bitterly that they would have won the match had Mossie O'Riordan's 'goal' been correctly given.

They even went so far as to have a motion passed at the Munster Council that all goal-posts be equipped with corded rather than wire netting so the situation could never arise again of a ball rebounding back into play, as they claimed it had in Limerick.

A year on, the Rebels were determined to set the record straight. For the Cork team and supporters alike, revenge was the primary motivation as they prepared for the 1950 Munster Final in Killarney.

•••●•••

July 23, 1950, Munster Senior Hurling Final v Cork.

The mood in Killarney had been souring with every passing hour.

Staggering supporters seeped from packed pubs onto the streets and the usual pre-match to and fro banter was tainted by alcohol-fuelled belligerence.

Many were only topping up from the previous night when every single hotel room in Killarney had been filled, but the Cork trains that had arrived very early that morning had also deposited a thirsty cargo.

Some were already spoiling for trouble by the time they finally left the pubs and weaved their way to the ground, and the scene that greeted them there quickly turned an already strained atmosphere a lot uglier.

The Fitzgerald Stadium stewards were utterly unprepared for the deluge of supporters that descended on them, and a terrible crush quickly developed around every gate and stile that led into the ground.

Both stands were already full before the minor match even took place, and when the stewards tried to turn back any more fans from entering through those gates, chaos quickly took hold.

One gate was ripped from its hinges and a torrent of supporters quickly flooded through it, while hundreds more desperately scaled the walls.

The official attendance was 40,000, but up to 20,000 more forced their way into the ground without paying and all around the stadium ugly scenes were breaking out between both sets of fans.

The hundreds who forced their way onto the sidelines were blocking the view of the fans who'd queued early to get a prime spot but who now had no option but to stand on their seats.

This, in turn, obstructed the view of those on the embankment behind the seating area, who now began throwing sods of earth, bottles and other missiles to persuade those standing to sit back down.

The anarchy spread to the pitch before the ball was even thrown in when a knot of Cork fans burst from the sideline and attacked Tipperary's Sean Kenny.

Alcohol was surely the spark, but Kenny's demeanour possibly threw petrol on an already flammable situation.

He gloried in his status as a hurling tough-man, and before matches liked to stride purposely about the field, flexing his thickly knotted muscles with a half-cracked glint in his eye.

A sideline full of Cork fans roaring abuse wasn't the sort of thing to unnerve Kenny, so he warmed up a couple of yards from them by violently slashing imaginary ground strokes with his trademark reckless grin.

Eventually a couple of Cork fans made a burst for him with arms and legs flailing, but just as Kenny freed himself and was about to use his hurley as a scythe, Cork's Jack Lynch ran between him and his assailants.

Of all the players on the Tipperary team to tackle, the inebriated Cork fans had chosen most unwisely. The 'Iron Man' wasn't the type to be trifled with, and Lynch's intervention was probably more of a saving grace for them than it was for Kenny.

The start of the match did little to cool tempers on the sideline. A wave of angry Cork fans swept onto the pitch again when Christy Ring was flattened in the opening minutes, and mini-invasions followed every other testy exchange on the field.

Despite the madness that was swirling all around them, the Tipperary and Cork players were somehow managing to produce an absolutely classic match of hurling that bore little similarity to the slug-fest in Limerick the previous year.

The ball was moving swiftly from one end of the field to the other as both teams strung attacking moves of real dash and pace together but, as the half wore on, Tipperary started landing the heavier blows.

Jimmy Kennedy was flitting here and there with his usual lethal elegance, and Paddy Kenny was busy confirming his status as one of the most promising young hurlers in the country.

He wasn't blessed with the same raw strength as his bull-dozing, older brother Sean, but he more than compensated with stealth and skill and was also able to generate enormously powerful shots with his distinctive left-handed stroke.

In a club match for Borris-Ileigh the previous year he'd struck a shot of such venom whistling past the ear of Boherlahan's Jimmy Maher that everyone who saw it agreed it would have killed the little man stone dead had it hit him in the head.

Cork goalkeeper Tom Mulcahy had no hope of stopping a similarly emphatic drive midway through the first half as Tipperary gradually took control of the match.

"Did you score that goal, little boy?" queried Kenny's marker, Gerry O'Riordan, as he congratulated the Tipp corner-forward with tasty dig in the ribs. "I hope you enjoyed it, because you won't be doing it again."

Kenny's goal helped Tipp into a 1-13 to 1-6 half-time lead, and, with every component part of the team ticking over nicely, they were starting to look comfortable.

Tony Reddin and the full-back line of Doyle, Brennan and Byrne had been supreme for the first half, but the vision that awaited them when they trotted back onto the field from the dressing-room suggested the second 30 minutes wouldn't be so straightforward.

The Cork fans had ripped up the stake-wire fence in front of the terrace and were now crowded right behind the goal and along the end line.

The four men were met with volleys of abuse as they took up their positions, but none was of the type to blink.

Reddin, especially, was determined not to be cowed. After the previous year's epic against Cork, Paddy Leahy had taken him aside and warned him that he had to toughen up and learn how to look after himself because Cork were "a rough shower".

As Doyle walked towards the baying mob he knew they probably thought he'd be the weakest link because he was the youngest, so he gripped his hurley hard, slung back his shoulders and made himself look as big as he possibly could.

One Cork supporter clearly remained unconvinced, because he lurched from the herd and made for Doyle with his fists raised.

He beckoned the 20-year-old to come hither, but when the undaunted Doyle stepped in his direction the would-be pugilist quickly danced his way further up the field and waved his fists in another Tipperary player's face instead.

Once again, when it looked like his invite was about to be accepted, he moved on and continued to weave and waltz his way around the pitch in this way with his dukes up without ever managing to actually deliver a blow.

Eventually a fellow Cork fan who had grown tired of his ineffective charade ran on and pulled him away by the scruff of the neck to a great chorus of cheers.

The start of the second half was delayed by yet another pitch invasion, and, when it finally got under way, Christy Ring dragged his team back into the contest by slaloming through the Tipperary defence in typical style and rifling the ball the back of the net.

Before Cork could build up any more momentum though, Paddy Kenny lashed home his second goal of the match.

As he wheeled past his marker O'Riordan, he roared: "I got that one too, Gerry, stick it up your backside!"

Cork kept coming forward in waves but were frustrated time and again by Reddin, who pulled off two miraculous saves from Lynch and Ring.

A by now totally frustrated Lynch decided it was time something was done about the cat-like goalkeeper, so he beckoned over wing-forward Willie John Daly and issued some specific instructions.

"Next time you get a ball around the middle of the field, lob a high one into the square and I'll take care of Reddin."

Daly nodded and a couple of minutes later carried out his orders to the letter. As Reddin waited to claim the dropping ball Lynch charged like a bull straight at the goalkeeper.

Reddin sensed the imminent danger, so immediately after catching the ball he sidestepped nimbly as Lynch crashed into the post and ended up in a crumpled heap in the back of the net.

The Cork TD and future Taoiseach's woes weren't over yet. Sean Kenny made it his business to exact retribution, and shortly afterwards nearly cut his victim in two with an almighty shoulder that sent Lynch flying over the sideline.

As the match drifted away from their team the Cork fans grew more and more belligerent, and when a Jimmy Kennedy point put Tipperary 2-17 to 2-9 ahead with just ten minutes remaining, hundreds invaded the pitch from behind Reddin's goal and forced referee Liam O'Donoghue to call a halt to the match.

The overworked Fitzgerald Stadium stewards had given up entirely by now, and it fell to the Cork players to try and persuade their countymen to leave the field.

Even fan favourites, Ring and Lynch, were having little joy talking sense into the maddened horde, the latter receiving a punch, which he returned with considerable interest.

After a 15-minute hiatus the match was eventually started again, but by now the area around Reddin's goal was completely lawless.

The crowd continued to press onto the field around the goalkeeper and his full-back line like the horns of an angry bull, and Reddin was pelted with stones, bottles and sods of earth.

At one stage someone flung an orange in his direction, and he infuriated his tormenters even more by deftly controlling it on his hurl and eating a piece of it before smashing the rest back to where it had come from with his hurley.

He made one flying save despite having a hat thrown in his face as he dived across the goal, and, shortly afterwards, a coat was thrown over him as he tried to clear the ball.

One Cork fan got more than he bargained for when he pulled Reddin back as he tore from his goalmouth after intercepting yet another attack. The goalie lashed back at his assailant and made a satisfyingly solid contact with his hurley that quickly set him free.

Reddin's resistance was finally broken when the crowd kicked a ball that was going wide back towards the goalmouth and Lynch doubled it home. The goal was allowed to stand, and Cork followed up with two quick-fire points to reduce the gap to just three.

By now the net behind Reddin had been pulled down and one of his goalposts shaken loose of its mooring, but the latest act of intimidation backfired badly.

A long delivery from midfield looked like it was on its way over for another Cork point until an unbowed Reddin yanked the loose pole towards him so the ball went narrowly wide instead.

The umpire was attacked by the mob when he failed to raise the white-flag, and Reddin had to step in with his hurley to shield the unfortunate man's head from the bottles that were winging their way towards him.

"Reddin," roared one red-faced Cork-man. "When that final whistle blows you're a fuckin' dead-man."

The match ended in fittingly chaotic fashion a couple of minutes later when O'Donoghue called for full-time instead of awarding Cork a '65 after Tipperary knocked the ball over their own end-line.

The very second the referee's whistle blew, Reddin raced towards the middle of the field because he knew what was coming next.

The Cork fans behind the goal tore after him in a great big angry surge and the goalkeeper might have come to a sticky end had it not been for the quick thinking and bravery of his Lorrha mentor, Fr. O'Meara.

The priest could see his friend was in peril, so as soon as Reddin started to run from his goalmouth O'Meara raced in from the sideline with a group of Tipperary fans who hastily surrounded the goalkeeper.

Quick as a flash, O'Meara gave Reddin's hurley to a Tipperary County Board official, put his clerical hat on the goalkeeper's head and dressed him in a short-coat to disguise him from his would-be attackers.

The subterfuge prevented Reddin from being immediately swallowed whole by the mob, but when they realised who the man standing in the midst of the tight knot of Tipperary supporters were, things threatened to turn ugly again.

The presence of two more priests alongside O'Meara was Reddin's only saving grace. Drunk as they were, attacking men of the cloth was still a step too far for most of the Cork fans who, instead, turned their attentions to Liam O'Donoghue.

Just when things were looking black for the referee, Christy Ring stepped between him and his assailants with his hurley raised.

Luckily for O'Donoghue, Ringy was regarded by Cork fans to be even closer to God than a humble priest.

It would be a whole two hours though before the irate crowd would disperse altogether, and all that time Reddin was forced to stay on the field until his safe passage from it could be guaranteed.

The mood around Killarney remained poisonous long into evening as skirmishes broke out in the streets around the stadium, and it was only when the Tipperary team's convoy had driven six miles outside the town that they felt safe enough to pull over, tie the cup to the roof of the lead car, and fly blue and gold flags.

Reddin might have escaped the mob in Killarney, but there was no avoiding the huge crowd that waited in Thurles to welcome home the triumphant Tipperary team.

The goalkeeper was flung into the air again and again by a hammock of hands, the happy Tipperary supporters oblivious to the pain their hero was in from all the blows he'd suffered during the match.

It would take a couple of weeks before the welts and bruises had faded fully. And as he watched them turn from blue to brown to yellow, Reddin could only smile at the wisdom of Paddy Leahy.

Cork were indeed a rough old shower. But the goalie knew too he was plenty tough enough to handle them.

••• ● •••

Jimmy Kennedy waited at Puckane cross-roads, his hurley and sliotar helping pass the time.

He belted the ball as high as he could into the air and, on its return, killed it stone dead with a deft flick of his stick that stole gravity's thunder.

Kennedy's wrists could make a hurley talk, and the sliotar was an attentive pupil.

Through constant effort he made the game look effortless. A portion of every day was spent pucking a ball against a wall and he never tired of the practise.

Strike, kill, catch. Strike, kill, catch. Strike, kill, catch. It was never monotonous because every stroke had its own reward.

The satisfying hum than ran from the hurley through his bones after a perfectly struck shot. The happy pleasure of bending physics itself to his will with ash and leather.

There was no shot too audacious for him. No target too difficult.

His favourite party piece at Tipperary training sessions was to take a free from the corner-flag, steal a yard with the rise, and then angle the ball through the needle-eye gap between the posts.

As he was about to drive the ball heavenwards again he was paused by the low burr of a car engine in the distance.

Moments later Tony Reddin's hackney car hove into view, the goalkeeper piloting it with the usual disdain for speed that was starting to frustrate the team-mates he drove to every match.

Reddin stuck his arm out the window and hailed Kennedy happily with a cap gripped in his outstretched hand.

The target was irresistible. Kennedy took aim and lanced a shot at the still 20 yards distant car that ripped the cap clean from Reddin's grasp and carried it into the ditch.

The car nearly went the same way, such was the driver's shock. Reddin was still shaking his head in wonder when he eventually rescued his cap.

"By God, Jimmy, that was the best shot I've ever seen in my life. The Galway boys are in some trouble!"

• • • ● • • •

August 13, 1950, Tuam.
All-Ireland Semi-Final v Galway

Jimmy Kennedy lay in a crumpled heap on the ground while around him legs strained, hurleys clashed and voices screamed bloody-murder.

From the very first whistle Kennedy had been cynically targeted by the Galway defence, but now his marker had stepped over the line altogether by cleaving him with a vicious blow of his hurley that almost sparked a riot on and off the pitch.

The Galway defender who struck him had a reputation for losing the run of himself entirely when his dander was up, and Kennedy was later told this natural inclination had been further encouraged by the consumption of a couple of brandies in the Galway dressing-room before the game.

If the corner-back had been acting under instructions to neutralise Tipperary's dangerman, then he had carried them out most effectively.

Kennedy made no impact on the match, and without their attacking talisman's usual contribution, Tipperary were lucky to survive.

It required another goalkeeping masterclass from Reddin, some backs-to-the-wall hurling by Doyle and his comrades in the full-back line and a three goal haul by Paddy Kenny to eventually see them through a bitter game of hurling.

After the match a pale-faced Kennedy quietly undressed with his head down, and when he removed his playing gear everyone else in the changing room was hushed too.

His body was covered in an ugly lattice of welts and bruises of varying angry hues. The damage was more than skin-deep though.

Something within Kennedy was broken that day, and he was never the same hurler afterwards. The man who had done more than anyone else to win the '49 All-Ireland Championship for Tipperary wouldn't bend a major match to his will again.

• • • ● • • •

September, 1950, All-Ireland SH Final v Kilkenny, Croke Park.

Kilkenny men fell to ground like dead wasps as Doyle swatted them aside and launched yet another lengthy clearance that brought roaring Tipperary fans to their feet.

Kilkenny had been targeting the two youngsters in the Tipperary defence all match – Doyle and Jimmy Finn - but with little joy.

Doyle was hurling his greatest match yet in the blue and gold, and 19-year-old rookie wing-back, Jimmy Finn, was also announcing himself as something special, too.

His neatly coiffed hair and unassuming expression gave the Borris-Ileigh youth the look of a choir-boy, but he didn't hurl like one.

He was a son of the soil like Doyle, and allied with that natural farmer's strength was a crisp, close style of hurling that saw him do everything with perfect economy of movement.

Finn was clearly blessed with considerable mental strength, too, because he didn't blink at the prospect of making his debut in an All-Ireland Final.

Not only was he making his championship bow on the biggest stage of all, he also had the task of marking Jim Langton, who was the embodiment of all that was good about Kilkenny hurling.

A snake-hipped stylist who could filch points from all sorts of angles, Langton was at the peak of his powers in 1950 and, in the opening exchanges, it looked like Finn was struggling to cope with him as the Kilkenny half-forward clipped over two early points.

Their individual battle would be a microcosm of the game itself though, because as the match progressed Finn's confidence and dominance grew and so did Tipperary's.

They were lucky to only trail by 0-7 to 0-5 after a dour first 30 minutes, but slowly took a strangle-hold on the match in the second half as their defence squeezed the life out of the Kilkenny attack.

Finn was winning everything that came between him and Langton now, and drawing great gasps from the crowd with the murderous ground-strokes that would become his trademark.

His perfect timing and length of delivery had been honed by years of practise hitting 'droppers' with his uncle when the pair would walk the fields herding cattle.

A 'dropper' was the art of dropping the sliotar to the ground and then meeting it on the pull a millisecond after it bounced.

If you timed it perfectly you could hit the ball an almighty distance, and, with constant practise, Finn eventually developed a hurling stroke of prodigious timing and power.

Their defence might have been hurling their men to a standstill, but, with Jimmy Kennedy uncharacteristically subdued, the Tipperary forward line was struggling to make much headway at the other end of the field.

With time almost up they finally landed the first really telling blow of the match when Paddy Kenny wriggled free from the formidable attentions of Kilkenny full-back Pat 'Diamond' Hayden and scored a rasper of a goal.

Tipperary fans were still on their feet celebrating it when Kilkenny's Jimmy Kelly delivered a 70-yard drive that went straight to the net after Tony Reddin was barged over the line by Kilkenny full-forward Jack Mulcahy.

Despite the obvious foul, the green flag was risen and Kilkenny had closed to within a point again – 1-9 to 1-8.

"For God's sake Con, Reddin was taken out of it before the ball came near him," roared Pat Stakelum at referee Con Murphy.

"I know Pat, but I'm blowing the final whistle now so don't worry," replied Murphy sanguinely.

The Cork-man was as good as his word, and while Reddin's puck-out was mid-flight three shrill blasts crowned Tipperary as All-Ireland Champions for the second year in a row.

Ireland had been conquered again. America was next.

CHAPTER 10

The pilot walked across the tarmacadam with his usual relaxed stride, but the men who waited to board his airplane were struggling to look so sanguine.

Most of the Tipperary players had never flown before, and their first experience of it earlier that day hadn't gone so well.

Not long after flying out of Shannon their plane was forced to limp back to the airport after developing engine trouble.

Those who hadn't been edgy before that first aborted attempt to make it across the Atlantic certainly were now.

As usual, Mickey The Rattler Byrne was doing his best to lighten the atmosphere with some typically witty repartee, but he was having mixed results.

There was no shortage of laughter, but it came a little too quick and rushed because his team-mates were anxious to hide their nerves any way they could.

As the captain climbed the stairs to the plane he was halted in his tracks by a shout from The Rattler.

"Hey, captain, I hope this one flies a bit better than the yoke ye had us on earlier."

The pilot turned and looked down at the faces looking up at him, some smiling at their team-mate's impertinence, others still pinched with tension.

"Don't worry gentlemen, you're all in very safe hands. Try to relax. As I always say, if your time is up, there's not much you can do about it anyway."

"That's all very well," fired back The Rattler, "but if your time is up, we're all in trouble!"

• • • ● • • •

The mood amongst the Tipperary players lightened considerably once the Sabena DC6 had climbed skywards and levelled out at 18,000 feet.

The Rattler led the charge again and got a sing-song going with the aid of the trusty harmonica that was never far from his lips whenever the Tipp hurlers travelled together.

One by one the Tipperary players sang their party pieces, much to the bemusement of the passengers who had boarded the plane in Brussels and Manchester.

The only person who wasn't smiling was the member of the Tipperary party who lost his upper dentures in one of the plane's toilets after rushing into the cubicle to relieve a bout of air-sickness.

After informing his team-mates of his unhappy accident with a dismayed lisp, the man's humour wasn't helped much when The Rattler immediately launched into a rousing rendition of 'All I want for Christmas is my two front teeth'.

After a brief stop-over in Gander, Newfoundland, to refuel, the plane continued on to Idlewild Airport in New York where it made a fairly dramatic landing.

Just after it touched down on the runway, one of the wheels hit a small pothole and all the Tipperary players were thrown forward violently in their seats.

That fright was quickly followed by a more pleasant shock. As they alighted from the plane they were greeted by hundreds of well-wishers, flashing cameras and a squad of newspaper reporters.

The visit of the Tipp hurlers was big news, but the eager reporters were left more than a little stumped when team captain Sean Kenny began answering their many questions in Irish.

The players were booked into the Henry Hudson Hotel on West 57th Street for their two-week stay, slap-bang in the middle of Manahattan.

The two 'babies' of the team, Doyle and Finn, were quartered together and neither felt more assured than the other in their strange new surroundings as exotic sounds and smells drifted in through their hotel-room window.

Sleep didn't come easily for either of them that first night, but they did a bit better than some of their colleagues further down the corridor.

Tommy Doyle and The Rattler were woken at 2am by a staccato of desperate knocking on their bedroom door.

When Doyle gingerly eased the door ajar, he found himself looking into the frightened eyes of a pale-faced Tommy Ryan.

"What do you want at this hour of the night?"

"For God's sake, just let me in would you?"

Doyle obliged and a few seconds later Ryan's confused looking room-mate, Jimmy Kennedy, also arrived on the scene.

"What's the matter with you at all?" asked Kennedy.

"Did you not see what I saw?" replied Ryan.

"See what?" chorused his increasingly impatient friends.

"There was a black man with a hacksaw trying to cut through bars outside our window. I got out of there as quick as I could."

Ryan's team-mates were inclined to believe a vivid nightmare was the likeliest explanation, but none of them walked too confidently into the bedroom to examine whether the window bars had indeed been tampered with.

There was no sign of any damage, but Ryan was adamant he saw what he said he saw, and refused to sleep another night in the room.

If New York City seemed like a strange and forbidding place for some of the team that night, it was an entirely different story the following morning.

The team were driven to City Hall for an audience with New York Mayor Vincent Impellitteri, and the last few hundreds yards of the route was lined with thousands of cheering Irish-Americans.

A brass band accompanied a tenor singing 'Where the River Shannon Flows' as the team was introduced to the Mayor on the steps of City Hall. For the second day running the Tipperary hurlers were front-page news.

There was still a week to go to the 'Away' League Final against New York, but the players had plenty to keep them occupied in the meantime.

The Tipperary diaspora in New York couldn't do enough for their hurling heroes, and the players were showered with gifts and invitations to dinner.

There was no shortage either of people willing to show you the sights of the Big Apple, and the Grand Marshall of the Tipperary Men's Association in New York, Mick Flannery, made a point of taking the two youngsters, Doyle and Finn, under his wing.

On their second night in the city he brought them in his car on a tour of the hot spots of Manhattan Island.

Back home in Glenbane night-time was only dimly lit by paraffin lamps and a turf fire, so the 40 million lightbulbs that lit up Broadway struck Doyle dumb.

As Flannery's car cruised along, the sights that slid past the window were from another world altogether.

The pavements choked with a rush of humanity. The roads gridlocked with snub-nosed Buicks, elegant Cadillacs and sporty Chevrolets. The noisy shooting galleries and arcades. The theatres sprinkled with star-dust. The neon-lit Burlesque clubs that set young Irish minds racing.

For men used to the quiet countryside and small towns of Tipperary, New York was plugged into a different voltage altogether. The place was a sensory overload. Some of the Tipp players were frazzled by it, others energised.

Mickey Byrne, Tommy Doyle, Paddy Kenny and Jimmy Kennedy very much fell into the latter category.

A couple of days before the match against New York they accepted an invitation to appear on the WNBT Television programme, Broadway Open House that was broadcast to millions of homes across America.

The men took to the limelight like naturals. Doyle could sing like a lark and belted out 'Ireland, I love you', 'Acushla Macree' and 'My Heart's in Old Killarney' while the others supported him with harmonica, button-accordion and backing vocals.

The hyperactive host of the show, singer-comedian Jerry Lester, even found himself upstaged by the none-too-bashful Mickey The Rattler who wasn't the slightest bit overawed by a live studio audience.

The men caused such a stir that offers flooded in for them to tour the country as a musical act, and, by now, everyone wanted a piece of the Tipperary hurlers.

They accepted an invitation to visit West Point Military Academy where they played an exhibition match in front of 2,000 army cadets.

Younger soldiers who were being trained for mortal combat watched open-mouthed as the stick-bearing Irishmen tore into one another with a relish that soon had the spectators whooping and hollering in disbelief.

When the team got back to New York a beer company offered the very princely sum of $100 a man to be photographed drinking their beverage, but County Board secretary Phil Purcell knocked the proposition on the head because it ran contrary to the amateur code of the GAA.

His team-mates might have missed out on massive pay-day, but Tony Reddin came away from a New York with a priceless gift.

When he was in the city he was befriended by a Tipperaryman, Chris Cooney, from Moycarkey, who decided to do all he could to help the goalkeeper address his hearing and speech defects.

After a consultation with a specialist an operation was ruled out, but a hearing aid was recommended, a device that still wasn't available in Ireland.

The hearing aid that Cooney purchased for him was attached to a sizeable box that had to be carried everywhere in a special holster, but this was a small inconvenience as far as Reddin was concerned when weighed against the benefits.

For the first time in his life he was able to hear clearly and was finally free from the disability that, until then, had made him such a shy man who preferred to hover in the background rather than push himself forward.

Despite all the distractions, the League Final against New York was still very much the primary focus for all the players.

The prospect of going home beaten was unthinkable, and the fact that the New York team was a formidable outfit helped to concentrate minds.

The Americans boasted men like Kilkenny's Terry Leahy, Waterford's Phil Grimes and Kerry's Jimmy Smee, who had all been stars back home in Ireland before they emigrated, and the New York County Board had gone to considerable lengths to make sure their team was as well prepared as it could be.

The players were paid to take four weeks off work to train collectively, so by the time the match came around they were a very fit, well-drilled team.

The match was given a big billing in the New York press, but previews such as this one from esteemed sports columnist Bernard Peyton Junior suggested the American journalists weren't quite sure what to expect:

'NY and Ireland Will Vie at Old Hurling Sport – One of the Roughest of Games Pits Tipperary and Local Team at Polo Grounds.'

"Nearly a ton and a half of Irishmen from Ireland will engage a similar amount of Irishmen from New York at the Polo Grounds today in whacking at a horse-hide ball, ten inches around and at each other in an old-time, rough-and-tumble sport called hurling."

••• ● •••

Sunday, September 24, Polo Grounds.
National League Final v New York.

As the Tipperary and New York teams prepared to march around the Polo Grounds, John Doyle's eye was caught by New York captain Jimmy Smee who was fixing a pair of over-sized shinguards into his socks.

He tapped Mickey Byrne on the shoulder and pointed over at Smee. "What do you make of those things?"

The Rattler's face was immediately creased by those well-worn laughter-lines.

"Hey, Jimmy," he shouted over at Smee.

"You shouldn't have bothered with those yokes. We start from the head and work our way down." Considering The Rattler's reputation as a hard man, the New York captain wasn't sure whether to laugh or bless himself.

If the 30,000 enthusiastic fans who had paid in to watch the match were hoping for a tough, no-holds barred contest, they weren't disappointed.

The Polo Grounds was the home of Major League Baseball team the New York Mets, and the shortness of the pitch meant that the play was always crowded and the physical exchanges constant and robust.

Great clouds of dust rose up from the bone-dry surface wherever the players strained and tussled for possession, and the spectators lost sight of the ball altogether whenever it landed around the grassless baseball pitcher's mound at one end of the stadium.

The mound offered a unique challenge for Tony Reddin because it was placed just before his goalmouth.

The sliotar bounced unpredictably off it, and it also made diving to save shots a more painful business than usual. He learned that the hard way when he ripped his two knees asunder and had to scrape the clay clear from the wounds.

Despite the challenges posed by the under-sized pitch, the oppressive heat and their determined opponents, Tipp lead by 1-7 to 1-1 at half-time.

It looked like they were going to ease to a comfortable win when they increased the margin to eight points in the second half. The Polo Grounds erupted though when New York scored two late goals to close the deficit to just two points.

The Tipperary players were out on their feet by now, but were saved by the final whistle that brought the curtain down on a 1-12 to 3-4 victory.

The win was celebrated in fairly novel fashion that night. Part of the evening's entertainment was a Men's Beauty Pageant that all the Tipperary hurlers entered.

The judges were three female TV stars, but the eligible bachelors hoping to impress the glamorous trio were left disappointed when the only two married men on the team, Tommy Doyle and Mickey Byrne, were declared joint-winners.

The Beauty Pageant judges weren't the only women who took an interest in Tommy Doyle on the trip.

The Rubber Man had a reputation for being a little bit naive, which is probably why he thought nothing of it when a woman who was dolled up a little excessively engaged him in conversation outside of the Henry Hudson Hotel one night.

His tickled pink team-mates immediately copped that she was a prostitute touting for business, and got an even bigger laugh when Tommy shot the breeze with her for a few minutes before wishing her a warm good-night and rejoining his friends.

"Lads, I think that woman knows me," said Doyle to his smirking pals. "She was fierce friendly anyway. Isn't it a small world all the same?" His team-mates didn't have the heart to set him straight.

Their American sojourn was coming to an end, but there was time for one last adventure. The entire team was invited by the New York Chief of Police to attend the Heavyweight Boxing World Title fight between Ezzard Charles and Joe Louis in Madison Square Gardens.

This was a particular treat for Tommy Doyle whose own boxing gym at home in Thurles, was adorned with posters of Louis, but he was left disappointed when Charles fought his way to a unanimous victory over his ageing hero.

On October 4, the Tipperary team sailed for home aboard the SS Washington, 19 days after they'd first landed in New York.

The trip had done much to enhance their reputation at home and abroad, and in '51 they'd gild it even more by completing the three-in-a-row that would forever frank their status as one of the all-time great teams.

CHAPTER 11

As soon as Jimmy Finn spotted Paddy Leahy striding with intent towards the car, he leaped out of the driver's seat as quickly as he could.

He and Doyle had been chatting up their girlfriends in Chris Cooney's impressive V8-powered hackney: Jimmy and Maura Fitzgerald in the front seats, Doyle and Frances Finn in the back.

Cooney was one of the drivers who used to ferry the Tipperary players to and from matches and had parked his car as usual in Liberty Square while everyone ate their post-match meal in the Glenmorgan.

John and Jimmy's romantic endeavours had been spotted by some of their older team-mates who decided to have a bit of fun at the pair's expense.

"Hey, Paddy," shouted Sean Kenny over at Leahy, who was busy clearing his plate. "Young Doyle and Finn are cavorting with a couple of women in Cooney's Car. They'll have no strength left for hurling if you don't sort that out."

Leahy immediately rose from his seat and made for Cooney's Car. Finn saw him coming and scarpered, but Doyle didn't and paid the price.

Leahy flung open the back door of the car, unceremoniously grabbed Doyle by the forelock and pulled him head first from the car to a chorus of cheers from the Tipperary players that had gathered to watch the show.

"Young Doyle, don't ever let me catch you acting the maggot like that again when you're meant to be representing your county," said Leahy in as stern a tone as he could muster.

A scarlet Doyle mumbled an apology and was oblivious to the wide grin that creased Leahy's face when he turned on his heel and marched back to the Glenmorgan.

●●●●●●●

Doyle and his team-mates were hailed as heroes when they arrived home from the States, but they were afforded little time to walk on air before being hauled back to earth with a resounding thud.

Three weeks after their return they played Wexford in the first round of the 1950-51 National Hurling League and were beaten by 8-8 to 6-6, their first defeat in the League or Championship for 28 months.

Wexford had been hurling nonentities until they'd caused a massive stir earlier that year by reaching the Leinster Final and pushing Kilkenny all the way, and Tipperary hadn't heard the last of them yet.

That loss ended their hopes of a successful League title defence, but, as the '51 Championship approached, they proved they remained as formidable a team as ever by retaining the Monaghan Cup.

Played in the 30,000-seater Mitcham Stadium in London every year, the Monaghan Cup was a fund-raiser for the London County Board and the highlight of the social and sporting calendar for tens of thousands of Irish emigrants in England.

The '51 Final was hailed in the press as the greatest game of hurling to have ever been played on foreign soil as Tipperary defeated the reigning League Champions, Galway, by three points.

Doyle starred at full-back that day but was back in his more familiar left corner-back berth for the first round of the Championship against Waterford.

Tipp were expected to win easily because Waterford were missing some of their best players, including inspirational centre-back Vin Baston, but, in the end, they were lucky to escape with a 2-10 to 1-10 victory.

Waterford were a much lighter and smaller team than Tipp, but they were a skilful outfit who kept Tipperary off-balance by moving the ball quickly and changing the direction of their attack with whipped, wristy ground-strokes.

Tipp probably would have lost were it not for a tour de force performance from Seamus Bannon who, once again, proved he was the most versatile player on the team.

In his style of play Bannon was similar to Doyle. He tore into every physical contest with an abandon that brought great roars of approval from the crowd and there was a great dash and drive to everything he did.

He could play well in almost every position on the field, and saved the day for Tipp when he moved from midfield to full-forward and inspired a second-half surge that just about got them over the line.

The victory came with one considerable casualty though. The Iron Man from Borris-Ileigh, Sean Kenny, proved he was made of flesh and bone after all when he sustained a serious knee injury.

It would never heal properly. Tipperary hurling had just lost one of its greatest warriors.

Even without their inspirational captain they had a comfortable eight-point win over Limerick in the Munster Semi-Final, but a different challenge entirely was looming on the horizon.

Once again Cork would provide the opposition in the Munster Final, and, after the epic encounters of the previous two years, the match was given a breathless billing.

It would more than live up to it.

$$\bullet\bullet\bullet\,\bullet\,\bullet\bullet\bullet$$

July 29, 1951.
Munster SH Final v Cork.

The stewards in the Gaelic Grounds in Limerick had a well-earned reputation for ruthlessness and they were showing just why.

Whenever a skirmish broke out in the crowd, or a knot of supporters attempted to force their way onto the pitch, order was quickly restored by any means necessary.

The stadium was already wedged to capacity a full three hours before the match was due to start, leaving thousands more locked outside.

Only those who had been willing to queue for four or more hours before the throw-in managed to make it through the turnstiles.

The authorities in Limerick were determined there wouldn't be a repeat of the lawless scenes witnessed in Killarney the previous year, but the fans locked outside weren't about to accept their fate meekly either.

An organised charge at one of the gates sent it flying open and a desperate surge of supporters began forcing its way into the ground.

The stadium announcer called for reinforcements and dozens of stewards immediately rushed to fill the breech. Fists flew and heads were cracked until eventually the hard-pressed stewards managed to force the gate shut again.

The stewards were so zealous that even some members of the press struggled to gain admittance to the stadium.

One only made it past the gauntlet when he persuaded the Order of Malta to pretend he was one of their first-aid men, while another successfully masqueraded as a member of a fife and drum band.

One concession was made to the disappointed fans who were refused admission. The stadium's loudspeakers were turned outwards and a commentary of the match was relayed to those camped outside the grounds.

Little of it was heard though, such was the thunderous noise coming from inside the stadium as the combatants earned sustained volleys of throaty roars.

Eventually it all became too much for one frustrated fan outside the ground who flung the bottle of stout he was drinking over the perimeter wall in disgust.

Had he known what became of it, he probably would have been pleased with himself. It struck neither friend nor foe, but a Clare man by the name of Martin Moloney, who was surely punished by the Gods for taking a seat that could have been filled by a Tipp or Cork fan.

The unfortunate Mr Moloney had to be taken to Barrington's hospital to have six stitches applied to the wound on his forehead. His humour surely wasn't helped by the fact that he missed one of the greatest ever games of hurling.

It was Christy Ring's finest hour in the blood and bandages of Cork, but even his heroics weren't enough to lower Tipp's colours. Ring was irresistible, but the Tipperary full-back line of Doyle, Brennan and Byrne also chose the day to produce their most defiant performance.

Even their stubborn resistance didn't look like it would be enough to save their team though such was the pace with which Cork began the match.

Ring started at midfield rather than in his usual wing-forward berth and, in the opening quarter of the match, seemed to be constantly involved in the play.

He was winning hard ball, jinking and juking his way through the Tipperary defence with those swivel-hipped runs and lashing in shots from all angles.

Against any other team he would have scored a couple of goals in the first half alone, but, once again, Reddin's unnatural agility was breaking his heart.

He might have been keeping Ring at bay, but the goalkeeper was finally bested by a scorcher from Tom Crotty that put Cork 1-4 to 0-5 ahead.

A desperate rearguard action from the Tipp full-backs and some typically opportunistic scores from Paddy Kenny were keeping Tipperary in touch, but it was obvious that, if something wasn't done soon about Ring, there would be only one outcome.

Tommy Doyle decided he was the only man for the job. He raced over to the sideline to volunteer himself for the thankless task, but Paddy Leahy informed him action had already been taken. Mick Ryan would move from centre-forward to midfield and pick up Ring.

Leahy made the call despite not getting the full backing of all of his fellow selectors who wondered loudly how a natural forward like Ryan could possibly contain Ring.

It was clear to Leahy though that no man could possibly hold Ring on this day if the tenacious Seamus Bannon couldn't, so the only solution was to distract him instead.

Ryan was a skilful hurler who was capable of making and creating scores, and Leahy reckoned that attack was the best form of defence. Ring mightn't be so inclined to roam and run forward if he was leaving a man free who was capable of hurting the Cork defence.

The ploy worked a treat. Ring's overwhelming mastery of the match waned as he was forced to track the elusive Ryan rather than concentrate solely on his own attacking schemes.

Ring was still at the heart of most of Cork's best moves, but Ryan was also hurling a lot of ball and would ultimately play a crucial role in the winning of the match.

The growing influence of Phil Shanahan in the Tipperary midfield also helped level the balance of power. Nicknamed 'The Gorgeous Gael', Shanahan was a handsome man and so was his brand of hurling.

He had a stylish, sweeping stroke that enabled him to land points from distance, and two typically sweet strikes brought Tipperary level. They moved two points clear by half-time, but neither Ring nor Cork were finished yet.

Early in the second half they won a free 30 yards from the Tipperary goal. This was Ringy territory.

Running at the ball in a straight line he scooped it forward a good five yards without breaking stride before launching himself at the sliotar like a human slingshot.

A mixture of hopeful anticipation and dread silenced the crowd as he started his run and when ash met leather a resounding THWACK echoed clearly around the stadium.

Reddin must have been the only man who saw the ball in flight because no one else on the goal-line moved. Even his supernatural reflexes weren't quick enough though. He got the tip of his hurley to the ball but that wasn't enough to prevent it ricocheting past him into the net.

"Doubta Ringey Boy!" roared the Cork fans as the Gaelic Grounds erupted in acclamation of the strike.

When two more Cork points from Ring and Willie John Daly put Cork three ahead Tipp were teetering on the brink, but Paddy Leahy had another trick up his sleeve.

The order went out to the six forwards to begin swapping positions incessantly, and with the confused Cork defenders pulled this way and that, Tipp made the most of the space that was created by scoring two quick-fire goals.

Mick Ryan had a hand in both. A smart pass set up Ned Ryan for the first, and then Sonny Maher scored the second when Ryan's attempted point was blocked down into his path by Cork goalkeeper Jim Cotter.

Tipp were three points ahead but, during the final seven minutes of normal time and another seven of extra-time, Cork applied ceaseless pressure.

Two pointed frees from Ring closed the gap to the minimum and still Cork kept pressing. They nearly surged ahead when Ring unleashed a stinging ground-stroke, but the ever alert Reddin saved.

As he cleared the ball a hurley flashed past his head like a tomahawk and ended in the back of the Tipperary net.

"Who's hurley is that?" demanded Reddin. "It's Ring's isn't it?"

"Ah, Jaysus, Reddin, don't do anything with it now," said Tony Brennan.

"I'm not going to do anything to it, but Ring isn't coming in for it. This is my goal, and he's not coming past me."

Ring didn't force the issue. He must have known by the look in Reddin's eyes it would have been a fruitless venture so he made do with a replacement hurley that was thrown in from the sideline.

A couple of minutes later the umpire beckoned over Reddin. "Tony, there's a Cork County board man here who wants Ring's hurley."

The goalkeeper didn't even turn around to see where the request had come from. "Tell him he'll have to wait until after the game."

With time almost up Cork had a chance to equalise when they won another free, but Ring struck it wide with his new, unfamiliar hurley. Reddin belted the puck-out down the field and Paddy Kenny clipped over a point that edged Tipp two clear.

Cork summoned one last charge. In the seventh minute of injury time they won a free in the middle of the pitch. The only option was to float it in and hope the sliotar could be doubled to the net.

Christy Ring, Willie John Daly and Tom Crotty lined up on the 21 yard line. Facing them stood Doyle, Brennan and Byrne on the edge of the small square, their knuckles whitening as they tensed their bodies for the test to come.

As soon as the free was struck the Cork-men charged and the Tipp defenders rushed to meet them. Red and blue jersies crashed into one another in an almighty collision of flesh, ash and bone.

When the sliotar dropped from the heavens it landed in the midst of a ruck of flashing timber and straining limbs as the stadium trembled to the half-mad roars of 43,000 souls.

Men swung hurleys like they were scything corn and the sliotar spun this way and that off sticks and shins.

Time seemed to slow down as everyone waited for the decisive stroke. After a couple of seconds of frenzied chaos it finally came when the ball was spat over the end line by a splintering clash of hurleys.

A waving pair of white arms signalled a wide, Cork's defeat and Tipperary's third Munster title in a row.

●●●●●●●

The 1951 All-Ireland Final captured the public's imagination like none before it, but few people were talking about Tipperary.

Their opponents, Wexford, were a much more glamorous proposition entirely. In little over a year they'd transformed themselves from hurling no-marks into one of the most exciting sides in the country.

There had been no warning of the team's sudden coming as a genuine hurling force. They last time they'd won an All-Ireland had been in 1910, and, since then, the county had been more renowned for its footballers than its hurlers.

Even beating Meath in the first round of the 1950 Leinster Championship was regarded as a mild shock at the time, but people were forced to take them seriously when they ran Kilkenny to three points in the provincial final that year.

They proved that was no fluke by reaching the 1951 League Final, but it wasn't just the fact that this talented team seemed to have suddenly fallen from the sky that made them such an intriguing bunch.

Even the brand of hurling they were playing was novel. At the time ground hurling and overhead pulling was the norm, but the Wexford players preferred to get the ball into their hands whenever possible.

Attempting to catch a high-ball amidst a thicket of swinging hurleys was something that just hadn't been done up until now, but many of the Wexford players were also fine footballers and it was an instinct that came naturally to them.

Purists would cock their noses and remark 'that's just not hurling', but the sight of men like Bobby and Billy Rackard plucking the ball from the heavens and launching huge clearances downfield thrilled the crowd.

The eldest Rackard brother, Nicky, was the real star though. Sixteen stone in weight, well over six feet tall, blond-haired and handsome; he was an impressive sight to behold.

The big full-forward was even more formidable when he got a sliotar in his over-sized hand and ran at opposition defenders who were invariably flattened like road-kill. And when he opened up those wide shoulders and let fly on the ball, the net usually shivered violently half a second later.

His star appeal was burnished even more by the fact that he was from

Killane and had grown up in the same house that was the former home of John Kelly, the leader of the 1798 Rebellion.

For Wexford fans these hurlers that had come from nowhere were the very reincarnation of those heroic freedom fighters. To a man they were impressive physical specimens who hurled with a rare dash and threw themselves into the fray with a reckless abandon.

Tipperary might have been the established power, but the rebels of Wexford weren't to be taken lightly.

•••●•••

September 2, 1951.
All-Ireland SH Final v Wexford.

Anastasia Rackard sat rigidly in her seat and fingered her rosary beads nervously while everyone around her in the Hogan Stand stood and roared.

Her sons Nicky, Bobby and Billy were leading the Wexford team pre-match procession around Croke Park, but any pride she felt had been drowned in a sea of nervous tension.

Why had she come here? She'd made a point of never watching her boys in action before and was regretting breaking that rule for the first time in her life.

She made a silent vow to herself that from now on she'd stick to her usual routine of spending the day at Tramore beach in Waterford whenever the boys were playing a big match in Croke Park.

Down on the field the Tipperary and Wexford players marched in the colours of their provinces rather than their counties. The blue and gold of Tipp and purple and yellow of Wexford were deemed too similar, so Tipp wore blue jerseys and Wexford donned green.

Ireland was basking in an Indian summer and, as the players marched around the field, their unfamiliar jerseys were already stuck to their backs with salty sweat.

The atmosphere in the stadium raised the mercury another couple of degrees. Tipperary fans were outnumbered five to one by Wexford supporters, and the two pike-men that marched in front of Nicky Rackard and his team-mates echoed the defiance that rolled down from the packed stands and terraces.

The match was only a couple of minutes old when every Wexford man and woman in the stadium was given cause to leap from their seats and empty their lungs.

A long-ball into the Tipperary square was collected by Reddin, but half a second later he was skewered like a trainee matador by the charging bull Rackard who bundled man, ball and all into the back of the net.

The big Wexford full-forward was only getting started. He flashed over two points and then smashed home a second goal after another charging run skittled Tipperary full-back Brennan.

Tipp were five points down and reeling, but things could have been much worse. In those chaotic first 15 minutes Reddin somehow saved two more murderous strokes from Rackard.

After the full-forward's second goal Paddy Leahy ran in from the sideline and called Doyle, Brennan and Byrne into a huddle while Reddin took his time retrieving the sliotar from the net.

Grabbing Doyle and Byrne by their jerseys, he issued an urgent order: "The next time Rackard gets the ball, the two of ye are to come in from the sides and give it to him as hard as ye can."

"But, shur, what about our two men," replied Doyle. "He only has to throw it out to them and it'll be an easy goal."

"I'm telling ye now, Rackard isn't going to pass the ball to anyone. Don't worry about the other two, just stop Rackard."

Doyle and Byrne exchanged dubious glances, but when Leahy gave an order you did well to follow it to the letter.

When Rackard won the next ball that came his way and turned to run at Brennan again he was immediately crucified by a pincer attack from Doyle and Byrne that stopped him dead in his tracks.

Paddy Kehoe and Tim Flood were free either side of him in splendid isolation, but Leahy was right, Rackard didn't pass it.

His instinct every time was to continue taking the water-buffalo route to goal, but now there were three hungry lions tearing lumps from him every time he won the ball. With Rackard's considerable threat neutralised, the game swung decisively Tipperary's way.

Paddy Kenny had been keeping them in touch with some sparkling points against the run of play in the opening quarter, but, in the final 10 minutes of the half, they upped it a couple of gears and goals from the three Ryans – Mick, Ned and Tim – helped them into a 3-6 to 2-6 half-time lead.

Despite dominating for most of the first half Wexford were trailing, and that harsh reality seemed to drain them of much of their confidence and brio.

It didn't help either that their goalkeeper, Ray Brennan, had a disastrous second-half performance, conceding four goals because of an unfortunate habit of blocking the ball back out to onrushing Tipperary forwards.

At the other end of the field Wexford repeatedly went for goals instead of taking the points on offer. Even when the not-so-loving embrace of the Tipp full-back line earned Nicky Rackard a series of 21-yard frees, he was in turn frustrated by Reddin who saved a a couple more raspers from the Killane man.

The final score of 7-7 to 3-9 in Tipperary's favour wasn't wholly representative of the balance of play, but there was plenty of honour in defeat for the men of Wexford.

Wing-back Wilkie Thorpe, in particular, showed his class when he waved away a first-aid medic after Paddy Kenny's head-wound had been bandaged and insisted on helping Tipperary's man of the match to the sideline himself.

Wexford had fought valiantly, but no one could dispute that Tipp were deserving victors.

Thousands of supporters travelled to Thurles to welcome home only the second Tipperary team to win three All-Irelands in a row and few doubted they were capable of even greater feats. After all, they were still a young team with their best years ahead of them.

Sport is unpredictable though. Many years would pass before Tipperary fans would have cause to cheer in September again.

CHAPTER 12

May, 2011, Banagher, Offaly.

Tony Reddin is 92 years old now but his handshake is firm, his eyes twinkle brightly and he still walks with the light step of a born sportsman.

Some say that good humour is the key to good health. An afternoon spent in Tony Reddin's company is enough to convince you it is.

A half-smile is forever playing on his lips and it broadens into a creased grin or an infectious laugh with little invitation.

He'll tell you he has every reason to be happy. Since making the fateful decision to cycle across Portumna bridge from Galway into Tipperary in 1947 his life has been blessed.

Crossing the Shannon transformed him from a relatively anonymous hurler into the greatest goalkeeper the game has ever known, but it did so much more for him too.

He might have always remained the shy and socially reticent 'Thaudy', had hurling for Tipperary not boosted his self-confidence and given him the opportunity to be fitted with that hearing aid in New York in 1950 which helped him overcome his deafness and speech difficulties.

He wouldn't have met his wife Maura either, or had the nine children that have brought so much joy to his life. He was Galway's gift to Tipperary hurling, but Tipperary gave him plenty in return.

These days, home is Banagher in Offaly where he has lived since work with Bord na Mona brought him there in 1963, but one room of the house remains a little corner of Tipperary.

The blue goalkeeper's jersey he wore for Lorrha is framed alongside a number of photos of the great three-in-a-row Tipperary team.

The portrait that commemorated his selection on the hurling team of the Millennium has pride of place on another wall, but your eye is drawn most by the impressive collection of medals artfully arranged and hanging in a glass cabinet.

They've been cared for so well that they look newly minted, but the memories of the men he won them with shine even brighter for Reddin.

When he talks about that band of brothers his bright eyes occasionally moisten, his voice raises a couple of octaves and the cups of tea his wife Maura has brewed for us rattle in their saucers when he thumps the table with his fist to emphasise a point.

The good china threatens to hop off the table altogether when conversation turns to Reddin's Praetorian Guard – the full-back line of Doyle, Brennan and Byrne.

"Doyle just knew the right thing to do all the time even though he was young," says Reddin. "He was a big man too, fierce strong."

"He was great when he came in for that replay against Cork in '49. He was as quick as lighting and he was unbelievably strong altogether for a young lad. He was pure determined and if a man was coming in soloing towards him he'd get it.

"Himself and the other two gave me great protection and they were a brilliant full-back line to play behind. Mickey The Rattler was a great man to pull altogether, and once he did the ball would be gone.

"If anyone hit me Rattler would get awful wicked. He'd come straight in with the handle of the hurl.

"One day a Cork fan threw a Cork flag up on top of the net. Didn't Rattler go at it with his hurley and not only did he knock it down and make bits of it, he tore a big hole in the net too.

"Tony Brennan was a mighty man, too. He was just physically very strong and nothing came through him. They all gave me great protection."

Any opposition forward that did make it past that formidable full-back quickly found out that Reddin was well able to look after himself too.

He might have been a shy man off the field in his early years with Tipp, but he overcame that natural inclination when he pulled on the blue and gold.

"The lads were telling me I was too quiet altogether and that I should be pulling like a savage and breaking hurls," recalls Reddin with a laugh.

"I was too quiet alright in the '49 draw against Cork when Ring clattered me across the legs, but I learned after that.

"They were telling me I should be tough. Paddy Leahy was telling me that Cork forwards were tough and I should be standing up to them. So that's what I did.

"Christy Ring gave me plenty of deadly shots but he hardly scored a goal against me for a good ten years. That used to drive him mad.

"He was a tough auld yoke and a few times he'd hit me a shot or I'd turn him upside down. But, then, when we played together on the Railway Cup he was always fierce friendly."

Christy Ring's antipathy towards Reddin when they were in opposition was understandable. Few men did more to frustrate him than the Tipperary goalkeeper.

The harder Ring struck the ball, the more spectacular was Reddin's save. Cork fans were convinced the Tipperary goalkeeper had super-human powers, and, in a way, he did.

One positive consequence of his hearing and speech deficiencies was that all his other senses were heightened.

He'd amaze friends with his telescopic eye-sight, which remains razor-sharp to this day, and his coordination and reflexes were cat-like.

Reddin was able to get his hurley to shots that other goalkeepers wouldn't even see go past them on their way to the net, and his wrists were so quick, and his touch so refined, that he had an amazing ability to kill the ball dead.

He still has a total recall of every great save he made in those tumultuous years with Tipp. When he describes them he rises to his feet, holds an imaginary hurley in his hands and tenses his body as if readying it to make the save again.

"I'd never block it out to where a forward running in could pick it up," he says. "In ten years I never did that. I'd always kill the ball.

"I always tried to stay on my feet as well, whereas the likes of Brendan Cummins is always falling. He makes a save, and then he falls. He shouldn't be falling.

"If you fall after you make a save then you're helpless. To make sure I would never fall or trip I took out the studs from my boots and replaced them with strips of leather. That way I was quicker and my feet never caught in the ground."

Strangers regularly call by the Reddin home. Some just want to shake the hand of the greatest goalkeeper the game has ever known, others stay for hours to talk about the old times. All are received with grace and good humour.

He made more great saves against Cork than any other county, but when a man with a southern lilt to his accent visits he knows what they want to talk about most is the shot they're convinced he didn't save.

For people of a certain age the infamous 1949 replay between Cork and Tipperary is still a bone of contention.

Cork fans swear blind Mossie O'Riordan's second-half shot rebounded back into play off the horizontal stanchion that held up the net, whereas Tipp supporters insist it cannoned off the cross-bar. To this day people still visit Reddin in search of the definitive truth.

"I love to talk about that," he chuckles. "They're always asking me that question but I honestly don't know if it went in or not.

"I was four yards out from the goal. There was a tussle for the ball and everyone was rooting for it when Mossie Riordan came in and hit it a right slap.

"I got my hurley to it but Mossie had hit the ball so hard that it broke the hurley. After that it either hit the crossbar and came back out or it hit the lower crossbar that was holding up the net.

"I'm convinced it hit the crossbar because it bounced back out the field so far. If it had gone in for a goal and hit the lower cross-bar, it would surely have bounced back out lower than it did."

His answer mightn't please Cork fans, but then he was rarely flavour of the month with that tribe anyway.

They made that much obvious down in Killarney in '49. Hardly surprisingly, the memory of that fraught afternoon remains vivid for Reddin.

"A friend of mind travelled down the night before to Killarney and heard a few Cork lads say in the pub 'if we knock out the goalkeeper we'll have it won.' They'd even been talking about it the night before," he says with a shake of his head.

"After half time I came back out and I said to myself, 'Jesus Christ would you look at all the people down around the goal'.

"They'd pulled up the stake-wire and come in on the field right behind the goal. They were leaning on the goal-post and it got loose.

"Christy Ring was trying to keep the people back but they wouldn't move. Then Jack Lynch tried to talk to them but he got hit in the face and he hit someone a good belt back.

"At this stage now I couldn't even look behind me because they were throwing stones and bottles and all sorts of things.

"I got stones down on top of my head, I got a cap thrown in my face when I was trying to make a save and then, when I went to clear a ball, someone threw a coat over me.

"I was trying not to look behind me, but the next thing I noticed, wasn't the net gone. There was no net now at all only the two poles, and one of those was fierce loose in the ground.

"At one stage Cork got the ball in midfield and drove it for a point. By now I could move the pole over and back because it was so loose, so, as the ball was coming in, I moved the post a little so that the ball went wide instead of going over for a point.

"The Cork supporters went roaring at the umpire to put up the flag for a point and one of them hit him a belt. I was so afraid he was going to get a bottle down on top of the head that I covered his head with my hurley.

"T'was good enough for the Blackcoats. That's what they get for loosening the pole in the first place."

He knew that they were going to make a charge for him as soon as the final whistle blew. Surely he was petrified he was about to be pulled limb from limb?

When the question is aired his wife, Maura, is tickled pink: "Tony afraid? You must be joking. That man was never afraid of anything in his life."

Reddin backs up his wife's assertion with a broad grin.

"I was more annoyed than anything that they wouldn't let me off the pitch because I wanted to go get my dinner. I was kept abroad on the pitch for over two hours though because there were still Cork fans milling about the place.

"All the other Tipperary lads got their dinner and didn't realise I was still stuck on the pitch. They were all ready to get in the cars and get going when they were told I was still abroad on the pitch.

"I was bloody starving and wanted my dinner but shur t'was all eaten on me at that stage.

"I got off the field in the end thankfully, but we had to hide the Cup and not fly any colours or anything until we were six miles outside the road. It was only then we pulled over and tied the Cup to the roof and drove on to Thurles with it."

Were he hurling today the playing rules would provide him with far more protection than he was used to in the 1940s and 1950s, but he's happier to have played in an era when no quarter was asked nor given.

"It's a different sport altogether now. There's a lot more loose ball being played and it's not nearly as tough as it used to be.

"They're not playing tough at all now. They're letting lads rise the ball whatever way they want and hit it over the bar.

"That's not good enough at all. You should be lying in to your man and not giving him an inch. Kilkenny are one of the few teams that get in close enough. They're not afraid to let you have it. That's the way it should be. The likes of John Doyle never gave his man an inch."

When he mentions Doyle's name he gives a rueful shake of the head and his eyes take on a far-away look.

Doyle's was the latest in a long line of funerals of former team-mates he's attended in recent years. There aren't many of his friends left from the three-in-a-row team now, but he'll always cherish the memories of what they achieved together.

"Doyle was a great man, but they were all mighty men on that Tipperary team," says Reddin. "It was an honour for me to have hurled with them."

The honour was their's too.

CHAPTER 13

Paddy Leahy's kitchen door flew open and Doyle stomped into the room in his usual rush to reach his desired destination quickly.

He made a beeline for the same spot he always did – a fold-up canvas chair that was placed in front of the kitchen window so you'd have a good view of whoever or whatever was passing on the road.

"Young Doyle, any news?" enquired Leahy, as he busied himself buttering a few slices of bread to go with his tea.

"I'll tell you now in a minute Paddy," replied Doyle as he opened the Irish Press *with a flourish that made the newspaper snap.*

This was their routine most days. After they'd been to the creamery Doyle would drop by for a cup of tea, read the paper, and deliver his verdict on the news of the day.

He'd do his best to figure out Leahy's position on an issue, and then take the opposite viewpoint in the hope of getting a rise out of his host.

"The Springboks are playing Munster down in Limerick next weekend Paddy. I was thinking of heading down myself."

Leahy's buttering paused for a second as he cast a worried look in Doyle's direction. Was he being serious or just stirring the pot?

The GAA had Vigilance Committee members at every major rugby and soccer match whose job it was to spy out any hurlers or footballers who might be in the crowd.

If one was spotted, he'd be reported and handed a lengthy suspension from playing Gaelic Games.

The thought of his star defender being banned for something as stupid as attending a rugby match filled Leahy with dread, but he knew there was little point expressing his concerns.

If he told Doyle not to go, then he definitely would. And there was a good chance Doyle had no intention of going anyway and was just looking for a rise.

"Did you hear what I said?" shouted Doyle again over his shoulder. "I'm going to go watch the Springboks. What do you make of that?"

Leahy took a big bite of the buttered bread and washed it down with a careful sip of the piping hot tea before eventually delivering his verdict.

"Shur, hopefully, it'll be a good game so."

Doyle threw Leahy an annoyed look, rolled up his paper roughly and stomped his way back out the kitchen door.

He'd be getting no satisfaction out of the old man today.

•••●•••

As it happened Doyle did go to watch the all-conquering Springboks narrowly beat Munster in Limerick in December, 1951, and it wouldn't be the last time he'd flout 'The Ban'.

He often spoke out publicly against the growing influence of soccer and rugby and was utterly opposed to the opening up of Croke Park to rival sports, but his actions didn't always tally with his utterances.

He was a big Manchester United fan, and broke the ban once again in October, 1968, when he went to watch the reigning European Champions play Waterford at Lansdowne Road in the first round of the European Cup.

By then his own inter-county career was over so he wasn't taking all that big a risk but, in 1951, there would have been serious consequences had a Vigilance Committee member spotted him at the Springboks match.

Doyle was feeling invincible though. He was 21 years old and had just won his third All-Ireland Championship in as many years with Tipperary and his second county title with Holycross after a comfortable victory over neighbours Clonoulty-Rossmore in the '51 final.

Success and high achievement was all he knew and all he expected, but he was about to learn the hard-way that nothing lasts forever. It's the punch you don't see coming that does the most damage and, in the Munster Final of '52, Tipperary were flattened by an unexpected haymaker.

They went into the match against Cork more sure of themselves than they'd been in any of their previous three victories. Wexford had been beaten again in a classic League Final, and Waterford crushed by 17 points in the Munster semi-final.

Tipp were hurling better than ever, whereas Cork seemed a team in transition. Players like Paddy Barry, Liam Dowling, Tony Shaughnessy and Gerard Murphy were new to the scene, but Tipp were to find out the hard way that Cork's young pups didn't lack for bite.

●●●●●●●

July 13, 1952.
Munster SH Final v Cork

Salty pearls of sweat clung to Sean Og Murphy's brow and his fists squeezed to the rhythm of his quickly beating heart.

The Cork County Board secretary looked around at the tense faces that lined the walls of dressing-room.

For a few seconds the only sound was the clack of his shoes on the hardwood floor as he paced over and back with all eyes on him. Then he began.

"We've always respected Tipperary, but we've never feared them. Though they may be our greatest rivals, they've never been our superiors.

"Whatever they have achieved, we have bettered. Today they think they're going to turn the tables.

"Are you going to be the Cork team that lets that happen? The first Cork team to lose to Tipperary for four years running?

"The Cork team that allows them to equal our glorious four All-Irelands in a row? The Cork team that allows them to win a 17th All-Ireland while we make do with 16?

"Or are you going to go out there and defend the honour of your county by showing that a Cork man never lies down before anyone, least of all a Tipperary man?

"Are you going to remind them why it is always they who should fear us?"

The air was splintered by a chorus of war cries.

●●●●●●●

Christy Ring pinballed his way through the Tipp defence before somehow getting his shot off despite shipping an almighty blow.

The referee's whistle blew for the foul, but half a second later Liam Dowling dived full length to get his hurley to Ring's shot and deflect it into the net.

The umpire hesitated, but Ring didn't. He picked up the green flag himself, waved it vigorously then ran towards the referee with his eyes ablaze and roared "GOAL!" in the official's face.

The referee's mind was made up for him. The goal stood and, by now, Tipperary's six-point interval lead had been whittled to the minimum.

Cork had all the momentum and the Tipp defence was struggling to contain them. Tommy Doyle had been forced off in the first half with a head wound so severe even The Rubber Man couldn't bounce back from it, and Jimmy Finn had been a sick man before he ever went on the field.

A brace of points from Ring put Cork ahead and then two more from Dowling and Seanie O'Brien stretched the advantage to three with ten minutes to play.

For once Paddy Leahy didn't have a ready answer for the crisis engulfing his team, and there were none forthcoming from his fellow selectors either.

"Have any of you anything to suggest at all?" demanded Leahy.

"Philly O'Dwyer, can you think of anything?"

All O'Dwyer could summon was a defensive shrug of his shoulders.

"Christ Almighty. And you a teacher."

Leahy took the initiative himself and jogged out onto the field to relay new orders to his struggling defenders but was intercepted on his way by Ring.

"Too late, Paddy."

"I think you're right, Christy."

Ring was indeed correct. Tipp did manage one last charge, but Gerry 'Bowler' Doyle's fierce ground stroke went over the bar instead of under it and Cork triumphed by 1-11 to 2-6.

The three-in-a-row champions had been dethroned, and an era of ill-luck and underachievement ushered in.

••• ● •••

Cork held the whip-hand again in 1953 when they deservedly defeated Tipperary in the League and Munster Finals, but it looked like Tipperary were on the march again in '54 when they beat Kilkenny in the League Final.

The Tipp players awoke to monsoon conditions on the morning of the match, presumed the game wouldn't go ahead, and instead expended their energies by having a massive pillow-fight that turned a floor of Barry's Hotel into a feather-filled snow-globe.

Kilkenny were hot favourites to win the match and insisted it should go ahead despite the inclement conditions, but they were made rue their eagerness because Tipp were in the mood to swing their hurleys as hard as they had their pillows and stormed to a 3-10 to 1-4 victory.

Clare were bested in the provincial semi-final and Tipp seemed set for victory over Cork in the Munster Final when they led by a point a minute into injury time.

Their advantage would have been more comfortable had a second-half Seamus Bannon goal been allowed to stand, but the referee Bill O'Donoghue brought play back and awarded a free in to Tipperary instead.

It looked like they'd still manage to hang on for a deserved victory though, until Ring won a ball out on the wing and somehow managed to get a shot off despite falling under the combined weight of Doyle and Pat Stakelum.

It was trailing wide, but Tony Reddin made the fateful decision to claim it anyway. As he attempted to catch the sliotar it hopped off his breast-bone and into the path of Paddy Barry who had the simple task of flicking it to the back of the net.

Ring followed it up immediately with a pointed free, and Tipperary were beaten again.

••• ● •••

Doyle was Tipperary captain for the only time in his long career in 1955 and, once again, the portents were promising when they won the League; Wexford the victims on this occasion.

Cork had put together their own three-in-a-row of All-Ireland titles between '52 and '54, but were surprisingly beaten in the first round of the '55 Munster Championship by a Jimmy Smyth-inspired Clare team.

Despite that result Tipperary were expected to handle the Banner comfortably enough in the Munster Semi-Final but they, too, suffered a sensational defeat, thanks mainly to some abysmal shooting by their forwards.

A Championship exit at the hands of Clare was regarded as nothing short of a disaster, but it still wasn't the bitterest defeat that Doyle would suffer that year.

There was never any love lost between Holycross and Thurles Sarsfields, but their meeting in the '55 Mid-Tipp Final was an even bigger grudge match than usual because of the farcical events of the previous year.

Both teams had been due to contest the '54 Mid-Final, but Sarsfields refused to fulfil the fixture because they objected to the choice of Templemore as the match venue.

Holycross had played all their Championship matches against Sarsfields in Thurles since 1946 but had lost in 1952 and 1953 and felt a change of venue might do them some good.

An entrepreneur by the name of Jim Cahill was keen to promote Templemore as a venue for hurling matches and offered an under-the-counter payment of £20 to Holycross if they pushed to have the Mid-Final held in the town's pitch.

When word was leaked to Sarsfields of the cosy arrangement they refused to play in Templemore unless they were paid £40 expenses.

Even when Cahill agreed to their demands they pulled out of the fixture because they objected to a remark by the Holycross County Board delegate, Bob Stakelum, that the Holycross club "wanted for nothing because they had their parish and their Parish Priest behind them".

Sarsfields perceived this to be a slur on their own Parish Priest as well as the Archbishop himself and, on a point of principle, refused to hurl against

1.

2.

3.

4.

5.

6.

7.

8.

Dunlop's Studio, Thurles

9.

10.

11.

12.

13.

14.

15.

16.

17.

18.

19.

20.

21.

22.

23.

24.

25.

26.

TiPPERARY 5·13
LiMERiCK. 2-4
22-7-62.

27.

28.

30.

31.

32.

34.

35.

36.

Holycross who were awarded the Mid-Tipp title by a walkover.

When Holycross went on to beat Roscrea in the County Final every Thurles Sarsfields' supporter said they'd won the Championship by default, so, when the two teams prepared to meet in the '55 Final, the match had more needle than a seamstress.

The ante only increased when Tipp star Paddy Kenny controversially transferred from Borris-Ileigh to Sarsfields and, by the time the match came around, the impending contest was the talk of the county.

Ten-thousand fans somehow shoehorned themselves into the cramped facilities of Gaile hurling field for the match. Every vantage point was taken, dozens even climbing the trees that surrounded grounds so as to have a clear view of the action.

Such was the enmity between the teams that they each marched behind their own pipe band, and the County Board felt it had no option other than to employ the services of a referee from Limerick for fear a local man could be accused of bias.

The referee was busy early because the Holycross defenders made a point of targeting Sarsfields' new recruit Kenny. It did them little good. Sarsfields rattled in three goals in the opening minutes and Kenny scored two of them.

Doyle was then delegated to mark his county colleague and, with Sarsfields' most dangerous gun successfully spiked, Holycross slowly hauled themselves back into the contest.

By half-time they trailed by just two points – 3-5 to 3-3 – but the match turned decisively Sarsfields' way in the second half when Doyle was sent off.

As he was tearing out of the defence with the ball in hand, Kenny raced after him and hit him a couple of clatters on the top of the head with the flat of his hurley as if he was hammering a reluctant nail.

Doyle swung back with his own stick and blood spurted from the point of impact where he met Kenny just above the eye.

There had already been a couple of other testy encounters in the second half, and the Limerick referee had enough. Doyle was sent to the line, but he didn't go quietly and eventually had to be ushered away by his own mentors.

Reduced to 14 men, Holycross stood little chance and, in the end, were beaten by five points – 3-10 to 3-5.

That defeat marked the end of an era for Holycross hurling club and the beginning of a glorious one for Thurles Sarsfields, who would win 10 of the next 11 county hurling titles.

For the rest of his hurling career Doyle would be consumed with the challenge of beating the greatest-ever club team in the history of Tipperary hurling, but not even his considerable will would be enough to bring another county championship to Holycross.

He might have had little success on the hurling field in 1955, but, off the field, the year did end with one considerable victory for him.

At the age of 25 he became a married man.

CHAPTER 14

Thurles, 1951

Anne Reidy, Mary Maher and Eilish Costigan strolled gracefully through Thurles, resplendent in their green and cream Ursuline Convent school uniforms.

Their Alma Mater was renowned for moulding elegant young ladies and, with scarcely a hair out of place, the three friends were fitting testaments to that reputation.

Holding an animated conversation while walking is a talent perfected by teenage girls, and whispered gossip and peals of laughter perfumed the air around the trio as they happily made their way along.

When Mary absent-mindedly fixed her hair behind her ear, her wrist-watch caught the sun like a flickering molten mirror.

The watch was her pride and joy and a source of envy for her friends. Her boyfriend, Paddy Kenny, had bought it for her in New York when he'd visited the Big Apple with the rest of the Tipperary hurling team the previous Autumn.

It had caused quite a stir among her class-mates when she displayed it for the first time, but not as much as the nylon stockings her boyfriend had also brought back from the States.

Such luxuries were unheard of in Ireland at the time, and Mary's status amongst her peers was immediately elevated.

Anne liked to throw her eyes to heaven and shake her head in amusement when the topic of conversation regularly turned to the other eligible young men on the Tipperary team, but even she couldn't help occasionally glancing green-eyed at her friend's watch.

As the trio walked from Liberty Square onto Friar Street, Mary suddenly silenced her two companions with a couple of urgent nudges.

"Look, look, look. That's John Doyle from Holycross on the other side of the street."

Anne quickly turned her gaze to the young man she'd heard so much about from some of her besotted classmates, but what she saw didn't living up to the billing.

Doyle was dressed in his working clothes – a shapeless shirt tucked into a grubby pair of well-worn trousers – and his hair was an unruly black thatch atop his head.

"I thought he was meant to be a good-looking fella," said Anne.

"He is," insisted her two companions in unison.

"Well, I'm not too impressed anyway," replied the 16-year-old dismissively, her tone one of bemused disappointment.

● ● ● ● ● ● ●

Doyle may not have wowed Anne Reidy that day on Friar Street, but she certainly made a big impression on him when their paths next crossed.

It was another sticky day in the hot summer of '51 and Anne and a large group of her friends from Thurles were cycling to Holycross to swim in one of the bathing spots there that dotted the meandering River Suir.

Along the way they met Doyle, Philip Maher and a couple more of the Glenbane gang coming in the opposite direction.

As the two groups drew closer Doyle only had eyes for the pretty blonde and, when they passed one another on the road, he braked to a halt and turned to watch her onward journey.

A few seconds passed before he found the courage to make a decision that would change his life.

"Hey, Sean," shouted Doyle at the receding group of cyclists, "come here for a second, will ya?"

Sean Gleeson was one of Anne's friends and travelling companions and Doyle recognised him because he hurled for Thurles Sarsfields.

They were barely well acquainted enough to nod at one another when they passed on the street, so, as Gleeson swung his bike around and slowly cycled back towards Doyle, he could only wonder why he had been summoned.

"Well, John, what's the story?"

"Will you ask yer wan will she go to the cinema with me on Friday night," replied Doyle, the words tumbling out of his mouth in a rush as he nodded in Anne's direction.

Gleeson cycled back to where his friends waited 20 yards further up the road, his face creased with a crooked smile.

"Hey, Anne, the county hurler wants to know if you'll go to the flicks with him on Friday."

Anne blushed red to a chorus of 'oohs' from her friends as she quickly nodded a panicked acceptance that sent Gleeson on his way back to Doyle with the good tidings.

The matchmaker was furnished with a meeting place and time and then Doyle directed a hesitant wave in Anne's direction before hurriedly remounting his bicycle to head on his way again.

Anne watched him disappear into the distance, her face still hot with embarrassment. She needed a swim in the cooling Suir now more than ever.

• • • ● • • •

The first thing Anne Reidy quickly learned about John Doyle was that he was a man of few words.

On their first cinema date the opening credits of the film were a blessing when they came because long, uncomfortable silences were only broken infrequently by stilted conversation.

At first she thought that maybe he was full of himself and didn't feel obliged to make an effort, but eventually she realised that, despite his fame, he was actually quite shy.

Once he became more confident in her company the second thing she noticed about him was that he was stubborn and head-strong.

'No' wasn't a word that John was all that accustomed to hearing. He liked to set the agenda, and if someone offered a different opinion to his own they were expressing the wrong one.

It wasn't long, though, before he discovered that his new girlfriend wasn't the sort to indulge him in the way most other people did.

Anne Reidy was very much her own woman, and not the slightest bit afraid to express a contrary opinion, or put John in his place if necessary.

• • • ● • • •

Anne checked her watch yet again and tapped her foot impatiently as she watched John from the passenger seat of his car.

He'd said he'd only be a minute, but at least 20 had passed by now as he stood talking to some cousins of his that he'd spotted while they were driving through Liberty Square.

That was it, she'd had enough. As she stepped from the car she slammed the door behind her with as much force as she could muster and marched purposefully down the street.

A few minutes later the Morris Minor pulled up alongside and John wound down the window with a confused look on his face.

"Where are you going?"

"I'm going to the pictures, like we were supposed to for the last half hour," snapped Anne.

"Shur I was only talking there," replied John defensively.

"Well, you left me sitting in the car there and it was the height of bad manners. I'm not used to that."

Anne got back into the car but no matter how much she explained why his behaviour was out of line, she could tell by the expression on her boyfriend's face that he couldn't quite see what it was he'd done wrong.

• • • ● • • •

Doyle's year-long romance with Anne looked like it had come to an end when she successfully applied for a job in Shannon Airport Duty Free after completing her Leaving Cert.

In the Ireland of 1952, there was scarcely a more exciting or glamorous job for a young, ambitious woman.

Ireland was still very much an insular and inward-looking country, but the booming Shannon Airport was a window to a much more cosmopolitan and modern world.

Visionary businessman, Brendan O'Regan, had established the world's first ever Airport Duty Free facility at Shannon just two years previously, and it was an immediate and high-profile success that made headlines around the globe.

Anne couldn't persuade her boyfriend though that this was the opportunity of a lifetime. As far as Doyle was concerned she was deserting him, and there was no good reason why she couldn't just get a job in Thurles instead.

The day before Anne travelled down to Shannon they met in Liberty Square in Thurles, and the formal handshake of farewell they exchanged had a feeling of finality about it.

● ● ● ● ● ● ●

"Excuse me, Miss, how much for this?"

When Anne turned around the first surprise she got was that such a soft voice had come from such a big man.

That was just a mild tremor though compared to the shock she experienced a second later when she recognised who her customer was.

Her father, Ger, had fostered a love for all types of sport in his three children and, from a young age, Anne's greatest hero was the heavy-weight boxing champion of the world, Joe Louis.

It wasn't just his fistic prowess that captured her imagination; the fact that he came across as a bit of a softie outside of the ring only endeared him to her more.

That's just who stood in front of her now. The 'Brown Bomber' himself.

His plane had been delayed and, over the course of the next hour, he chatted happily with Anne and her colleagues in the Duty Free shop until he was finally called to board.

Before he left though he purchased a small china figurine and shyly presented it to Anne.

"Oh, Mr Louis, you shouldn't have, thank you so much."

"My pleasure, Miss. But by the way, the name is Lou-ee, not Lou-is."

● ● ● ● ● ● ●

Joe Louis wasn't the only star Anne met while working in Shannon Duty Free. On another occasion she spent some time with Liz Taylor and her two young sons when their flight was grounded.

The job was everything she hoped it would be – exciting and glamorous – and she soon made fast friends with her co-workers who all palled around together like one big happy family.

At first Anne moved in with her uncle-in-law in Ennis but, as soon as a room became available, she moved into a hostel in Shannon with the other girls who worked in Shannon Duty Free.

It was a totally different life than the one she'd known growing up in Thurles, but one constant remained – John Doyle.

When they shook hands that day in Liberty Square she was sure that the romance was over so, when she received a letter from him a few weeks after moving to Ennis, she was shocked.

Not so much by the fact that he was still interested, but that he'd gone to the effort of writing a letter. No more than most other Irishmen of the time, Doyle wasn't usually the sort to bare his emotions.

Shortly after he'd put pen to paper he drove down to see her, and from then on he'd regularly make the considerable journey south in his new Morris Minor.

The good-looking couple would go dancing together in Cruise's Hotel in Limerick and, at the end of the month, would take a spin out to Ennis when Mick Delahunty was in town.

Mick Del's Dance Band was the most famous in Ireland at the time. They'd travel to a different town almost every night of the week and hundreds of smartly dressed young men and women would flock to hear them play.

From nine at night until three in the morning, the dance-floor would be packed with jiving couples as the band played the upbeat saxophone-led music that the Glenn Miller Orchestra had made famous in the United States.

After Doyle had dropped Anne home in the wee hours of the morning he'd drive back to Tipperary and make it back just in time to ditch his good suit and start his working day by milking the cows.

He didn't always bear this considerable commitment stoically. Every time he visited he'd urge Anne to return home to find work in Thurles, but she wasn't for budging.

Both would occasionally grow frustrated with the other's stubbornness and the whole thing would be called off for a few weeks until they inevitably got back together again.

Anne wasn't the type to mope and feel sorry for herself when the couple would occasionally go their separate ways.

She and her friends enjoyed a lively social life in Shannon, especially when BOAC, the forerunner to British Airways, sent their top pilots there to learn how to fly the world's first fleet of jet-engine passenger planes.

Looking sharp as tacks in their crisply cut uniforms, the pilots would regularly hold dinner-dances in Bunratty Castle and issue an open invitation to the female members of staff in Shannon Airport.

As dashing as the English pilots were though, none of them could hold a candle to John as far as Anne was concerned.

Her friends in Shannon had been hugely impressed by her tall, dark and handsome admirer when he first made the trip down and, by now, Anne was totally smitten.

She went to watch him hurl for Tipperary whenever she could get the time off work, and every absence between visits from him seemed to grow longer and lonelier.

Both were growing more and more frustrated with the intermittent nature of the relationship and, when John's father, Tim, passed away in December 1953, his desire to anchor his life only grew more pronounced.

Tim died after a year-long battle with stomach cancer and, a few weeks later, Doyle also lost the nearest thing he ever had to a mother – his Aunt Mary.

At the age of 23, he was alone in the world with no parents or siblings. Anne was the only real constant, and he was determined to make her a permanent fixture in his life.

••• ● •••

May, 1955

Anne had been having a bad day at work and waiting for the phone to ring in the airport lounge was doing little for her humour.

John would ring at an agreed time during the week but, in order to be in a position to take the call, Anne would need to get her friends to cover in work and hope the manager didn't spot her slipping away.

The phone finally rang and Anne quickly picked it up.

"Hello, John?"

"Yeah, it's me, how are ya keeping?"

"I've been better," sighed Anne.

"What's the matter?"

"Ah, I'm just fed up of this place."

There was a pause on the other end of the line while Doyle took a deep breath.

"Shur maybe we'll get married altogether so, will we?"

There was an even longer pause now as a stunned Anne took a moment to gather herself.

"Are you serious?"

"I am."

"Oh my God. Alright so!"

•••●•••

Doyle might have gotten Anne to accept his proposal of marriage, but her parents weren't convinced it was such a good idea.

Their daughter was still only 20, and Ger and Sis Reidy thought she was too young to marry.

Her father was a native of Clare so Anne enlisted the help of one of the county's most famous men, Canon Michael Hamilton, to persuade him to give the marriage his blessing.

Canon Hamilton was one of the leading figures in the GAA at the time and a family friend.

The idea of playing the 1947 All-Ireland SF Final in the Polo Grounds in New York had been his, and he also made headlines when he performed the first official opening of Cusack Park in Ennis by throwing in the football from a light aeroplane that flew above the pitch.

With a man as formidable as Canon Hamilton on her side, Anne couldn't fail and, sure enough, after the pair visited her parents in Thurles together her father finally granted the marriage his blessing.

Anne didn't want to have the service in Thurles Cathedral because John's fame would turn it into a public event, and decided instead she'd like to get married in Clare because she always had a natural affinity for the county of her parents.

Canon Hamilton brought her to the Church of the Seven Wells near Sixmilebridge and, with the venue picked, the date itself was quickly settled on – October 1 – just five months after John had proposed.

There was one more hurdle to overcome first though. Doyle needed to a letter of release from his parish, which required a visit to the daunting Parish Priest, Father Byrne.

Now in his nineties, Fr Byrne was very much of the fire and brimstone order of clergy and ruled Holycross with a rod of iron.

He was nearly as passionate and hard-line about Holycross hurling as he was Catholicism, and before every match the club played he'd enter the dressing-room to give the team the same final instruction.

"No one is to let down the parish so I don't want any dirty play from ye men. But if they start it, make sure to give 'em back plenty of it."

When Doyle was sent off in a club match one day, Father Byrne denounced the decision as an absolute disgrace from the pulpit the following Sunday. He was one of Doyle's biggest fans, but that didn't make the thought of visiting him any less nerve-wracking for John.

There was nothing that frightened Doyle on a hurling field, but like everyone else in Holycross he was intimidated by the stern-faced Parish Priest.

He came away empty-handed from his first visit, Fr Byrne informing him that all he needed to get married was his Baptismal Certificate. Anne sent him back a second time for the letter of release, but by now Fr Byrne was inflamed by the thought that anyone should even question Doyle's freedom to marry.

"Go back and tell them I said it's perfectly alright for you to get married wherever you like," said the PP in a tone that brooked no argument.

Unfortunately for John and Anne, Fr Byrne's verbal blessing wasn't enough, and Bishop Rodgers in Ennis informed them that he wouldn't allow the marriage to go ahead unless all their papers were in order.

The couple were thankful yet again for some good clerical connections when Dr Christy Lee, who was Diocese Administrator in Thurles and a big GAA man, successfully interceded on their behalf with Bishop Rodgers.

After everything that had gone before it, the wedding itself was the easy part. The only disagreement the couple had in the run-up to it was whether to go on honeymoon for one or two weeks.

Doyle insisted he couldn't leave the farm untended for two whole weeks, but his fiancée dug her heels in and eventually got her way.

After the 11am church service the newly-married couple had their wedding reception at the Ardhu Hotel in Limerick. As per the tradition of the time, it didn't last all that long.

There was dinner and a few happy dances afterwards, but by 4pm it was all over and the couple climbed into Doyle's car and set off on honeymoon as their cheering friends and family waved them off.

● ● ● ● ● ● ●

The gravel that crunched noisily under the Morris Minor's wheels was all the more audible because of the silence inside the car.

The further they drove down the avenue, the higher the towers and turrets of Ashford Castle loomed over them and the smaller John and Anne felt.

Just as they pulled into the forecourt, the main doors of the Castle swung open and, a few seconds later, so did the mouths of the newly-married couple.

Men in full evening dress escorting ladies in ball gowns emerged from the castle and made their way regally down the sweeping stone steps that led to the forecourt where the humble Morris Minor was parked.

"Jaysus Christ Almighty," said Doyle slowly.

The look on his wife's face quickly told him that she felt just as much out of place as he did.

He gunned the engine and gravel spat from beneath the wheels of the car as Mr and Mrs Doyle beat as hasty a retreat as they could.

● ● ● ● ● ● ●

The honeymooners instead pointed their car towards Galway where they checked into the Great Southern Hotel on Eyre Square for a week before moving on to Dublin for the second leg of the holiday.

Doyle had booked them into the Castle Hotel on Great Denmark Street, which was a favourite amongst the Tipperary hurlers because you'd get two dinners on one plate such was the generosity of the chef.

He had another motive too, though. It was right next door to Barry's Hotel, which had become the Tipperary team's HQ whenever they hurled in Croke Park.

• • • ● • • •

Anne walked down to the hotel lobby to see if her husband had completed his phone-call home yet.

She was quickly learning that a farmer's thoughts never stray too far from his holding.

At the same time every day since they'd come on honeymoon he'd phoned his cousin Gerry 'Bowler' Doyle who was looking after the farm to check on the condition of a sick bullock.

As she reached the bottom of the stairs she was stopped dead by the sight that greeted her in the lobby.

Her husband was cracking jokes with Pat Stakelum and a couple more of his Tipperary team-mates.

When the laughter suddenly stopped Doyle turned around to face his wife with the guilty expression of a schoolboy caught stealing chocolate by a shopkeeper.

Before she could take another step he quickly walked over and intercepted her at the bottom of the staircase.

"Anne, can I have a quick word with you back in the room?"

When the door closed behind them Anne asked the obvious question.

"What are Pat and the lads doing here?"

"They're after persuading me to play a match in Croke Park," replied Doyle.

His wife's eyebrows arched and so did the tone of her voice.

"I don't believe you! You promised me that you'd give up the hurling entirely after we got married. And now you're telling me that you're going to go hurling on our

honeymoon?

"I have to play," replied Doyle, with defensive shrug and his palms opened. "It's the St Brendan's Cup Final against New York and I'm the team captain this year. This is my last chance to win something as Tipperary captain."

Doyle's explanation did little to soothe his wife's temper, nor did his insistence that she'd have to come to the match and watch it.

After just two weeks of marriage Anne was beginning to realise that marrying John Doyle the man also meant marrying John Doyle the hurler.

CHAPTER 15

As soon as Doyle appeared over the gate a great cheer went up from the men and boys kicking the ball around Maher's top field.

He'd only arrived back from his honeymoon the previous night and some had wondered if he'd join them like he usually did for the 'Sunday League' game.

When he emerged from the house with the familiar pep in his step, the few who had doubted him were quickly admonished with a chorus of 'I told you so's' from the majority who knew he wouldn't be able to resist.

Unlike most Sundays, the hurleys and sliotars had been left at home and the men were instead playing a game of football with a set of rules very much open to interpretation.

It was nominally a soccer match, but there were few holds barred and the occasional high catch and rugby tackle were being thrown in here and there for good measure.

Not long after he'd joined his friends in their sport the returning hero was laid low in spectacular fashion.

He made the fatal decision to stoop to head the ball when Mikey Ryan had already made up his mind to kick the thing as hard as could.

Boot met nose with a sickly crunch and Doyle fell to ground in a heap with blood already gushing angrily from the point of impact.

The nose was in smithereens and, as his friends stood around their fallen comrade who was out cold on the ground and spouting blood, they all shared the same thought: How were they going to explain this to the new wife?

••• • •••

Her husband's broken nose wasn't the only unpleasant surprise that greeted Anne on her first day in her new home in Holycross.

She had never before set foot in the house so it came as a real shock to discover there was no running water or toilet in it. Water had to be drawn from a well a mile away in Tubberadora, which required a couple of round trips a day.

She was almost as dismayed to see that a house that hadn't benefited from a woman's touch in twenty-five years wasn't even equipped with any sort of oven.

Instead, a large pot that hung from a hook over the open fire was used to make the same meal every day – boiled hairy bacon, cabbage and spuds.

The bacon was bought in Jim Hayes' shop down in Holycross village where pigs would be killed, butchered and then treated heavily with salt and put in barrels of brine to persevere the meat.

Even if you regularly changed the water in the pot while you boiled this bacon, it still tasted so salty it would nearly strip the roof of your mouth raw.

When Anne saw the soot-blackened boiling pot in the fireplace of her new home for the first time she immediately set John straight: "I'm telling you right now that I'm not cooking in that thing."

"What do you mean you're not cooking in it?"

"I don't care if we have to go hungry for twelve months, I'm not cooking in that dirty thing."

Her new husband could see he wasn't going to win this argument, so he immediately arranged the purchase of a spanking new Rayburn cooker.

Two days would pass before the stove arrived and, in the interim, John's uncle, Tom, who was also living in the house at the time, was given the task of preparing the meals in the much-maligned pot.

When the Rayburn was eventually installed Anne quickly set about changing the culinary habits of the household.

The salty bacon was no longer a daily staple and, instead, the extremely impressed men of the house were treated to luxuries such as lamb chops and Sunday roasts.

The condition of her new home or the dietary habits of her new husband weren't the only culture shock for a woman who had no real idea of what being a farmer's wife entailed.

She quickly discovered it was a life of constant gruelling physical labour, but if any of her neigbours thought the 'townie' wouldn't be able to hack it, they were soon put to right.

A formidable woman, Anne was determined not to be cowed by her new circumstances, so she threw herself wholeheartedly into every new challenge, even if this enthusiasm was a double-edged sword.

The more tasks she mastered, the more she was left with. Where before John would rush home after every match he played for Tipperary to milk the cows, now he could leave that job to his wife.

He was also able to rest on the morning of a big match because Anne and their neighbour, Mikey Ryan, would look after the milking so he'd be as fresh as possible for the game.

The pair would head out to the fields at 6am with a couple of flashlamps to herd the cows and, while Anne would milk them, Mikey would take every filled churn one by one to the creamery.

If Tipperary were playing a match in Dublin that day, they'd have to have everything done in time to make the 9.10am train from Thurles.

During the summer Anne's young brother, Ray, would cycle out from Thurles to give a helping hand on the farm when he was on holiday from Kiltegan seminary in Wicklow where he studying to be a St Patrick's missionary priest.

An outstanding hurler himself, he captained the Tipperary minor team to All-Ireland success in 1955 and was on the senior panel from '56 to '60 even though his studies only allowed him to hurl from the months of June to September.

Like his sister, he had little experience of farm work before Doyle started making good use of him during those summer months but, though the work was hard, it was always made enjoyable by the banter he exchanged in the fields with his brother-in-law.

By then Ray was hurling for Sarsfields when their rivalry with Holycross was at its very zenith, and the repartee always had a little extra cut and thrust to it the week before the two teams played a match.

"By Jaysus we'll be giving ye plenty of timber next Sunday, Ray. We're after getting a new supply of hurleys in and we've told the referee to take it easy on d'oul whistlin'.

"Don't bother coming into town, John, ye'll only make a holy show of yourselves again. You'd be much better off now staying at home."

Saving the hay was always more important than hurling though. Whenever Ray would mount his bike and head for home Doyle would make sure to shout the last word as his brother-in-law cycled down the road.

"Whoever wins that feckin' match tomorrow, you be here on Monday morning regardless."

Ray might have been getting the better of Doyle and his Holycross team-mates in the blue of Sarsfields, but beating him one-on-one was a different challenge entirely.

• • • ● • • •

After Doyle had mopped his plate clean with a heel of bread he nodded across the table at his brother-in-law.

"Are you ready so? The football is in the corner there."

Ray knew the routine by now. After lunch every day Doyle and he would head out to the small field behind the house and make two sets of goal-posts thirty yards from each other with a couple of jumpers or gallons.

The game was a simple one. The first to score ten points was the winner.

Ray was a handy footballer as well as a hurler and, like he did most days, he took an early lead.

What came next was just as predictable. Trailing by 7-5, Doyle gave the ball an almighty hoof that sent it a good 20 yards beyond Ray and into a ditch.

By the time Ray recovered it and looked back down the field, Doyle's two goal-posts had come in a good yard at either side and the target he was now faced with was barely broader than the man himself.

"Ah, for God's sake, John, would you not play fair?"

"Jaysus, if there's one thing I can't feckin' stand it's lads feckin' cribbin'," shouted Doyle back at him. "Just kick the feckin' ball."

A few minutes later Ray caught Doyle's winning tenth point behind his goal.

"You could never bate me," roared Doyle down the field, before marching off with his usual determined stride, another foe vanquished.

•••●•••

Even with the help of his wife, brother-in-law and neighbours, Doyle was finding it more and more difficult to combine the demands of farming, hurling and a family life.

He'd increased his dairy herd and purchased more land so the couple's workload was increasing all the time, and, by 1957, the first two of their eight children – Margaret and Johnny – had been born.

Even though he was still only 27, Doyle agreed with his wife that it was time to give up inter-county hurling, a decision that was made easier for him by the fact that Tipperary showed little sign of recapturing the sort of form that had brought them three All-Irelands in a row between '49 and '51.

In 1956 they earned the nickname 'The Lead Losers' because of catastrophic second-half collapses against Wexford in the League Final and then against Cork in the Munster Semi-Final.

In the League Final they led by 2-10 to 0-1 at half time but their defence was overrun in the second half as Wexford scored 5-8 with just four points in reply to turn a 15-point deficit into a four-point victory.

Much of the blame for the defeat was laid at the door of the full-back line and goalkeeper Tony Reddin, who was at fault for two of the goals, and would never play a major match for Tipperary again.

The defeat to Cork wasn't quite so spectacular, but no less devastating. Tipp led at half-time by 2-6 to 0-1, but only scored a point in the second half and lost by 1-11 to 2-7.

Once again Tipp felt hard done by a refereeing decision when Paddy Kenny had a last-minute goal disallowed because a Cork defender threw a hurley at him just before he struck the ball.

Rather than wave play on and allow the goal to stand, the referee blew for a free, which was saved by the massed Cork defenders on the goal-line. Gerry 'Bowler' Doyle let fly on the rebound, but his shot rocketed over the bar instead of under it, just like it had in '52.

Tipperary did manage to beat Kilkenny in the 1957 League Final, which earned them another trip to New York but, once again, their championship was ended by another calamitous defeat to Cork.

Tipp totally dominated possession and territory in the first half, but some abysmal shooting, combined with lax defending, meant they went in at the break trailing by 3-1 to 0-8.

At half time the team selectors made the strange decision to replace Tony Reddin's goalkeeping heir, Blackie Keane, with another Championship rookie, Eddie Moloughney.

Christy Ring won the ball straight from the throw-in at the start of the second half and sent a high ball scudding towards the Tipperary goal which Moloughney thought was trailing wide but, to his dismay, curled just inside the post for another soft goal.

Most of the blame for the defeat was pinned on the goalkeeping calamities by the local press, but a number of other under-performing players also came in for some criticism, including Doyle.

Cork's Paddy Barry had scored three goals off him, and there was a widespread view that he was now a pale shadow of the young buck who'd taken the inter-county scene by storm in his late teens and early twenties.

He took the barbs personally and, by the time he boarded the flight to the USA in October for the St. Brendan Cup against New York, he was clear in his mind that it would be his last match in the blue and gold.

He hadn't reckoned on the persuasive powers of Paddy Leahy. The Tipp team returned home from America by boat and, after five days on the high seas and a series of pep talks from his mentor, Doyle's mind had been changed for him.

While he'd been away his wife had to deal with a family emergency single-handedly. Their son, Johnny, had become very ill, so much so that it was deemed too much of a risk to even move him to Dublin.

He'd developed a sudden allergy to milk that left him with a raging fever, and for a couple of fraught days it was touch-and-go as to whether he'd survive.

Doctor Paddy Molony came out from Thurles and stayed with the sick infant and his worried mother through the night when the fever was at its worst, and, after a trying week, baby Johnny finally pulled through.

Anne had been unable to contact her husband to tell him of the crisis, so, when he returned home and told her he'd gone back on this decision to quit inter-county hurling, her reaction was predictable.

The dismay she felt was tempered slightly by one concession he was willing to make – he'd no longer hurl League matches.

In those days a successful League campaign would stretch from November until May so this promise was a significant victory for his wife.

It would also prove to be a short-lived one.

• • • ● • • •

When Anne Doyle looked out the window and saw John deep in conversation with Paddy Leahy by the front-yard wall, her heart sank.

She immediately knew the concession she'd fought so hard for was about to be blown to the four winds.

Anne had almost as much regard for Leahy as her husband did, but enough was enough. She marched outside to say her piece.

"Paddy, he's not hurling in the League. I'm just not able to cope here without him."

Leahy gave a loud exhalation and shook his head sadly.

"Well, the Lord have mercy on my mother. She had our togs and stockings ready every single Sunday and sent us off hurling with a smile on her face, God be with her."

Anne remained undaunted.

"God be with her is right. Now she's six foot under shoving up the daisies and I have no intention of going the same way early.

"If you want my husband that badly you can get someone from the County Board out here to milk the cows on a Sunday when these League matches are on and then he can hurl as much as you want."

Doyle remained mute while the two most important people in his life argued. His silence spoke volumes, the decision had been made.

Hurling had won again.

CHAPTER 16

Leahy drained the last finger of whiskey in the tumbler, his eyes narrowing for a second when the firewater hit the back of his throat.

He looked over at his host, Jimmy Finn, cracked a roguish smile, and reached his hand across the table.

Finn accepted the handshake with an almost rueful shake of his head. The deal had been done. He'd agreed to come out of retirement and hurl in the first round of the Championship against Limerick.

Leahy had got his man again, but Finn had been much harder work than Doyle.

Three times he'd driven out to Borris-Ileigh and three times Finn had welcomed him with a warming tipple or two. But it took a fourth visit before he finally got the answer he was looking for and could toast a victory.

Finn hadn't come home from America with the rest of the Tipperary team the previous Autumn. He'd stayed in the States for another three months working on the famous Man O' War horse farm in Kentucky.

He'd had an offer to stay, too, and when he arrived home to a cold, wet Ireland in December he spent a good while wondering whether he should have accepted it.

Whatever it was that brought him back, it certainly wasn't the hurling. Just like Doyle, a combination of six unsuccessful championships in a row and the demands of farming had convinced him it was time to move on.

Finn might have thought he was finished with Tipperary hurling, but Leahy wasn't about to let him go.

He was convinced he knew how to re-energise both him and Doyle, and, in the process, revitalise Tipperary.

Mission completed, he drove back to Holycross with a warm feeling in his belly that was part-whiskey, part-optimism.

●●●◉●●●

As the 1958 Championship loomed, Tipperary were rarely mentioned in dispatches as genuine contenders.

Doyle and The Rattler Byrne were the only men still on the panel who'd won All-Ireland medals in '49, '50 and '51, and there had been a rash of retirements after the calamitous defeat to Cork in the '57 Munster Semi-Final.

Everyone else might have viewed Tipp as an outfit in terminal decline, but not Paddy Leahy.

He could see an exciting new generation of hurlers emerging in the county, but he knew, too, a successful new team could only be built on solid foundations.

That's where Doyle and Finn came in. A dominant half-back line is the most important component in any hurling team, and Leahy planned to unleash both of his veterans on the flanks of his defence.

Finn had cut a frustrated figure at full-back for the previous couple of seasons and Leahy figured a return to his natural home on the wing would get the best from him again.

Doyle might been known only as a corner-back at inter-county level, but Leahy knew from watching him hurl with Holycross that he had both the athleticism and natural skill to flourish further out the field and that the new challenge would energise his prize pupil.

His faith in two of his veteran defenders remained undimmed, but not in a third. Pat Stakelum had been Tipperary's greatest-ever centre-back, but Leahy could see that he was slipping.

Stakelum had lost a yard of pace and was no longer able to sweep across the half-back line with the same effortless authority he did in his pomp. Dropping him was a huge call, but Tony Wall made it an easier one to make.

The Thurles Sarsfields man had been a member of the team since '54, filling shifts at corner-back, wing-back and even in the half-forward line.

His best position was centre-back, though, and his performances there for the all-conquering Sarsfields team already bore the mark of greatness.

Wall was an army officer and a perfectionist in his approach to the game. He was utterly dedicated to being the best hurler and athlete he could be.

He didn't drink or smoke and any day he didn't train collectively with

Sarsfields or Tipperary he'd make sure to train by himself.

He had a voracious appetite to educate himself on the best practices of fitness and coaching and collected every piece of literature he could that was being published on the subject in the USA.

As far as Wall was concerned, only by breaking down the game of hurling into its component parts and analysing every one of them in forensic detail could you hope to become the best hurler you could possibly be.

As a centre-back he had to contest a lot of clash-balls both overhead and on the ground, so he figured it was vital that the hurley he used would be stronger and heavier than the one his opponent would wield.

His hurley always weighed between 23 and 24 ounces, which was considerably heavier than most, but, with constant practise and arm-strengthening exercises Wall was eventually able to wield it as easily as his opponent could a lighter hurley.

The pole of the hurley was never less than one inch thick so the bas was particularly heavy and allowed him to get enormous distance on ground strokes and smash an opponent's hurley to smithereens in 50-50 contests.

He always made sure to lace up his boots a full 15 minutes before a match so, if one of the laces snapped, there would be plenty of time to re-lace the boot with a spare he carried.

And, during the summer when the ground hardened up, he'd remove the cogs from his boot and replace them with three-quarter inch bars of leather, onto which he nailed circular pieces of leather with a hobnail or stud in the centre.

He studied his opponents in minute detail too, and if they happened to get the better of him in an exchange by using a particular technique, they'd rarely pull the same trick successfully a second time.

Wall would have analysed where he had gone wrong and devised a solution. He was constantly learning from experience and forever refining his game.

In style he wasn't quite as flamboyant as Stakelum had been, but he was no less effective.

His ability to read the play enabled him to sweep across the entire half-back line to great effect, and, when he won the ball, his deliveries into the forward line were low and angled so as to give his team-mates the best chance possible of claiming possession cleanly.

He didn't earn the same renown as a hard man that some of his defensive colleagues did, but no one put in more crunching tackles in the blue and gold than Wall.

It was an era when the frontal charge was still a legal tackle, and no one could effect a shoulder into the chest with the sort of devastating timing and power that Wall could.

If you ran at the centre of the Tipperary defence, it was an invite to end up in a crumpled heap on the ground with your rib-cage feeling like it had been tickled with a sledgehammer.

Paddy Leahy knew that a defensive trio of Wall, flanked by Doyle and Finn, would be hugely formidable – the perfect combination of athleticism, skill, intelligence and raw strength.

But, even with that half-back line in place, there was still a lot of work to be done. So many of the '57 Championship team had retired that an almost entirely new side had to be constructed.

Tony Reddin had never been adequately replaced, and in '58 Moycarkey goalkeeper John O'Grady was finally given the chance to stake his claim.

He'd played with Doyle on the All-Ireland minor winning team of '47 and was captain when the minors were triumphant again in 1949 but never made the step up to the senior team because he moved to Cork where he taught in Sullivan's Quay CBS until 1955.

With Doyle and Finn relocated to the half-back line, there were a couple of vacancies to be filled in the full-back line, too.

That old war-horse, Mickey The Rattler Byrne, was still manning the right-corner back berth with his usual tenacity, and after a few false starts earlier in the decade, Doyle's childhood friend, Mikey Maher, would finally make the full-back position his own in '58.

Maher wasn't the most elegant hurler in the world, but he cut a formidable figure on the edge of the small square. Over six foot tall, broad-chested and with legs like tree trunks, there was no going through him, and it was a long way around.

He knew his limitations, took a sensible, safety-first approach to defending, and wasn't the least bit shy about being utterly ruthless when the situation demanded it.

Ruthlessness was a quality that Kieran Carey didn't lack either. The rugged Roscrea defender had been recommended to Leahy by Jimmy Finn after he'd impressed in a club match against Borris-Ileigh, and was such an instant success in '58 that Doyle's relocation would hardly weaken the full-back line at all.

Leahy didn't have too many concerns about midfield either. John Hough had won an All-Ireland medal in '51 and was still going strong, and Theo English was developing into one of the outstanding midfielders in the game.

As soon as an opponent sized up English he would have known he was in for a hard hour's hurling. The squat and powerful midfielder was built like a super-middleweight boxer with bulging biceps, a broad chest and thick neck.

His home place in Marlfield just outside Clonmel wasn't renowned as a hotbed of hurling, but English was always obsessed with the game.

When he was just 14 years old he borrowed a neighbour's bike and cycled the 30 miles to and 30 miles back from Thurles to watch Cork play Limerick in the Munster Final even though he wasn't big enough to sit on the bicycle's saddle.

He showed the same single-mindedness when it came to developing his own hurling talent.

Hurlers from South Tipperary were always at a disadvantage because they were traditionally perceived to be of inferior stock than the men from Mid and North Tipperary, so, if you wanted to make it onto the county team, you had to be something special.

English was ferociously determined to do whatever it took to make the breakthrough and did his own private training four evenings a week for 46 weeks of the year. He didn't drink or smoke, and on the week of a match always made sure to be in bed before 10pm every night.

Because of this professional approach the Marlfield man was a formidable athlete. His primary role was to keep the ball moving quickly through the middle of the field but, over the course of a match, he'd buzz all over the pitch to great effect.

Much like Tony Wall, he was fastidious in his approach to the game. He always had a stock of five hurleys that he trained with alternately so that, if he broke one or two on the day of the match, he'd have a replacement he was accustomed to.

Those same hurleys were made by his own hand and were of such a high quality that before long he was kept busy making them for many of his Tipperary team-mates as well.

English was one of those invaluable players you could be sure would put in a consistent shift every time he played, but though Paddy Leahy was happy enough with the way his team was taking shape from goalkeeper to midfield, he wasn't so confident about the make-up of his attack.

Paddy Kenny and Mick Ryan had left the panel after '57, and most of the scoring burden now rested on the slim shoulders of 19-year-old Jimmy Doyle.

The Boy Wonder had announced himself as something special the previous year with two crucial points in the League Final against Kilkenny, but it was still asking a lot of a youngster just a year out of the minor grade to lead the attack.

The burden didn't weigh heavily on Jimmy. He was born to be a hurler and had been preparing himself to play for Tipperary for as long as he could remember.

His father, Gerry, had been the reserve team goalkeeper on the All-Ireland winning Tipperary teams of 1937 and 1945 and his uncle, Tommy, was the great Rubber Man himself, so Jimmy came from good stock.

The environment he grew up in couldn't have been more conducive to nurturing a young hurler either. His home – Number 2, Church View, Bohernanave – lay right in the shadow of Semple Stadium, which was Jimmy's field of dreams for as long as he could remember.

When his father hurled for Tipperary he would don his hurling boots in the house and walk across the road to Semple for training, and the sound those boots made on the concrete stirred the young boy's imagination like nothing else.

When he was only two years old he asked his father could he have a pair of hurling boots himself. Gerry Doyle was a cobbler and only too happy to satisfy his son's request.

After he arrived home with the lovingly crafted minature boots his son spent the rest of the day click-clacking his way happily over and back across the kitchen floor with a tiny hurley in his hands and a huge smile on his face.

Jimmy's sole interest was hurling. When he'd come home from school his pet sheepdog, Pal, would be waiting for him at the gate with his hurley in his mouth and the two of them would immediately head for the Thurles Sarsfields pitch which was adjacent to Semple Stadium.

Pal was Jimmy's training partner and did more than anyone to help hone the sublime first touch and mastery of all the skills that would make his master one of the greatest hurlers to ever play the game.

Running at top speed Jimmy would puck the ball high up into the air, and if he didn't catch it first time, or kill it dead on his stick when it returned from orbit, Pal would snap it from him.

For hours and hours he'd repeat this drill and, though Pal was a willing accomplice, it was always the dog's enthusiasm that flagged before the boy's.

Jimmy's other favourite drill was to practise his shooting on the run and free-taking by banging the sliotar over a big green door at the back of the Town End terrace of Semple Stadium that backed onto the Sarsfields' pitch.

He was a natural left-hander and there was a lovely smooth motion to his swing because his father Gerry had made sure he held the hurley left hand on top rather than fall into the trap many citogs do by trying to hold the hurley with the same grip that right-handers use.

Jimmy would stay belting the sliotar at that green gate until dusk fell while, back home, his mother would have do his school homework for him because her son refused point blank to spend his time on anything other than honing his hurling skill.

At night time he'd lay his little hurleys out on his bed, sleep on them like a mattress, and place his sliotars under his pillow. When his mother kissed him goodnight she'd remove them, but as soon as she left the room he'd put them all back again.

For most Tipperary boys the county hurling team were faraway heroes they only heard about from their fathers, or were lucky to see from a distance at the occasional match, but Jimmy was on first-name terms with all of them.

His father, Gerry, helped County Board Secretary, Phil Purcell, train the three-in-a-row team, and Jimmy would watch every session intently from behind Tony Reddin's goal.

Even at the age of 10 he was taking it all in with a clinical eye, dissecting every player's strengths and weaknesses and soaking up every trick of the trade like a thirsty sponge.

Whenever there was a match in Semple Stadium he'd squeeze his way into the ground through one of his many secret entrances and, when the match was over, he'd hide beneath a row of seats until all the stewards had finally locked up and left.

With the stadium deserted, Jimmy would race out onto the pitch with his hurley and sliotar and recreate the most dramatic moments from the match he'd just watched.

The only time he didn't do this was when Cork came to town because then all his energies would be focused on stalking Christy Ring. Most Tipperary fans hated the sight of the man who broke their hearts more often than any other hurler, but to Jimmy he was a god.

The Cork team would congregate at the Glenmorgan before matches, so Jimmy would always be there waiting.

He was a small, unassuming-looking little boy with a knack for blending into the background unnoticed. So, when the Cork players started filing into the guesthouse he'd drift in with them and get as close to Ring as possible.

He'd follow them up to Semple Stadium too, and would stand behind whichever goal Ring was playing to in the first half and then make his way down to the other end of the field for the second half.

And, when the match was over, he'd ghost his way past the stewards and sometimes make it all the way to the Cork dressing room where he could watch his hero from close quarters again.

He'd be loitering in the background once more by the time the Cork players ate their post-match meal in the Glenmorgan and, when he noticed that Ring was in the habit of mashing all his food up together before spooning it down, that was the only way Jimmy would eat from then on.

Jimmy aspired to be as good a forward as Ring himself some day, but Tony Reddin had a different path mapped out for him. The youngster's precocity hadn't gone unnoticed by the goalkeeper who was convinced he was the natural heir to his No. 1 jersey.

He took the boy on as his apprentice, and at every session Jimmy would stand behind Reddin's goal fetching any ball that went over the bar or into the back of the net.

Standing in one spot wasn't Jimmy's style though and, when the play would be down the other end of the field, he'd solo a sliotar out to where either John Doyle or Mickey Byrne were standing in their corner-back position and arrow balls over the bar from the tightest of angles.

"Hey, Reddin," roared Doyle over at his team-mate one day when Jimmy sent another ball fizzing over the black spot. "You can give over trying to make that young lad a goalkeeper. He'll be winning matches for us at the other end of the field."

Doyle would be proven right with time, but Jimmy did make his first appearance in the blue and gold as a goalkeeper when, at the age of 14, he played between the sticks for the Tipperary minor team that lost the 1954 All-Ireland Final.

He made his debut for the county senior team in a League match against Galway when he was just 16, and before he was done with the minor grade, he had inspired Tipperary to three consecutive All-Ireland titles.

In 1957, he played in the Munster Championship for both the Tipperary minors and seniors on the same day. He was captain of the minor team but didn't start the Munster Final against Cork because Paddy Leahy had also selected him in the senior team.

As the senior team prepared for their showdown against Cork in the hotel across from the Gaelic Grounds, Jimmy asked Leahy could he go and watch his minor team-mates in action.

Leahy gave him his permission, but probably wouldn't had he seen Jimmy grab his hurling boots on his way out of the hotel.

The Tipp minors were leading by five goals at half time, but Cork being Cork produced a marvellous rally to reduce the deficit to four points. Jimmy immediately laced up his boots and declared himself available to the minor team management.

He scored a point as soon as he came onto the field and then set up a goal and scored a couple more points to see the minor team home safely. Half an hour later, he started for the Tipperary seniors.

Jimmy was a special talent alright, but he was a fragile one, too. No defender could hope to better him in a contest of skill and pace, but plenty were willing to try an obvious alternative.

Jimmy barely weighed 11 stone and didn't have a malicious bone in his body. In an era of hungry defensive lions, he was a vulnerable gazelle.

In full flight no one could get close to him, but for all Jimmy's prodigious gifts, and the fame he'd earned for his underage exploits, plenty of Tipperary fans wondered could he survive and thrive at senior inter-county level.

If he couldn't, it didn't look like the glory days would be returning to Tipperary any time soon.

••• • •••

June 1, 1958, Cork.
Munster SH Quarter-Final v Limerick

Tony Wall took the centre of the dressing room and regarded all the expectant faces looking up at him.

This was the moment he'd been thinking about all week. His first team-talk as Tipperary captain.

There were eight men in the room about to make their championship debuts and it was his job to send them out onto the field in as positive a frame of mind as possible.

Just as importantly, he needed to show the handful of veterans that he was now a team leader and no longer one of the rookies.

Usually little was said in the dressing room before matches, but he felt a weight of responsibility to lay down a marker.

Something strong. Something bold. Something to stir the blood of every player in the room.

He clattered his hurley off the floor, pointed it towards the dressing room door and roared: "Go out there now and kill those fuckers."

In an instant, the expectant atmosphere that had been building in the dressing room was drained as if someone had just pulled a giant bath stopper.

Wall couldn't have shocked his team-mates more had he gone around to them one by one and slapped them in the face with a big wet fish.

No one had ever used the word 'fuckers' in the dressing room before, and coming from the austere army officer it had even more of an impact than it would had anyone else uttered it.

Wall knew he'd made a terrible misjudgement, but there was little that could be done now. He stumbled over a few less profane words of encouragement and then hurriedly led his dumbstruck team-mates out the dressing room door.

As Jimmy Finn jogged out onto the pitch he winced with pain. The previous evening he'd badly sprained his ankle while breaking-in a horse, and he knew the injury was going to be tested to the full because he was marking Limerick's flying half-forward, Vivien Cobb.

He called over at Doyle: "Hey, John, any chance you'd mark Cobb and I'll take your man?"

"I will in me arse," replied Doyle. "You can mark him yourself!"

Even with that ankle injury and only one week of training under his belt since returning to the panel, Finn totally subdued Limerick's chief danger man.

Cobb wasn't the only Limerick man neutralised. Their entire forward line found itself held firmly in a vice-like grip as Doyle and Wall also hurled like men possessed in the Tipp defence.

But every time they belted the ball down the field it was invariably returned with interest because the Tipperary forwards were failing to make any sort of impression on the game.

It was only when Jimmy Doyle arrowed a 21-yard free to the back of the net to draw Tipperary level with 15 minutes to go that they suddenly came to life.

The Limerick defence that had been in control until that point unravelled like a cheap jumper in the final quarter, and in the end Tipperary won by double scores – 2-10 to 1-5.

The result raised a few eyebrows. Limerick had been unlucky to lose the League Final to Wexford and were expected to get the better of this stitched-together Tipperary team.

Despite their win, no one was willing to announce the Premier County's rebirth as a force to be reckoned with just yet. The general consensus was that Limerick just didn't hurl on the day and, anyway, Cork were up next in the Munster semi-final.

••• ● •••

June 22, 1958, Limerick.
Munster Senior Hurling Semi-Final v Cork.

The 45,000 Tipperary and Cork fans in the Gaelic Grounds stood as one with their heads bowed as a familiar incantation echoed around the ground.

They were being lead in prayer by the stadium announcer who had informed them that a Cork supporter had just died in the stadium and a decade of the Rosary would now be said in his memory.

For a few minutes after the prayer had been completed a surreal atmosphere suffused the stadium because the usual pre-match singing and shouting suddenly felt disrespectful; the spell was only broken when the Cork team ran out onto the field and the presence of Christy Ring in their ranks roused great roars from the Rebel faithful.

There had been a doubt whether he'd play or not after sustaining a broken rib in a challenge match against Galway, but you'd have to snap a more substantial bone than that to keep Ring away from a championship joust with Tipperary.

Few of those who did start the match in the whole of their health finished it in the same condition. The general opinion might have been that neither Tipp nor Cork were as potent as they'd been at the start of the decade, but this match would be just as brutally confrontational as those epic clashes had been.

No man threw himself into the fray with more relish than Doyle, who had a worthy adversary in the Cork half-forward, Tom Furlong. There was little point asking for quarter because it wouldn't have been given.

One particular throw-in they contested in front of the packed stand produced the sort of salty exchange that makes the weak of constitution blanch and small children cry.

Doyle was already a fan's favourite because of his years of solid service as a corner-back but, by fulfilling his new brief in the half-back line with typical gusto, he was gilding his status even more.

Now he was constantly in the thick of the action rather than just repelling the occasional raid.

And when he'd arrive on the scene with his collar up, that mop of hair bouncing, and smash someone to the ground with a meaty shoulder-charge or storm from defence through a series of wicked challenges, the Tipp fans would jump to their feet and bellow to the heavens.

He was taking just as much punishment as he was dishing out, but his unflinching hardiness in the face of some eye-watering blows only endeared him to the crowd more.

Doyle was a great man for shivering an opponent to their very bones with a hefty shoulder, but his own style of play left him open to the same treatment.

He liked to course the ball out from defence along the ground and hare down the line after it, but along the way he was being lined up by opponents who prized the honour of flattening Tipperary's totemic defender.

Most of them would bounce off him like they'd just ran into the butt of an oak tree, but when he was occasionally levelled it was a great cause for celebration for the opposition's fans.

Their roars would soon be drowned out, though, by a din of acclaim for Doyle when he'd inevitably rise to his feet a few seconds after shipping a blow that would have killed a mere mortal twice over.

Doyle was well aware of the reaction he was getting from the crowd. He enjoyed the acclaim and even sought it out. If he had the option of running around an opponent or straight through him, the decision required little thought.

As a young cub on the three-in-a-row team he was happy to do a solid job quietly and with the minimum of fuss, but now he was in his prime and a more confident and flamboyant hurler altogether.

There was a derring-do and defiance about everything he did that electrified the crowd and lifted his team-mates, and, after all the years of subservience to

Cork since the '51 Munster Final, his super-charged will to win was just the tonic that Tipperary needed.

Alongside him in the half-back line, Tony Wall and Jimmy Finn were hurling with similar bite and brio and, despite facing a stiff breeze, Tipp had forged a two-point lead after 15 minutes.

But then the sort of calamity that had become a hall-mark of championship encounters with Cork struck again when goalkeeper John O'Grady conceded two soft goals.

The first was an innocuous shot from Christy Ring that floated over his head and into the back of the net; the second came after he'd made a fine save but then had his attempted clearance blocked and flicked to the net by Liam Dowling.

The goals sandwiched a brace of points from Ring and Terry Kelly, so, despite hurling more ball, Tipperary found themselves trailing by six points.

Unlike the previous year though, this time their heads didn't drop. Theo English was playing his best game ever in the blue and gold at midfield and scored a point just before the break that testified to Tipp's sustained resolve.

At half time Leahy made a crucial switch when Liam Devaney came on for Doyle's brother-in-law, Ray Reidy, who had started at midfield despite only a couple of weeks training since leaving Kiltegan Seminary for the summer.

Devaney went into the half-forward line, which released championship rookie, Donie Nealon, to midfield. The fastest man in the panel, Nealon was a tireless worker and, in harness with English, provided Tipperary with almost total midfield dominance.

Devaney would have started had he been fit, but even on just one good leg he gave the Tipp attack the sort of focal point it had badly lacked in the first half.

The Borris-Ileigh man wasn't the sort who'd run up and down the field for you all day, but if he got the ball in his hand at all he'd either produce a score from nothing or create an opportunity for a colleague.

He was a nightmare for opposition defenders because he could make them look silly with one moment of magic, and there was little point trying to rough him up because Devaney was a master of the dark arts and would give it back twice as hard.

He wasn't the biggest man in the world but he was a great ball-winner and now, when the Tipp half-back line drove the sliotar down the field, it wasn't coming back as quickly as it had in the first half.

The only problem was that it wasn't going over the bar either. Five wides were accumulated in the first three minutes of the half to a chorus of sighs and swears from the Tipperary supporters.

There was still four points between the teams when John O'Grady redeemed himself for the two goals he'd conceded in the first half. Cork corner-forward Liam Dowling ran onto the ball at full pelt and let fly on it, but O'Grady somehow killed the shot on his stick and then doubled on the ball in mid-air.

From that clearance Tipp reduced the deficit to three points, and then came the moment that effectively ended a great era for Cork hurling, and ushered in one for Tipperary.

Larry Kiely had been struggling to get any sort of change out of Cork's masterful corner-back Jimmy Brohan, but then he hit the jackpot in a big way when he turned inside the defender and unleashed a pile-driver from 30 yards that ripped past Cork goalkeeper Mick Cashman.

The roar that greeted the goal was a frenzied one. After six years of failure and frustration, the Tipperary fans were allowing themselves to believe their team were finally about to throw off Cork's heavy yoke.

Points from Jimmy Doyle and Liam Devaney pushed Tipp ahead with time almost up, but no lead feels less secure than a two-point one especially when Christy Ring is on the opposition team.

And when Tipperary's bogeyman won the ball in injury time and floated in a high ball towards the square the cheers on the terraces turned to a fearful hiss that sounded like air escaping from a giant tyre.

Liam Dowling's hand rose highest, but just when it looked like he was about to claim the ball he was heaved aside by the considerable bulk of Mikey Maher and the ball was batted clear.

A few seconds later the final whistle blew and the pitch was immediately swamped by thousands of joyful Tipperary fans who carried their heroes shoulder-high. Nothing had been won yet, but breaking Cork's spell was cause enough for celebration.

• • • ● • • •

Tipperary had decided to tog out in the Confraternity Hall in the centre of Thurles rather than in Semple Stadium itself before the Munster Final against Waterford.

The dressing rooms in Semple were small and pokey and Leahy figured the team would be able to get ready for the match in more comfort in the hall.

The only downside was that the players then had to force their way through the surging crowds that choked the road to the stadium and brave a gauntlet of back slaps and unsolicited advice along the way.

As Doyle and Ray Reidy walked together towards the stadium the throng of humanity suddenly became more compressed as a car attempted to make its way slowly through the crowd.

When Doyle realised it was being driven by RTÉ's match commentator, Micheal O'Hehir, he jostled his way over to the car and knocked on the window.

A smiling O'Hehir wound down the window when he saw Doyle's mischievous face peering through the glass.

"Hey, be sure now to mention me plenty of times today now, won't you Micheal?"

"Certainly, young man," replied O'Hehir. "What's the name?"

O'Hehir made sure of his victory by giving the accelerator a quick stab before Doyle could think of an adequate retort.

• • • ● • • •

As it transpired, O'Hehir had plenty of cause to mention Doyle in his dispatches, and so did every other journalist at the match.

The *Irish Independent*'s, John D Hickey was particularly effusive of the supremely dominant Tipperary half-back line, but Doyle in particular.

"All three were positively magnificent and it is no reflection of the prowess of Finn and Wall to say that they were overshadowed by Doyle – the hardihood of the man is astonishing," wrote Hickey.

"With an assurance that savoured of contempt, he hurled Mick Flannelly and Larry Guinan in turn into the ground and, as if seeking new worlds to conquer, he tore into other rivals as eagerly as if he had been starved of hurling for weeks, if not months.

"Not unnaturally he took a lot of punishment in a contest in which every man comported himself in exemplary manner, but each succeeding weal seemed but to strengthen his resolve to make all his other great games for Tipperary seem but trifling contributions."

With their defence utterly dominant, and their much criticised attack suddenly inspired, Tipp hammered the reigning provincial champions by 4-12 to 1-5 to claim their first Munster crown since '51.

After the slug-fest against Cork such a bloodless victory seemed almost anti-climactic, but Tipperary fans wouldn't have to wait long for another hard-hitting grudge-match to stir their tribal instincts because reigning champions Kilkenny awaited in the All-Ireland Semi-Final.

●●●●●●●

August 10, Croke Park.
All-Ireland Semi-Final v Kilkenny.

Tipperary goalkeeper John O'Grady glanced furtively around the dressing room to make sure no one's eyes were on him before quickly shoving the small bottle up the sleeve of his jersey.

He made his way to the toilet and locked the door of the cubicle behind him. He didn't want anyone discovering his little secret.

O'Grady was suffering from the worst affliction possible for a hurling goalkeeper – his eyesight was steadily worsening.

In the privacy of his own home he'd taken to wearing glasses, but he never donned them in public.

He'd waited long enough for his chance to claim the number one jersey for Tipperary, and if anyone saw him wearing spectacles then his last chance of winning an All-Ireland senior medal in the blue and gold would be gone.

He'd made some spectacular saves against Cork and Waterford, but if people realised he'd taken to wearing glasses he knew they'd only dwell on the goals he'd conceded in those matches when he'd misjudged a couple of high balls.

So he kept the glasses at home, and before every match secretly bathed his eyes in Optrex solution to make sure his vision was as clear as it possibly could be.

Keeping his condition to himself just added to the pressure he was under. As far as the Tipperary public were concerned Tony Reddin hadn't been adequately replaced and the jury was still out on O'Grady's ability to fill his sizeable boots.

The goalkeeper knew he had a point to prove against Kilkenny and he wasn't the only Tipp player who was having his credentials questioned.

Jimmy Doyle's exploits at minor level for Tipperary had earned him national renown, but now plenty of people were wondering whether the slimly-built teenager would be able to recreate those sorts of heroics in the rough and tumble of senior hurling.

He'd failed to make much of an impression against either Cork or Waterford, and it was clear that opposition defenders were targeting him for rough treatment because he wasn't the sort of player who'd fight dirt with dirt.

By the time the final whistle blew against Kilkenny, both men had silenced their doubters for good.

It had looked like Tipp were in trouble when they trailed their dominant opponents by four points after 25 minutes, but then Jimmy popped over a free and a minute later lanced another to the back of the net to draw the teams level.

By half time Tipp had eased a point ahead and Kilkenny had been sapped of much of their resolve. They summoned one last charge early in the second half when Dick Rockett fired in a shot worthy of his name, but O'Grady dived low to pull off a brilliant save.

From that moment on, Kilkenny didn't look like a team that truly believed they could win the match and, in the end, Tipp won comfortably enough by 1-13 to 1-8.

Jimmy Doyle had scored as much as the whole Kilkenny team combined but, for the second match in a row, most of the plaudits went John Doyle's way for another thundering display in defence.

When Kilkenny poured forward in the first 20 minutes it was Doyle who did most to stem their flow and, once again, he earned a glowing review from John D Hickey who was fast becoming the Holycross man's greatest cheerleader.

"What a heroic figure of the game John Doyle has become," wrote Hickey. "Time and again he came through forests of Kilkenny hurleys utterly indifferent as to his personal safety.

"The more opponents there are around him the better he seems to like it. It was an inspiring spectacle."

The Semi-Final against Kilkenny had been billed as the All-Ireland Final in all but name, and so it would prove.

Galway had qualified for the Final without even playing a match, and that situation was made look all the more farcical when the championship showpiece turned out to be as anti-climactic as everyone feared it would be.

Tipp led by 10 points at half-time and free-wheeled from there to a 4-9 to 2-6 victory in the second half without ever really having to hurl at full revs.

The underwhelming nature of the match did little to mute the celebrations of Tipperary's 17th All-Ireland Final though as thousands greeted the team at Thurles train station where flares and bonfires lit up the night sky.

When the players were presented one by one to the Archbishop on the Cathedral's steps, none received a greater cheer than Doyle. The man who had been determined to retire a year previously was now hailed as the greatest hurler in the land.

Tipperary hurling was back on top for now, but tragedy and disaster lay just around the corner.

CHAPTER 17

May 2011, Clonmel.

Father Ray Reidy has one of those infectious laughs you can't help but echo, and, when he reminisces about his brother-in-law, the laughter flows freely.

The fondest memories hark back to the summers he would spend helping Doyle out on the farm when he was on holidays from Kiltegan seminary.

The townie who knew nothing about farming was always the source of much amusement for Doyle, but his young helper was knocking just as much mirth from their unlikely partnership.

"I used to love his company in the field because he'd always be full of devilment and chat," says Fr Reidy with a happy chuckle.

"He'd always be hopping a ball with you, especially if there was a match between Holycross and Sarsfields coming up.

"He was a good man for the witty remarks too, which were always original. He had his own auld wit and he'd say some very funny things without even meaning to be funny."

It would be a real country, agricultural sort of thing.

"I remember there was this one man he didn't like who was tall and thin with spiky hair. One day when we were working out in the field and Doyle was giving out about him and said: 'I'll meet that lad one day and I'll break him in two like a feckin' big thistle'.

"And, if you knew your man, it was the perfect description entirely for him. And Doyle, with the jaw set and he thinking about your man. He was funny without even meaning to be.

"Another time, I remember talking to him about hurling starting again. He was going hurling for Munster and it was, maybe, Februrary and hurling had been finished since November.

"He was giving out about heading off to play a match in Ballinasloe against Connacht and, as he was heading out the door with a scowl on his face, he said: 'I feel like a big dirty auld spider crawling out of his hole after the winter'.

"And that's exactly what he looked like. T'was fierce funny altogether. He had these spakes that he just came out with naturally. Between thistles and spiders!"

Doyle's sense of humour wasn't apparent to everyone who crossed paths with him because he was only really at ease around his closest friends, and that was a small enough circle.

He wasn't inclined to let his guard down in unfamiliar company, so those who weren't all that well acquainted with him found him a bit standoffish.

"You'd want to know him alright," agrees Ray. "He had this reputation of not suffering fools gladly, which he didn't I suppose, but shur the people who knew him best would only laugh at him.

"I suppose though he wouldn't always be the friendliest guy. John was usually surrounded by fellas who were mad to talk to John Doyle and could blather away and have great craic.

"But if John wouldn't have much interest in you he wouldn't make much of an effort.

"What people didn't realise though is that Doyle was a shy guy. He did lack confidence. Simply because he was an only child from a rural area like Holycross and was only a year or two in secondary school.

"He'd have been shy and wouldn't have put himself forward socially. He would have had a few insecurities.

"As he got older he got more confident and got into politics and that, but I would feel that the shyness was always still part of his personality.

"If he got going and was in good form then the auld wit and craic would come to the fore and the inhibitions would fall away. But that shy side was always there."

It manifested itself in the Tipperary set-up too. He was content to stick to his own small clique of Michael Maher and Kieran Carey rather than mix too freely amongst the group.

He also shirked from assuming an overt leadership role in the dressing-room, even when he was the longest-serving and most famous player on the team.

"I never remember him speaking in the county dressing room," says Ray, who somehow combined his studies for the priesthood with hurling for Tippeary for five years.

"Mikey Maher would have been more of a leader-type in the sense that he would have found words easier, as would Tony Wall.

"The most Doyle would say now and again would be a few sentences and it would generally be along the lines of 'this crowd need to be shown plenty of timber. There'll be no standing back today.' That would be it, up he'd get and out he'd go.

"He was a great leader without saying a whole pile though. The way he'd stand up straight and set the jaw out in a fierce determined fashion.

"You'd be glad to get in behind Doyle because the very way he'd look around the place was inspiring. His whole personality communicated great determination.

"He'd often do a great gaisce in the beginning of a match by coming out with the ball and having a few lads hopping off him and the whole crowd would cheer.

"His hair would be bouncing and fellas would be falling off him and, quite often, Doyle would lash it 70 or 80 yards up the field and the whole crowd would cheer, 'G'wan Doyle!'

"Players like Tony Wall, Jimmy Doyle and Theo English were all very skilful, but Doyle's persona on the field was different to anyone else's. A bit like Ring for Cork.

"Brian Lohan would be probably the nearest thing to him in terms of a modern-day hurler. The Clare crowd would rise to Lohan coming out with the ball in the same way that the Tipp crowd would react to Doyle."

Reidy was probably the only man that Doyle ever took it easy against on the field, but it only happened once.

When he was just 15 he lined out at corner-forward for Rahaelty in a Junior football match against Holycross and was horrified to see his marker was the famous John Doyle who by now had already three All-Ireland medals to his name

To Reidy's surprise Doyle hardly laid a finger on him during the game and there was little of the ferocious physicality that he'd witnessed from Doyle in the blue and gold of Tippperary.

So lax was the county star in fact that the 15-year-old was even allowed enough leeway to score a point in the second half. A whole new perspective was cast on the experience though when Ray found out a couple of weeks later that Doyle had recently begun doing a line with his sister.

Doyle didn't make any such allowances for his brother-in-law in later years though when he was a member of the all-conquering Thurles Sarsfields' hurling team that continually got the better of Holycross.

"John had to win," says Ray. "He was a tough man and he was very strong physically, but he was fierce competitive, the bugger. He never gave in.

"That Sarsfields team became a great side whereas Holycross fell away and in the early '60s and, in the end, Doyle would be trying to beat us on his own.

"He'd start centre-back, then he'd come up centre-forward, then he'd go back centre-field and he'd be giving out and effing and blinding at the referee, effing and blinding at us, and effing and blinding at his own fellas.

"You could be 10 or 11 points ahead and the game would be over as a contest, but Doyle would hurl his heart out from the first very whistle until the very last.

"He might have been 10 points down at the final whistle but he was never beaten. He couldn't throw in the towel really.

"I'd say he found those years hard to stomach because he came onto a very successful Holycross team and it would have been very frustrating for John to go out and play for a team that didn't have a great chance.

"When they hurled against us they'd go well for half-an-hour but then Jimmy Doyle would get a few scores and we'd pull away. Sarsfields had just too many good hurlers.

"The next day the whole thing would be forgotten though. He'd let a few swears and that would be it."

Once his hurling career ended that will to win and desire to have his own way still found expression in the committee rooms of the GAA where, over the years, Doyle held a number of different positions at club, divisional, county and national level.

"He'd a very strong personality and, at meetings and arguments and things, it would come out alright," says Ray with a knowing chuckle.

"I don't know how you'd describe a strong personality, but Doyle had a fierce passion and feeling for things, and the language could be strong too, of course.

"Because of his standing as a hurler, if he was in favour of something at a meeting you'd have an awful job to get something else passed.

"He would have been very much a mo-direach man. If he could jump queues or twist fellas' arms he always would.

"He wouldn't have been a great man to strategise, he wouldn't have been far sighted. He would have been much more concerned with something that he'd want for today or tomorrow rather than worry about what might be required further down the line.

"The whole thing of looking forward as to what things might be like in 10 years time, or be visionary in terms of bringing the GAA forward into what the world might become, wouldn't be his thing."

There were few things in life Doyle enjoyed more than a good argument, and whenever Ray visited his sister and her husband in Glenbane he knew it was only a matter of time before Doyle would drag him into some sort of debate.

The most divisive issue between the pair for a long time was the opening up of Croke Park to other sports. Ray was in favour of it, Doyle dead set against it.

"I was saying time moves on and what the hell do you have to worry about if a bit of soccer and rugby is played there. Shur, isn't it great to have them asking them can they come in? If we put them in there we can show the place off to the world.

"Anyway I was there one night shortly before they voted on the issue in Congress and Doyle was watching an Inter Milan v AC Milan derby in the European Semi-Final.

"That particular night the match had to be abandoned because of crowd trouble. Doyle turned to me and said: "And they're the shower that you want to let into Croke Park.""

"He just folded the arms then. The argument was won as far as he was concerned. You couldn't beat him!

"But even though he was very strong on the whole Croke Park thing he'd still be there glued to the television watching soccer matches and rugby matches. With Doyle, quite often the way he behaved contradicted what he said, which I always enjoyed.

"He was always very black and white on a range of issues, but he was a great man to get on with things too. He had a very short memory about these sort of things and always moved along quickly, even after the opening of Croke Park.

"And, in his playing days, if he had row in a match, or had given or taken a belt, by the following day it would be all forgotten. There was never any auld bitterness or nastiness in him that way."

The bigger the character the bigger the void they leave when they eventually pass on, and it's clear that Ray deeply misses the company of his brother-in-law.

In the end, all we really leave behind are the memories others have of us, and though John Doyle isn't walking the earth any more he's still making his brother-in-law laugh like no one else could.

"He told me this story once about one of those trips he was on to the US with the Tipperary team," says Ray, that familiar chuckle bubbling up again as the memory forms in his mind's eye.

"Because the Irish over there wouldn't get home that often, they'd ask the players to bring back gifts to Ireland for their relatives.

"Doyle used to get things to bring home for people every time he went out and this one fella gave him a suit to bring home for a brother of his.

"But, by the time Doyle came home, he couldn't think of who the suit was for and he was terrified that when he was back in the States again, he'd meet this man who'd given him the suit.

"I asked him what he ended up doing with the suit for a finish, and he said, 'I just started wearing the 'effin yoke out on the tractor'.

"The thought of him out on the tractor in that suit, God help us! But that was typical Doyle.

"He was just a gas man altogether and great fun to be around. That's what you'd miss most now that he's gone – the craic you'd have with him."

CHAPTER 18

Jimmy Finn woke in a hospital bed, his senses scrambled by the strange surroundings and the searing pain that lanced through his head.

For a second he forgot where he was and how he'd got there, but then it all came flooding back again.

He'd received an accidental belt of a hurley in a club match against Roscrea and, after he'd had the deep wound above his eye stitched up in Nenagh hospital, they sent him on his way with a clean bill of health.

He'd gone from there to a dance in Holycross, but, before long, it was clear something wasn't right. The pain in his eye was growing more and more severe. He didn't know it, but his retina was haemorrhaging blood.

He was driven back to Nenagh Hospital and, when they saw how much his condition had deteriorated, they immediately put him in an ambulance and sent him to Limerick hospital.

He woke up in a hospital bed, his head split in two by a piercing pain and his eye covered by an outsized bandage.

He'd lain there now for two weeks, and whenever he even moved slightly in the bed the pain was nigh unbearable.

He winced again when the door to his room opened and the surgeon who'd treated his eye walked in. Even a slight change in the environment around him sent a dart of pain coursing from the eye.

"Right, Jimmy, let's have another look at the eye."

The surgeon removed the bandage, peered closely at the damaged eye and tutted worriedly to himself.

"Ok, Jimmy, I want you to cover your good eye and read as many of the letters on this chart as you can from the top line down."

As the surgeon held the chart of in front of him, a deep frown slowly creased

Jimmy's brow.

Well, Jimmy, what do you see?

"I don't see anything, Doctor. Nothing at all."

The surgeon slowly put the chart down, a look of sad resignation on his face.

"I'm very sorry, Jimmy."

••• ● •••

At the age of 28, Jimmy Finn's county hurling career was over. The macula in his retina had been badly damaged and he'd never fully recover the sight in the injured eye.

Before suffering the injury he'd helped Tipperary to a National League Final victory over Waterford and a win in the first round of the Championship against Limerick, and, even without their inspirational wing-back, Tipp were hotly fancied to beat Waterford again in the Munster Semi-Final.

Goalkeeper John O'Grady was also no longer part of the team either. He decided to retire on the high of the '58 All-Ireland triumph, before his eyesight worsened any further.

His replacement, Terry Moloney, was a former underage star who'd won an All-Ireland minor medal two years previously, but he was about to find out the hard way that Senior Munster Championship hurling had a habit of chewing up and spitting out inexperienced young goalkeepers.

July 13, 1959, Cork
Munster Semi-Final v Waterford

The only sound in the Cork Showgrounds horse-shed that the Tipperary team were using as a dressing room was the gusting wind that whistled and huffed through every crack and crevice.

The damp air was heavy with the earthy smell of mouldering straw and horse manure, but that was a small discomfort compared to the deep shame every man in a blue and gold jersey was feeling.

Doyle sat on a bale of hay and stared glaze-eyed at the ground with his head in his hands. All around him his team-mates too looked like men who'd come home from work to find their house burned to the ground.

It was half time in the Munster Semi-Final, and the All-Ireland champions were trailing Waterford by the scarcely believable score of 8-2 to 0-0.

Their opponents had hurled with the gale-force wind at their backs in the first half and made the most of it by summoning a hurling storm that had blown Tipperary to smithereens.

You could never be sure what you were going to get from the talented but enigmatic Waterford hurlers but, whatever their expectations, the Tipperary players had never seen anything like what had hit them coming.

The quick-witted and spring-heeled quartet of Frankie Walsh, Phil Grimes, John Kiely and Larry Guinan had toyed with the All-Ireland champions like master matadors with an ageing bull.

Every swift dagger thrust drew great spouts of blood and increasingly raucous olé-s from the Waterford fans who could scarcely believe what they were witnessing.

The Tipperary players themselves were no less shocked. They trooped towards their makeshift dressing room at half time with their chins stuck to their chests because they were too ashamed to look towards the crowd.

As Paddy Leahy followed his charges, a sudden violent gust snatched his hat from his head and carried it hopping and skipping across the muddy Showgrounds paddock as if it was keen to flee the scene of the crime.

And, as he watched it on its way, he knew the fedora had been lost as surely as Tipperary's All-Ireland title was.

There was little to be done now other than to try to rouse the team enough to salvage some bit of honour, but, as he looked around the dressing room he saw little cause for optimism.

No one could bear to look in his direction and Jimmy Doyle was crying openly and would continue to do so every night for a full week.

Terry Moloney was just as upset and his voice cracked as he broke the silence in the room: "I'm not going out for the second half. I've had enough."

Leahy looked hard at his goalkeeper but could see there was little point arguing with him. The young lad was broken and there would be no fixing him just like there would be no saving the match.

It finished 9-3 to 3-4 and, when Micheal O'Hehir was told of the scoreline while wrapping up his commentary of the Leinster Semi-Final between Kilkenny and Dublin, he urged his listeners to take it with a pinch of salt, for it couldn't possibly be true.

•••●•••

The scale of the defeat to Waterford took much of the good from the previous year's success.

There had been no shortage of people saying at the time that it had been an average Tipperary team that had won the All-Ireland Championship in '58, and now they had all the proof they needed to back up that assertion.

Even when Tipperary travelled to the States again in the autumn of '59 and hammered a strong New York team in the St Brendan Cup Final, the victory did little to salve the sting of the humiliation suffered at Waterford's hands.

So, when 1960 swung around, Tipperary were a team with a point to prove, and they wasted no time doing just that by outclassing Cork 2-15 to 3-8 in the National League Final.

A Cork team that was relying more heavily than ever on an ageing Christy Ring fought with typical tenacity but, in the end, couldn't cope with the Tipp's effervescent half-forward line of Jimmy Doyle, Liam Devaney and Donie Nealon.

Cork were made look slow and cumbersome in the closing minutes by Tipperary's younger legs and, when the final whistle blew, there was a definite sense that the balance of power between the two great rivals was beginning to shift decisively.

•••●•••

Anne Doyle anxiously checked her watch and peered out into yard to see if there was any sign yet of her husband and Kieran Carey.

She'd made it back from the National League Final against Cork an hour earlier, but there was still no sign of the two men and she was starting to worry if they'd make it to Cashel at all now in time for the Adam Faith concert.

The visit of the English chart-topping popstar had been the talk of the county for weeks, and it would be a killer to miss the thing after looking forward to it for so long.

The relief she felt when the two men eventually arrived in the door evaporated as soon as she saw the state Carey was in.

He'd received a blow from Christy Ring that had split the top of his head wide open and the stitches that had been hastily applied after the match didn't look like they were up to the job.

"God Almighty, Kieran, are you alright?"

"Ah, not a bother on me, Anne, shur tis only an auld scratch," said Carey with his usual crooked grin.

"Will we still be able to go to see Adam Faith?"

"Of course we will," replied Carey. "Shur he'll hardly go on stage without us, will he?"

The fun-loving Carey wasn't the sort of man who'd let a head wound get in the way of a good night out and, anyway, he had his eye on a girl by the name of Nancy who he knew would be at the concert.

Adam Faith lived up to his billing, but the night still wasn't the relaxing and carefree break from life on the farm that Anne had hoped it would be.

Her evening took a turn for the worse when she was tapped on the shoulder by a wealthy local landowner and cattle dealer who was renowned in the area for being an unabashed womaniser.

So rakish was his reputation in fact, that when he'd call to the Doyle farm to buy some livestock Anne would order her husband to deal with him out in the yard rather than bring him into the house.

She couldn't escape him now though, because her grinning husband was quick to grant the man permission to escort his wife to the dance floor.

And, when the music slowed and her suitor pulled Anne closer, Doyle found even more merriment in his wife's discomfort. Even when she noticed that the cock-sure Don Juan was wearing odd socks, it did little to lighten her mood.

The ordeal only came to an end when Kieran Carey took it upon himself to rescue her. With a face like thunder she returned to her waiting husband who innocently enquired: "What's wrong with you at all?"

•••●•••

Tipperary hammered Limerick 10-9 to 2-1 in the first round of the Championship and then proved definitively that the defeat to Waterford the previous year was a freakish one by comfortably beating them in the Munster Semi-Final.

The two Doyles, John and Jimmy, were once again afforded the lion's share of plaudits, but the 6-9 to 2-7 victory also marked the coming of age of two men who would play a huge part in Tipperary's successes in the coming decade – Mick Burns and Sean McLoughlin.

Burns had no shortage of doubters when he'd first arrived on the scene the previous year to replace Jimmy Finn in the half-back line.

Weighing little more than ten stone he was a flyweight compared to the strapping Finn and didn't at all conform to the rugged profile that Tipperary fans preferred their defenders to fit.

But what the Nenagh man lacked in physique he made up for in pace, stick-work and vision and, over the course of his career, he helped redefine the position of wing-back.

Hurling would change during the 1960s from a ferociously physical and occasionally dour game that heavily favoured ground-hurling into a more open and expansive one where skill could flourish more easily. Burns was very much one of the new breed who would thrive in this slightly more forgiving environment.

He wasn't the sort of player who'd win the ball amongst a ruck of players, or smash someone to the ground with a meaty shoulder charge, but he was such a consummate hurler he rarely found himself in a situation that required those abilities.

He always played a yard in front of his man and had the pace to beat him to the ball and the stick-work to claim it cleanly almost every time.

And though he didn't look like he had much power in his narrow shoulders, he was one of the cleanest strikers of the sliotar in the game and was well able to drive the heavy sliotar of the times over the bar from 80-plus yards.

He rarely cleared a ball for the sake of it. Much like Tony Wall, he'd hit an angled ball into space that a forward could run onto rather than deliver it to them in a static position that made life easier for their marker.

Sean McLoughlin would benefit many times from Burns' ability to angle a ball from the right-wing back position into the left corner of the attack. Though he wasn't an orthodox or even hugely skilful hurler, he became one of the most feared predators of the era.

In his youth he'd been a long-limbed and extremely quick wing-forward who'd starred on the 1952 Tipp minor team, but his evolution as a hurler was redirected when his leg was smashed by a dirty stroke in a club match against Holycross.

It took two years of convalescence before he could start hurling again. He never fully recovered the burning pace that had been such a feature of his play but, instead, reinvented himself as a target-man corner-forward.

He'd loiter in around the small square and stand shoulder to shoulder with his man rather than take off on angled runs away from him because he never again wanted to be left open to the sort of blow from behind that had shattered his leg.

He was tall, powerful and exceptionally good at cleanly catching high deliveries, which made him a fantastic target-man. It was another special ability, though, that earned him a well-deserved reputation as one of the most ruthless finishers in the game.

Because McLoughlin was a champion handballer, he could hand-pass the ball almost as hard as he could hit it with his hurley which, in the tight confines of a crowded square, was a hugely valuable ability.

Over time he developed a style that would be illegal in the modern game whereby he'd drop his hurley when a high ball was delivered in towards the square, catch the sliotar with both hands gaelic football style, and then palm a shot past the goalkeeper from close range.

The arrival of Burns and McLoughlin on the scene were two more significant pieces in the impressive jigsaw that Paddy Leahy was assembling but, while Tipperary were unearthing new hurlers all the time, Cork's well of hurling talent seemed to be drying up.

Some of the young players they'd blooded in the League had looked out of their depth against Tipperary in the League Final so, as the Munster Final approached, the Cork selectors decided to put their faith in some grizzled veterans instead.

The forward line in particular was manned by battle-hardened men like

Christy Ring, Liam Dowling, Joe Twoomey and Paddy Barry, who weren't in the habit of bowing down meekly before the blue and gold.

The 1960 Munster Final was their last stand, and it would be a bloody and brutal one.

• • • ● • • •

July 31, 1960, Thurles.
Munster Senior HC Final v Cork.

The muggy air was split asunder by a neon flash of lightning that was almost immediately followed by a percussive clap of thunder.

Seconds later Thurles Sportsfield was lashed by sheeting rain that drenched everyone not lucky enough to have the luxury of a seat in the stand.

It was as if the gods themselves were spoiling for a fight, and the mood in the Cork dressing room was no less abrasive.

Christy Ring had just delivered a stirring speech that had brought the blood of his team-mates to a bubbling boil but didn't overly impress the team's padre, Fr Carthach McCarthy.

"You didn't find those words in the Bible, Christy," said Fr McCarthy in as disapproving a tone as he could muster.

Ring cast a jaundiced eye at the man of the cloth. "No, Father. But the men who wrote the Bible never had to play Tipperary."

Were a chapter of that particular book to be devoted to the 1960 Munster Final, it would have been filed somewhere in the Old Testament where taking an eye for an eye was all the rage.

There had been a few unsavoury incidents between the teams in the League Final, and the adversaries didn't take long to pick up where they left off that day.

Tipperary's teenage midfielder, Tom Ryan, had been one of the stars of that match but was a marked man now. An early blow from Terry Kelly split his head open and, though he somehow played on for the rest of the match, his evening would be spent in the Hospital of the Assumption in Thurles.

Even the chief enforcers in the Tipperary defence were finding out the hard way that Cork were amped to the max. A tangle between Kieran Carey and Liam Dowling ended emphatically when Dowling pole-axed the corner-back with a box that left him stretched out on the ground for a couple of minutes, before he fully recovered his senses.

There was a rabid physicality to every challenge that brought as many boos as cheers from the crowd but, in between the crunching tackles and off-the-ball niggles, both teams were producing some spells of quality hurling.

Cork produced most of it in the first half and got off to the perfect start when Doyle's nemesis, Paddy Barry, escaped his clutches to score a goal in the very first minute.

But, despite dominating both possession and territory for much of the first half, Cork trailed at half time by 3-4 to 2-4, thanks to the opportunism of Jimmy Doyle and Sean McLoughlin at the other end of the field.

The hostilities didn't ease in the second half and the biggest flashpoint came when Doyle and Paddy Barry decided to throw down their hurleys and duke it out like gentlemen.

Doyle might have been the most impressive physical specimen, but Barry quickly made it apparent he had the more refined pugilistic skills and popped a couple of stiff jabs into his opponent's face before Doyle swung an awkward haymaker that was some way shy of hitting its target.

Up in the stand Anne Doyle covered her eyes out of pure embarrassment rather than fear for her husband, who was plainly no Joe Louis.

He was saved by referee Gerry Fitzgerald who jumped between the two brawlers, told them to cop themselves on, and took their names before starting the match again.

As the second half wore on, the more youthful legs of the Tipperary players began to tell and another goal from McLoughlin helped them into a five-point lead with time almost up.

An injury-time goal from Cork briefly flung the fat back into the fryer, but a minute later the final whistle signalled the end of the match, a 4-13 to 4-11 victory for Tipperary, and a watershed moment in the rivalry with Cork.

For so long equals, Tipp were on the cusp of an unprecedented period of mastery over their neighbours.

• • • ● • • •

The Tipperary players gathered in a ragged semi-circle in Thurles Sportsfield were all in various states of exhaustion.

Those still standing were taking in great lungfuls of air with pained expressions on their faces and few more were on their hands and knees heaving up whatever was left of their lunch.

"Get back on your feet," roared the portly red-faced man they'd all come to hate with every fibre of their beings. "I'm not finished with you all yet."

Drill Sergeant Jack Behan O'Brien was an army colleague of Tony Wall's who'd been drafted in to get the team into the best shape possible for the All-Ireland Final against Wexford.

The hard-up Tipperary County Board could only afford to pay for collective training for the panel for the two weeks prior to the All-Ireland Final and were keen now that the players make up for lost time.

It was the Wednesday before the All-Ireland Final, and they'd trained hard for eight of the previous ten days.

It was pretty brutal stuff, too, because Sergeant O'Brien wasn't the type to take it easy on his men, an enthusiasm the Tipp players were convinced was partly fuelled by the fact he'd imbibed a couple of stiff drinks before every session.

"You and you come here," shouted O'Brien at John Hough and Donie Nealon. "Carry that man on your back and do a round of the pitch. The rest of you pair up and follow them. Go, go, go."

The Tipperary players didn't know whether to laugh or cry as Nealon hopped up on Hough's back and the big midfielder staggered away on tired and unsteady legs.

"In the name of Jaysus, what sort of fuckology is this?" gasped Doyle between heavy breaths to Kieran Carey

"I don't know," replied Carey, "but there's no way you're getting up on my back."

• • • ● • • •

September 4, 1960, Croke Park.
All-Ireland SH Final v Wexford.

Doyle felt like he'd been running through sand with weights strapped around his ankles. His legs were dead and as soon as he filled his lungs they ached for more air.

His mind knew what he should be doing, but his body was refusing to obey orders. He'd never met a man he couldn't out-run or out-last over 60 minutes, but there was still 20 minutes left in the All-Ireland Final and he was already totally spent.

And as he looked around the field, it was clear that rest of his team-mates were in just as poor shape. A Wexford team that was meant to be over the hill were making a Tipperary side with an average age of 24 look like old men.

Veterans of the '51 All-Ireland Final like Bobby Rackard, Nick O'Donnell, Tim Flood, Ned Wheeler and Padge Kehoe, were all proving they remained proud hurling warriors and that people had been foolish to write them off; but it was clear, too, that the labouring Tipp team was a pale shadow of the side that had won the Munster Championship.

They'd struggled to keep within two points of the Leinster champions by the break and could hardly raise a gallop after it, only managing another three points in the entire second half.

Theo English was the only one who seemed capable of keeping pace with the Wexford men, and it was hardly a coincidence that he'd missed the severe training sessions with Sergeant O'Brien because he'd been nursing an injury.

Tipperary's Championship had been bookended by an unexpected humiliation for the second year running. Wexford won in the end by 2-15 to 0-11 and were in no way flattered by a result.

As Paddy Leahy watched Wexford captain Nick O'Donnell lift the Liam McCarthy, he turned to his friend Jim Ryan and magnanimously said: "Well, it's for the good of hurling, I suppose."

Ryan didn't look nearly so convinced. "Maybe, Paddy, but how the hell are we going to face them at home?"

CHAPTER 19

Paddy Leahy held court in the centre of Thurles Sportsfield surrounded by his Tipperary team. Beside him stood a strongly-built man in his mid-40s dressed smartly in a three-piece suit, shirt, suspenders and tie.

"Lads," said Leahy, "this is Ossie Bennett. Some of ye know him already, but, for those of you who don't, Ossie trained Toomevara to the County Championship last year.

"He's going to be our team trainer for the rest of the year, and before we start tonight's session he wants to have a word with ye all."

Bennett took a couple of steps forward and clasped his hands behind his back, which accentuated his powerful shoulders and broad chest.

"Boys, I'm going to make a promise to ye all now," began Bennett in his lilting Cork brogue.

"If ye listen to what I tell ye boys, and if ye do what I say boys, I'll make ye all fitter, faster and stronger than ye've ever been before.

"Getting the most from the human body is a lot like getting the most from a car engine boys, and I know all there is to know about both.

"Everything we'll do here in training will be designed to get your heart revs up, because if you don't get the heart revs well up over 80, ye'll be good for nothing in a game of hurling."

"Actions speak louder than words boys, so I hope ye're all ready to get going, because I most certainly am."

Bennett took off his suit jacket, folded it carefully, handed it to Leahy and set off on a brisk run down the muddy field in his perfectly shone leather shoes, trousers, shirt, tie and waistcoat.

For a couple of seconds the wide-eyed Tipperary players stood rooted to the spot.

When he'd gone 20 yards Bennett began running in reverse and shouted back at *his new charges.*

"Come on, boys. Chop, chop!"

• • • ● • • •

Ossie Bennett's appointment as team trainer in the Spring of '61 was just the boost the Tipperary players needed.

The failures of the previous two years had weighed heavily on the young team and sowed seeds of doubt in their own ability, but Bennett's infectious positivity was the perfect antidote.

He was hardly your typical hurling trainer. A Protestant from Bandon, in Cork, he had never really played the sport himself but came from a long line of renowned athletes.

His father, Bill, was such a famed hurdler and jumper that he was picked as one of the elite athletes to lead the opening parade of the Tailteann Games in 1924.

Cycling and boxing were Ossie's favoured disciplines. He won over 100 cycle races in his youth and fought eight bouts as a professional boxer in places as far flung as Montreal and South America until the outbreak of World War II ended a promising career prematurely.

He worked as an engineer with the Limerick Steamship Company until he married in 1949 and moved to Roscrea where he worked in the local meat factory and gained his first experience of training hurling teams with the Coolderry club over the border in Offaly.

Toomevara took him on in 1960 as team trainer and caused a sensation by beating the all-conquering Thurles Sarsfields team in the County Final. Bennett had made his name, and Paddy Leahy brought him on board with Tipperary the following spring.

He had no formal training, and all of his theories on physical preparation were ones he'd invented himself based on the experience of his own athletic endeavours.

Few of them were all that rooted in any way on reliable science, and Tony Wall, for one, thought he was a complete bluffer and resented Bennett's arrival because Paddy Leahy no longer turned to him for advice on physical training like he once had.

But, while Bennett's methods mightn't have always been at the cutting-edge of physical education, there was no arguing with his results.

On his watch, the Tipperary players would develop a knack of peaking for big matches that had been markedly absent for the previous two years. Bennett's contribution went far beyond simply getting the players in good physical nick though.

His effervescent personality and enthusiasm made him a hugely popular figure in the dressing room, where the atmosphere was always lightened by the craic that could be knocked out of the Corkman.

He had an endless supply of colourful stories about his time at sea, his athletic exploits in his youth and his passion for vintage cars, and the players could never be sure whether he was telling the truth or spinning a yarn.

His enthusiasm for his job was something to behold too. He might have been a Cork-man, but the players were never in any doubt about his passion for Tipperary hurling and appetite for success.

He took a full part in all of his own training sessions, and though he was in his mid-40s and always dressed in a three-piece suit and smart pair of shoes, even the fittest players on the team struggled to match the pace he'd set.

Bennett wasn't just the team trainer, he was the self-appointed physiotherapist too. He claimed he'd inherited an ability to cure people of physical ailments from his grandmother, but some of the Tipperary players would prefer to grit their teeth and let time heal an injury rather than surrender themselves to him.

He had a pair of hands that could loosen the wheel nuts of a tractor, and his massage technique was to dig his steely fingers into a muscle as hard as he could and attempt to soften what he liked to call 'kernels'.

Some of the players swore by his methods, others just swore a lot when he laid his outsized hands on them.

There was no doubt, though, that he played a huge part in the successes to come, but he wasn't the only important new arrival in '61.

Toomevara corner-back Matt Hassett came into the team to replace the retired Mickey The Rattler Byrne, Donal O'Brien displaced Terry Moloney as goalkeeper and, most significantly of all, John 'Mackey' McKenna also burst onto the scene for the first time.

He scored two goals off Cork's renowned corner-back Jimmy Brohan in a tournament match in Buttevant, which earned him his first competitive start in the National League Final a week later against Waterford.

It was his first-ever visit to Croke Park and he made the most of it by scoring another brace of goals that helped Tipperary to a 6-6 to 4-9 victory and sealed his place in the team for the Championship campaign ahead.

The nick-name 'Mackey' was awarded in childhood when he earned his stripes in ferocious hurling battles played in Borrisokane square between the 'uptown' and 'downtown' kids.

The combatants enjoyed assuming the names of famous hurlers, and the young McKenna always insisted on being Limerick legend Mick Mackey. He also shared the same fondness for solo-running that his hero did, which helped make the name stick.

That's where the similarities between the two men ended, though, as far as their hurling traits were concerned. The original Mackey was a big, strong bruiser of a man, but McKenna was a flyweight in comparison.

His father knew that if young Mackey was ever going to make it as a hurler at the highest level he'd have to compensate for his lack of physique with unmatchable speed, which was a quality Mackey's father knew a lot about.

A renowned greyhound trainer, he set about using the techniques he used in that sport to turn his son into a formidable sprinter. The young Mackey was roused every morning at the crack of dawn and brought to the greyhound run the family owned where he'd sprint 30 yard dashes while his father timed him with a stopwatch.

All the hard-work paid off because Mackey developed a turn of pace that made him nigh unstoppable once he got the ball in his hand, and brought an entirely new dimension to the Tipperary attack.

• • • ● • • •

Mackey swallowed nervously as he walked towards the corner of Thurles Sportsfield where Doyle waited for him.

He'd only joined the Tipp panel the previous week, and this was his first time to go up against the great John Doyle in training.

He'd seen from a distance at the only other two sessions he'd taken part in that the Holycross man was as ferociously committed in a training match as he was in a Munster Final, which did little to soothe his nerves.

When he reached Doyle he nodded quickly at him and then turned to face the play with his hurley clasped hard in a pair of sweaty palms.

He saw Doyle's long shadow loom over him before he felt the weight of the Holycross man leaning down on his shoulder as he spoke into his ear.

"This is the place you'll prove whether you're up to it or not, Mackey. It doesn't matter what you did in the League Final, it's what you do in here that you'll be judged on. You'd want to be going at it hard, because I will."

Mackey managed another nervous nod and gripped his hurley even tighter.

A few seconds later it felt like he'd been hit by a cement truck when the first 50-50 ball came their way, but he gritted his teeth and gave as good as he got for the rest of the match.

When Paddy Leahy eventually called a halt to proceedings Doyle gave his team-mate a brief pat on the back on his way to the changing-room.

"Good man Mackey. Keep it up."

The five-foot, seven-inch McKenna walked off the pitch feeling six feet tall.

••• ● •••

July 30, 1961, Limerick. Munster SH Final v Cork.

"Holy mother of God, if that yoke snaps, he's a dead man," said Doyle to Mackey McKenna as they watched the show from their hotel window.

Dozens of men were attempting to break their way into the Gaelic Grounds by shinning up ropes attached to grappling hooks that had been thrown over the high wall at the back of the terrace.

A record crowd of over 60,000 people were already inside the ground a couple of hours before the match was due to start, but there was still another 15,000 locked outside and willing to do anything they could to make their way in.

The bitter nature of the matches the teams had contested the previous year had heightened anticipation of the latest instalment because there were still scores to be settled on both sides.

When the teams had met in the Oireachtas Final the previous October, Kieran Carey had earned infamy amongst Cork fans by breaking Christy Ring's jaw with a blow of his hurley, retribution for the head wound Ring had given him in the League Final.

The likelihood of some more testy exchanges between the protagonists only piqued the public's interest in the game, and those in the mood for blood would go home with their appetite sated.

For a while, though, it looked like there wouldn't even be a match. The Tipperary team were on the field for 20 minutes and throw-in time had almost passed before the bedraggled looking Cork players started to make their way onto the pitch in ones and twos.

Rather than tog out in the dressing rooms at the Gaelic Grounds they had made the fateful decision to stick to their usual custom of preparing for the match in the Railway Hotel and then travelling to the ground by car.

But, because the road to the stadium was so badly choked with supporters, their cars made painfully slow progress and, in the end, the players had no choice but to get out and force their way through the throng on foot.

When they eventually reached the stadium they were greeted with bedlam. A couple of the stadium's gates had been knocked down by the desperate supporters trying to make their way into the ground and the rest had been flung open to prevent a potentially fatal crush developing.

The Cork players had to force their way through the maddened crowd to get to the pitch, and, by the time they made it, they were hardly in the best shape or frame of mind to play a game of hurling.

It showed. By half-time Tipperary led by 3-3 to just as single point in reply and the match was already over as a contest.

Cork simply couldn't make any headway against a Tipp defence that was anchored by Doyle, who had been given the responsibility of playing at centre-back because Tony Wall had injured his knee in the Munster Semi-Final victory over Galway.

Cork had brought Paddy Barry out of retirement in order to unsettle Doyle further in his new position but, for once, Doyle comfortably had the beating of a player who had troubled him more than any other in the past.

Cork's last throw of the dice was to move Christy Ring onto Doyle in the second half. By now Ring was like a man possessed because losing gracefully wasn't a quality he cared for all that much.

Mick Burns felt his wrath when he attempted to skip past Ring with the ball in hand and received a lash of Ring's hurley for his temerity.

"God, Christy, aren't you the right brave man altogether to be hitting a young lad like that!" roared Doyle .

A few seconds later the ball came down between them and Ring proved he didn't discriminate on the grounds of age by pulling an even wilder stroke on Doyle, who immediately wrestled him to the ground.

Ring's strength was legendary, but Doyle somehow pinned him to the ground with his knees and began raining punches down on him from a height. The mistake he made was to stop punching him.

Satisfied that justice had been administered, Doyle pushed himself back to his feet but as soon as Ring was released he struck like a coiled snake and lashed Doyle across the side of the face with a one-handed stroke of his hurley.

Doyle collapsed in a heap and an already explosive situation went supernova as players from both sides ran in and a free for all broke out.

When corner-forward Billy Moloughney raced down the field to join the fray, Mackey McKenna roared after him: "For fuck's sake, Billy, come back, there are enough of them down there as it is."

Moloughney didn't listen to Mackey's advice and paid the price. As soon as he tore into the midst of the mass brawl he was felled by ferocious belt of a hurley across the forehead that split him open.

When he eventually rose to his feet he staggered unsteadily back up the field to his position, oblivious to the blood streaming down his face.

"In the name-a-jaysus what took you down there at all?" said Mackey. "Who hit you anyway?

"I don't know, Mackey," replied Moloughney, "but I'll say one thing for him, he hit me a right good shot."

Christy Ring was accused of delivering the blow by the *Irish Independent*'s John D Hickey but, while he was innocent of that particular crime, he certainly left his mark on Doyle.

For the rest of his life, Doyle would be reminded of Christy every morning he shaved because, reflected in the mirror, the crescent-shaped scar on his face looked like the letter 'C'.

He had to be taken to Limerick hospital to have the wound stitched up after Tipperary's 3-7 to 0-6 victory, and was joined in the ambulance by a more serious casualty – Jimmy Doyle – whose ankle had been broken by a wild stroke from Cork's Jimmy Brohan.

The trip was a wasted journey for both of them. Nothing could be done for Jimmy until the swelling in his ankle had gone down, and the stitches applied to Doyle's face did more harm than good.

His face swelled up grotesquely a few days later and, when Dr Moloney in Thurles examined him, he discovered that whoever had applied the stitches in Limerick had sown over some grass and dirt that was still in the wound.

A little antiseptic and new stitching had Doyle right as rain again, but, with just five weeks to go to the All-Ireland Final, the prognosis wasn't nearly so encouraging for his name-sake, Jimmy.

• • • ● • • •

Jimmy Doyle lay on the hospital bed and stared furiously at his swollen and discoloured ankle.

He knew it was badly damaged – shur the thing looked more like a hoof than a foot, but he said a silent little prayer to himself anyway that Surgeon O'Donnell would have good news.

As soon as the surgeon arrived into the room with an expression on his face that was half apologetic and half sympathetic, Jimmy prepared himself for the worst.

"It's not good, Jimmy, I'm afraid," said Surgeon O'Donnell as he gave the X-ray chart in his hand a regretful shake. "We're going to have to put that ankle of yours in plaster for a few months."

"Well, it's like this Surgeon O'Donnell," replied Jimmy, "if you don't take the plaster off before the All-Ireland then you're not putting it on."

O'Donnell was briefly taken aback before he recovered his usual clinical composure.

"Jimmy, there's no way on earth you're hurling in the All-Ireland. That's only a month away and you have a break and a fracture on that ankle.

"Well, then, you're not putting a plaster on it," said Jimmy defiantly. "I'll get it right for the All-Ireland Final one way or another."

"Okay, Jimmy. I'll put on the plaster and take it off two weeks before the match, but I'm telling you now there's no way you'll be hurling in it. What you're doing is a waste of time."

"I'll hurl in that match, you'll see," said Jimmy. "Just make sure you cut off that plaster three weeks from now because, if you don't, I'll cut it off myself."

O'Donnell looked Jimmy in the eye and could tell from his unblinking gaze that there was little point arguing any more.

"I'll tell you one thing, Jimmy. You'll hide it from everybody but you won't hide it from yourself. The damage that you're going to do to yourself will be with you for the rest of your life."

Time would prove both men right. Jimmy would hurl in the All-Ireland Final, but his body would pay a high price for his bravery.

●●●●●●●

Even with the plaster-cast on his ankle, Jimmy walked from his house to the hill of Killinan and back every night with the aid of a walking stick to try to strengthen the damaged joint.

And when Surgeon O'Donnell reluctantly removed the plaster a couple of weeks before the All-Ireland Final to reveal a still badly discoloured and swollen ankle, Jimmy simply strapped it up and started to work it even harder.

With a week to go to the All-Ireland Final he could manage to jog in a straight line again, but Paddy Leahy wasn't about to risk starting him unless he could prove he was able for the considerably more rigorous demands of an All-Ireland Final.

Jimmy wasn't Tipperary's only injury doubt for the match. Tony Wall still hadn't fully recovered from the knee injury he'd sustained in the Munster Semi-Final against Galway, and Kieran Carey had tweaked his hamstring when he unwisely agreed to take on Doyle in a sprint at training.

The trio were given one last chance to prove their fitness on the Wednesday night before the match when they were put through their paces by the Tipperary team doctor, Dr Herlihy.

Jimmy managed to keep pace with Wall and Carey as they jogged around Thurles Sportsfield, but when Dr Herlihy blew his whistle to signal an all-out sprint Jimmy immediately pulled up when he heard and felt a painful crack in his ankle.

He was sure his All-Ireland Final dream was over, and with tears streaming down his face he hobbled off the pitch and across the road home where he threw himself on his bed and bawled his eyes out.

That's still where he was an hour later when Dr Herlihy called over to the house and asked to speak to him.

"Jimmy, you failed the test but I'll tell you what I'll do," said Herlihy. "You'll make it provided you get permission from your father and mother for me to give you two injections into your ankle, one on either side.

"It'll deaden your leg from your toes to the butt of your knee, but the only problem is that if the ankle breaks again you won't know it's broken. It's up to you now, that's all I can do for you. What do you think?"

"I'll chance it," said Jimmy, quick as a shot.

"I don't care what you think, it's your parents who will decide," replied Herlihy.

Jimmy looked with pleading eyes at his father, Gerry, who had followed Dr Herlihy into the room.

"If he wants it, give it to him."

Jimmy was in.

• • • ● • • •

Paddy Leahy tapped his glass on the table to get the attention of his players and pointed to the clock on the wall of the lounge in Barry's Hotel.

"It's 10 o'clock, boys. Ye have a big day tomorrow and if ye want to hurl as well as ye can, ye need a good night's sleep."

No one grumbled about Leahy's early curfew. It was set in stone at this stage and part of the give and take between the chairman of selectors and his players.

Leahy would turn a blind eye to the few that liked a couple of pints the night before a big match to settle their nerves; and they did their part by keeping it to a couple and hitting the hay early.

He followed them upstairs himself an hour later but, before he made it as far as his room he was stopped in the corridor by a panicked-looking Jim Stapleton, one of his fellow selectors.

"Paddy, we have a problem," said Jim, his eyes like saucers.

"What sort of problem, Jim?"

"That young goalkeeper of ours has a big woman inside in the room with him. What are we going to do at all? We have no sub-goalkeeper or anything."

Leahy took stock of the situation and gave a considered verdict as he struggled to keep the corners of his mouth from curling upwards.

"Well, Jim, I'd say the only thing we can do is get down on our knees, say a Hail Mary, maybe throw in an Our Father, too, and hope that young lad doesn't hurt himself during the night."

●●●●●●●

Sept 3, 1961, Croke Park.
All-Ireland SH Final v Dublin.

As the Dublin players came out on the field and started to drift to their positions, Doyle cast his eye over them like a hungry wolf.

He had never before come up against the man he was slated to mark – Achill Boothman – and wanted to put a seed of fear in his mind before a ball had been even pucked.

Doyle knew quite well that his lofty reputation was enough to put the weaker of mind off their game and, when they came in to mark him for the first time, he made sure to stand as tall as possible, stick out the chest and darken the brow.

The sight of Doyle in full battle mode wasn't for the faint-hearted, but, as Boothman strolled his way, it was Doyle who suddenly had his composure cracked.

Boothman was small, prematurely bald and sporting a fairly spectacular gold earring that dangled insolently from one of his ears. He looked like nothing you were ever likely to meet on your way to the creamery in Holycross and, even as the ball was being thrown in, Doyle couldn't help but stare at him in wonder.

After the initial shock had subsided, it quickly became apparent that Boothman wasn't just an exotic looking fellow, he was a fairly spectacular hurler, too.

Had he played for one of the traditional powers he would probably have been regarded as one of the all-time greats but, for 60 minutes at least, he proved just how good he was by giving Doyle his toughest-ever match in Croke Park.

He was incredibly quick and roamed over and back across the pitch constantly, so he was always running onto the ball rather than waiting for it in a static position. And, when he won it, he had an unmatchable burst of speed that took him clear of his marker and the sort of snappy wrists that allowed him to easily clip over points on the run.

Doyle wasn't the only Tipperary defender struggling to contain his man. Dublin had other attacking speedsters in the shape of Achill's brother, Bernie, Larry Shannon and Willie Jackson, and all over the field they were proving, not for the first time that year, that they were one of the fittest teams to have ever played the game.

Under the guidance of their trainer, Mick Ryan, a PE teacher at North Strand Tech, they were the first hurling team to ever embrace collective gym-based winter-training. But, while they didn't lack for speed or endurance, they weren't equally blessed with composure.

Though they ran the Tipperary defence ragged in the first half they shot wildly or unwisely, and Tipp goalkeeper Donal O'Brien was proving he'd woken up that morning in fine fettle by making a series of confident saves.

By the break, Tipp led by four points but any prospect of the comfortable victory that everyone had predicted evaporated six minutes after half time when Willie Jackson finally broke O'Brien's resistance by lancing a spectacular shot to the corner of the net.

If Dublin hadn't really believed previously that they could win this match, they did now and three flashing points from Achill Boothman eased them two points clear.

After another spring-heeled run from Boothman had left Doyle in his wake yet again, he desperately issued orders to full-back Michael Maher: "The next time that little hoor comes running in here like that, you turn him and I'll deal with him then."

The extent to which Tipp's totemic defender was struggling, magnified the sudden peril the team found themselves in. For the third year in a row it was beginning to look like their Championship was about to end disastrously against opponents who'd been given little chance of beating them.

Had that happened, perhaps the team would never have recovered but, instead, destiny was directed down a different path when Tom Ryan was brought on as a sub for Mackey McKenna.

Ryan tore onto the field like a man possessed and his first act was to level Dublin defender Des Ferguson as he attempted to clear the ball.

As referee Gerry Fitzgerald walked over to the scene of the crime he was already reaching for his notebook, but Dublin's other corner-back – the legendarily ferocious Lar Foley – arrived on the scene first to administer his own brand of justice and, for his troubles, was ordered off the field along with Ryan.

The balance of power swung decisively with his departure. With Foley out of the equation Jimmy Doyle and Donie Nealon suddenly had far more room to manoeuvre on the right flank of the Tipp attack and three points from Jimmy and one from Nealon edged Tipp two points clear.

Boothman escaped Doyle again to reduce the deficit to a single point again, and Tipp probably wouldn't have survived were it not for two key decisions Paddy Leahy made on the sideline.

He took off Tony Wall, who was struggling with injury, brought John Hough on at midfield and switched Liam Devaney to the centre of the defence.

The Borris-Ileigh man was known to one and all as a half-forward or midfielder, so it wasn't an obvious switch, but it proved an inspired one as Devaney's ability to read the play and drive lengthy clearances turned back the blue tide again and again, while the experienced Hough brought some much-needed energy to the midfield sector.

In the closing minutes, when Tipp were under incessant pressure, Doyle also began to hurl with his trademark brio to finally subdue the electric Boothman but, still, Dublin could, and should, have won it.

All over the field the Tipperary players were out on their feet. Jimmy Doyle's damaged ankle had finally given way but he couldn't come off the pitch because Tipp had already used all their subs.

He somehow finished the match, but he wouldn't hurl again for six months and his damaged ankle would trouble him forever more.

Willie Jackson had a glorious chance to score a winning goal for Dublin at the death, but O'Brien charged straight at him and forced him to shoot early and wide.

Had Jackson the composure to take the ball around the keeper, he would have had the simple task of tapping it into the net, and Dublin would have been All-Ireland Champions.

It wasn't to be, and the hurling destiny of both counties was perhaps changed forever. Dublin would recede into the shadows, while the Tipperary players were now poised to write their names in vivid neon.

CHAPTER 20

Theo English turned to the two county minors, Mick Roche and Peter O'Sullivan, who had just mumbled respectful hellos after climbing into the back seat of his car.

"Lads, we're going by Holycross on the way to training to pick up John Doyle."

Mick Roche had been nervous enough at the thought of sharing a car with English, but the prospect of meeting a legend like John Doyle in the flesh suddenly made his mouth feel as dry as an old library book.

He exchanged a wide eyed glance with his team-mate that silently shrieked: "God Almighty, sharing a car with John Doyle!" As far as Roche was concerned, John Doyle was Tipperary hurling. The way he tore into every tackle with no fear, those thunderous clearances, the pure glamour of that thick, black hair bouncing over a face set with grim determination.

He'd only ever seen him before from a distance resplendent in the blue and gold, but now he was going to meet the man face to face.

He didn't know what to expect, but he was sure he wouldn't be disappointed.

By the time Theo piloted his car into Doyle's front yard the sort of heavy persistent rain that sends a dog scuttling, slouch-shouldered for cover, was falling.

Theo gave a couple of blasts of the car horn to roust his team-mate, and, a few seconds later, Doyle emerged from a cowshed looking little like the glamorous hero Roche had expected.

He was dressed in heavily soiled work-clothes and his face was framed by a wildly tousled head of hair and three-day stubble.

"I'll be with you in a minute, Theo," shouted Doyle as he marched across the farmyard and into the house.

He reappeared shortly afterwards with a hurley and two boots, his socks stuffed haphazardly into one boot and his shorts in the other.

After he opened the passenger door he flung the boots unceremoniously into the back-seat where Roche and O'Sullivan were sent ducking for cover.

When Doyle sat into the car he looked into the back seat at the startled minors in mock-surprise.

"God Almighty lads, I'm sorry, I didn't see ye there at all."

He winked at Theo and closed the door before turning around to examine the two young passengers again.

"'Tis a lovely evening for training lads, isn't it?"

For a second the only noise in the car was the rain that drummed heavily on the metal roof.

All Roche and O'Sullivan could manage in reply was a couple of quick nods that spread the grin on Doyle's face even wider.

• • • ● • • •

On Manhattan Island in New York City, between 34th street and 59th Street, and from 8th Avenue to the Hudson River, you'll find 'Hell's Kitchen'.

It earned infamy in the early 1900s as one of the most dangerous places in the world because it was ruled by a motley crew of violent Irish-American gangs who regularly settled their disputes by shedding blood on the streets.

The neighbourhood was first christened Hell's Kitchen by a veteran New York cop named Dutch Fred one night when he and his rookie partner watched a small riot on West 39th Street and 10th Avenue.

Shocked by the violence, his young partner turned to Fred and said: "This place is hell itself!" To which Dutch Fred languidly replied: "Hell's a mild climate kid. This is Hell's Kitchen."

There were plenty of hurling defenders in the 1960s capable of unleashing hell, but they, too, could only produce a mild climate compared to the heat the Tipperary full-back line generated for four campaigns between '62 and '65.

That's why they were first given the nickname Hell's Kitchen by *Irish Independent* journalist John D Hickey, and it immediately stuck because it was such an apt one.

After Tipperary were lucky to escape with a draw from the Munster Semi-Final against Limerick in 1962, Paddy Leahy decided it was time to shuffle his defence again, and Doyle was relocated from left-wing back to right corner-back.

The new full-back line of Doyle, Michael Maher and Kieran Carey was an instant success. Limerick didn't manage a single score from play in the replay until 12 minutes into the second half, and the performance of the newly-cast Tipperary full-back line that day was the template for many more like it to come in the future.

What made Hell's Kitchen such a difficult proposition for forwards was their potent mixture of power and cunning.

All three men had grown up on farms, and a life of hard labour had hardened them into athletes of supreme strength, which was a handy attribute to have in an era when the third man tackle was a legitimate defensive tactic.

If Doyle, Maher or Carey decided they didn't want you challenging for the ball, and attempted to hold you up with their hurley across your chest, there was very little most forwards of the time could do about it.

And, if they met you with a full-force shoulder charge, chances were you wouldn't be in the form to do a whole lot for some time afterwards. Maher was the strongest of the three and utterly immovable on the edge of the square. Christy Ring summed him up best when he remarked: "There's no change out of Maher".

If you weren't a player of courage then you had little business mixing it with Hell's Kitchen. Neither Doyle, Maher or Carey were in the business of saying 'excuse me' first before pulling on the ball, and if you didn't match fire with fire you'd be left charred by the experience.

When they came together for the first time as a unit in '62 both Doyle and Maher were 32-years-old and Carey was 29, so they were all hugely experienced hurlers.

They made the most of that to build up an immediate understanding, and the fact that Doyle and Maher had been hurling together since they were in short pants must surely have helped in that regard.

They covered for one another and they didn't get in each other's way. If a high ball was delivered into the Tipperary square whoever was closest to it would contest it with their man and the other two would hold back theirs.

Doyle was the most natural hurler of the three and the only one who could deliver 70-yard-plus clearances, but even if Carey and Maher weren't the most natural sticksmen in the world, they were smart enough to know their limitations and play to their strengths.

The trio were to the fore again in the '62 Munster Final when Tipperary hammered Waterford by 5-13 to 2-4, a victory that saw them straight through to the All-Ireland Final against Wexford.

Doyle was in line to become the first ever Tipperary man to win a sixth All-Ireland medal but, if he felt pressured by the chance to achieve such a feat, he soon had far bigger worries to occupy his mind.

••• ● •••

John and Anne were busily milking when their two young sons, Johnny and Michael, came racing into the cowhouse in an awful lather.

"Mammy, Daddy, we're after starting a right fire above in the haybarn."

They both rushed outside to see a thick plume of smoke rising from the barn that was packed to the rafters with hay.

"The new tractor," roared Doyle, and sprinted towards the barn that was being quickly consumed by a hungry blaze.

Doyle ran into the burning barn like he did every collision on a hurling field – with little fear for his own safety.

He braved the hot flames and managed to drive the tractor to safety just before the building was swallowed whole by the blaze, but there would be no saving a summer's worth of hay.

Two fire brigades were scrambled from Thurles, but had to relay their hoses all the way from Tubberadora Well. When they eventually started pumping water they discovered there were so many leaks in the rarely used old pipes they were next to useless.

The barn burned to the ground in front of a large audience. There had been a special Mass on the Rock of Cashel that day, and dozens of people on their way home stopped to watch the inferno.

Within a week, every bale of hay had been replaced by donations from local farmers and, when one donor was turned away because they already had more than enough, he returned the following day with a load of turnips instead.

John Doyle was a man who would have done anything for Holycross and, in a time of crisis, he found the parish had the same regard for him.

••• ● •••

As the All-Ireland Final against Wexford approached, the national media were of the opinion that Doyle wasn't done with fire-fighting just yet.

The Wexford full-forward line had murdered every full-back line they'd come up against in Leinster, and the consensus in the press was that they'd do something similar to Tipperary's.

The great Nicky Rackard was manager now rather than the team's full-forward, but his replacement in the number 14 jersey was no less a formidable a man.

Ned Wheeler had been wing-back on the Wexford team that lost the 1951 All-Ireland Final to Tipperary and the midfield powerhouse of the 1955, 1956 and 1960 All-Ireland winning teams, but, in '62, he successfully reinvented himself as a full-forward.

Like Rackard he was a colossus of a man at six-foot, three-inches in height and weighing almost 15 stone. He was a fine hurler, too, and the murderous over-head pulls he perfected to keep the ball moving in midfield were now a hugely effective weapon on the edge of the square.

Michael Maher was going to have his hands full keeping the blond-haired giant in check, but Doyle and Carey had equally taxing afternoons ahead of them.

Doyle was up against the canny 35-year-old veteran, Tim Flood, whose reputation as Wexford's answer to Christy Ring wasn't at all over-egged, and Carey would have to keep tabs on the swivel-hipped Oliver 'Hopper' McGrath who had been destroying defences all summer with his ability to twist this way and that and hit points while running at full pelt.

The showdown between the irresistible Wexford full-forward line and the immovable Tipperary full-back line was just one of many prospective duels that had captured the public's imagination, and the national press responded to the interest in the match by giving it more extensive coverage than they had any other previous All-Ireland Final.

●●●●●●●

John D Hickey pushed his spectacles further up his nose, as if by doing so he'd be able to see more clearly through the driving rain that was making a mockery of his car's window wipers.

It was an absolute dog of an evening and the Irish Independent journalist was beginning to doubt the Tipperary hurlers would dare venture forth into it for training.

If they'd cancelled their session then the long drive down from Dublin would have been a fruitless one.

Paddy Leahy and Ossie Bennett were peering doubtfully at the torrential rain and debating whether to send their players out into it when they saw Hickey pull up outside the Thurles Sportsfield.

Leahy turned to his men and quickly issued an order in a tone that brooked no argument:

"Lads, run out onto the field now and look lively about it. John D is down from Dublin and they'd only love to read in Wexford that the Tipp men are afraid of the rain."

The players, who hadn't fully togged out in the hope that the session would be called off, quickly pulled on their boots and started sprinting onto the pitch just as Hickey scurried from his car to the dressing room door.

All who passed the man from the Independent either greeted him warmly or nodded respectfully. A visit from John D was an occasion in itself.

Hickey greeted Leahy and Ossie warmly and gestured at the men braving the elements: "Well, it looks like you have them as a keen as mustard anyway, Ossie."

Ossie pondered Hickey's statement, hooked his thumbs inside his braces, and delivered his considered verdict in typically lyrical and confident fashion.

"John, as an engineer in the Irish merchant fleet for ten years I travelled the world five or six times. In those travels I met all kinds of men and groups of men, but never have I met such a fine bunch as the boys I am training.

"I am telling you nothing but the plain, honest truth when I say it is a pleasure to handle them. They are the finest set of lads anyone could hope to meet.

"I believe they are as fit a team as ever left Tipperary if not the fittest. It is my honest opinion that they will beat Wexford, and beat Wexford well. I could not see any team standing up to them at the moment."

As soon Ossie started speaking, Hickey produced his notepad and pen and began scribbling furiously. You could always rely on Ossie to give you good line.

"And how about you, Paddy? Are you just as confident as your trainer that ye'll beat Wexford handily?"

Leahy gave the journalist a conspiratorial wink.

"Ah, shur, I'd say we'll hardly keep it pucked out to them John."

Hickey smiled at the good of it. A Tipperary native himself, he and Leahy were old friends and he never tired of the man's mischievous banter.

"Nicky Rackard was saying something similar alright, Paddy," ventured Hickey with a grin.

"Well, I suppose after the recent visit of General Eisenhower to Wexford it's only natural that they would be on a war-footing," replied Leahy, warming to the cut and thrust.

"But much as I'd hate to disappoint my good friend Nicky, I would ask you to break the news to him, gently of course, that he's very much mistaken.

"Not this time, Nicky, it won't happen. Jimmy Doyle will bring back the Cup. Shur our County Board secretary, Pat Stakelum, already has a return ticket for it!"

Hickey chuckled as his pen raced across his notepad. There were few better men than Leahy to bring colour to a drab day.

••• • •••

September 2, 1962, Croke Park. All-Ireland Final v Wexford.

Wexford goalkeeper, Pat Nolan, looked at his full-back Nick O'Donnell like the man had just borrowed his car and crashed it.

There were only 80 seconds gone in the All-Ireland Final, but Tipperary had already scored two goals.

The first came when Billy Moloughney doubled a Donie Nealon centre to the net; the second when O'Donnell completely miss-hit the subsequent puck-out and sent it straight to Sean McLoughlin who smashed it past the helpless Nolan.

A different team might have folded after such a disastrous start, but Wexford possessed both great heart and experience and they grimly set about chiselling into the six-point deficit.

With the Wexford midfield and half-backs growing increasingly dominant, Doyle, Maher and Carey were coming under sustained pressure because every time they cleared the ball it was being returned with interest.

Doyle was keeping a tight rein on Tim Flood, but Hopper McGrath was twisting Carey into knots. And, when Ned Wheeler finally beat Michael Maher to the pull on a dropping ball, the net shivered and Wexford were level at 2-3 to 1-6.

Tipp regained their composure just before the break to hit three unanswered points, and a spectacular long-range point 12 seconds after the restart from Jimmy Doyle eased them further ahead but, shortly afterwards, the wing-forward was forced off with a broken collar-bone and the tide turned again.

A speculative 70-yard strike from Jimmy O'Brien went all the way to the net when his namesake – Tipperary goal-keeper Donal – was distracted by another great splintering clash between the two man-mountains Maher and Wheeler.

Wexford drew level and then hit the front for the first time thanks to a point from Wheeler, and when Tim Flood escaped Doyle for the one and only occasion in the match to push Wexford two points clear, the Leinster champions looked the most likely victors.

With the match threatening to slip from their grasp, Mackey McKenna knew it was shit or bust when latched onto the ball 50 yards from goal 10 minutes from the end. He did his father proud by setting off on a scorching solo run that left a clutch of Wexford defenders flailing in his wake and, after drawing out Wexford full-back, O'Donnell, he hand-passed the ball in to the now-unmarked Tom Ryan.

The Killenaule man was a mercurial character capable of anything on any particular day and never really fulfilled his enormous potential, but when Tipperary's need was greatest he delivered in spectacular fashion by unleashing a shot of such ferocious power that Pat Nolan hardly saw it pass him and was damned lucky he wasn't in the way of it.

Wexford hit an equalising point a minute later and, for the final 5 minutes of the match, both teams slugged it out like two tired and desperate heavyweights.

When the pitch of battle was at its fiercest, Liam Devanney fell in a heap in front of the Tipperary dug-out and roared 'cramp!'

Ossie Bennett raced onto the field in his Sunday best, grabbed Devanney's leg and stretched it as hard as he could.

"Ah, for God's sake, Ossie, tis the other leg," squealed Devanney with the pain.

An ageing team, Wexford were feeling the pace just as badly and, in the closing minutes, the young legs in the Tipperary forward line made a telling difference.

Ryan hit the post with another fierce shot when he really should have scored, but Donie Nealon and Sean McLoughlin made no mistake in the dying minutes with two late points that sealed an epic 3-10 to 2-11 victory.

As the players walked up the Hogan Stand steps to collect their medals, Michael Maher tapped Tom Ryan on the shoulder and had a word in his ear.

"Cripes, Tom, that was some goal. But if you'd steadied yourself you would have had a second one."

Tom looked at Maher askance and replied: "Shur, Mikey, if we needed it I would have gotten it."

Tony Wall accepted the Liam McCarthy Cup on behalf of the injured Jimmy Doyle and then brought it down to the bowels of the stadium where Jimmy waited on a stretcher because he refused to go to hospital until he got a chance to hold the Cup himself.

The two-in-a-row had been achieved and few inside or outside the county doubted a steadily improving team were capable of emulating the heroes of '49-'51 by stringing three All-Ireland titles together.

Tipperary's greatest bogey team had other ideas though.

••• • •••

If you lose to the same team three times in quick succession then you should surely have few complaints, but mention the 1963 Munster Final defeat to a veteran of the losing Tipperary team and you'll have ruined their day in double-quick fashion.

Waterford had already beaten Tipperary in the Oireachtais Final of '62 and League Final of '63 before completing the hat-trick of victories in '63 Munster Final, but the third defeat of that is still regarded as a criminal one by the men who played in blue and gold that day.

As far as they're concerned, in its own way it was just as freakish as the hammering Waterford handed to them in '59, and an even tougher one to accept.

Tipperary hadn't played all that well in the Munster Semi-Final when they'd laboured to a 4-7 to 1-11 victory over Cork, but there was still little reason to suspect the reigning All-Ireland Champions would suffer the total systems failure in attack that afflicted them in the Munster Final against Waterford.

Doyle and the rest of the Tipp defence did their part by holding Waterford to just three points from play but, at the other end of the field, the entire Tipperary forward line suffered a collective meltdown.

They hit 12 wides in the first half alone and their day was summed up by a bizarre sequence of play in the second half when Larry Kiely raced through on goal but struck the upright with his shot.

The rebound came to Donie Nealon but his drive hit the other post, and when the ball then bounced back into the path of Liam Devaney the net gaped in front of him but he somehow managed to drive the ball over the bar.

Tipperary had so many dangerous weapons in their forward line that even when one or two had misfired in the past others could be relied upon to shoot the team to victory.

In the '63 Munster Final, though, all six of them chose to share the same off-day, and Waterford took maximum advantage.

They had only a fraction of the chances at the other end of the field, but the steady free-taking of Phil Grimes was enough to clinch a 0-11 to 0-8 victory.

The three-in-a-row heroes of '49-'51 would never be emulated, but from the ashes of the '63 Munster Final defeat would rise one of the greatest hurling teams the game has ever seen.

CHAPTER 21

Hell's Kitchen Remembered

He's 81 years old now, but when Michael Maher shakes your hand you can still get a sense of the power that once made him such a fearsome prospect for opposition full-forwards.

The collective term for the Tipperary full-back line from '62 to '66 – Hell's Kitchen – makes the mind race in such a way that meeting the man who was at the very heart of it is a disarming experience.

Maher is quiet-spoken and unfailingly courteous, so it's hard to imagine him now as the defensive colossus who ruled the square in front of the Tipperary goal with utter ruthlessness.

He was that man though, and he doesn't mind at all that history has painted himself and his two corner-backs as such a fearsome combination. Invoke the term, Hell's Kitchen, in Maher's company, and he chuckles at the mention of it.

"John D Hickey put that name on us, fair dues to him," says Maher. "We never minded it at all either. There wasn't much said about it when we were playing, it was afterwards that people really started describing us as Hell's Kitchen.

"We were big and strong, I suppose, and protecting the goalkeeper was number one. We had no system as such, but we'd cover for each other when we could and get to the ball first if at all possible.

"Kieran Carey wasn't too spectacular in his hurling, but he was very strong. And Doyle was Doyle.

"At that time there was a big tendency to be too safe and play behind your man too much. But the place to be playing is to be out in front where you can get the ball, and that's the way we played it."

John O'Donoghue tended goal for Tipperary behind the Doyle-Maher-Carey combination from 1964 until 1966 after which Maher retired and Hell's Kitchen was no more.

For the three years that they stood in front of him as a threesome, he was glad of the protection they provided.

"Well, they tell me I wouldn't have been any good if it wasn't for them," says O'Donoghue with a laugh.

"It was certainly a great bonus for me though coming into the team as a 21-year-old to play behind a full-back line like them.

"It wasn't just that they provided great protection, they also trusted me enough to let the ball through to me and let me deal with it while they held back their men, which was a huge confidence-booster for me.

"As hurlers they were very much of their time. The rules of the day allowed defenders to be very physical, and they were all extremely powerful men.

"Maher had the coolest head of the three. No matter what was happening he kept his composure, and that's a great quality to have in a full-back.

"Carey was the toughest. He'd put his head where most men wouldn't even dream of putting their hands.

"Doyle was, comfortably, the best hurler of the three. He was obviously strong and tough as well, but the skill he possessed is something that a lot of people seem to overlook.

"He was a fantastic hurler, though, and a brilliant reader of the game. And, if he won the ball, there was no one going to stop him coming out with it because he was such a tremendously powerful athlete.

"They were all well aware, too, that they had the reputation they had and they played up to it, especially Doyle.

"At the start of a match, when the corner-forward came in on him, he'd say something like: 'Do you see that line, little boy? If you know what's good for you then you won't dream of going in past it.'"

There was nothing little or boyish about Wexford's Ned Wheeler when he came up against Hell's Kitchen in the 1962 All-Ireland Final. But even though he was six foot, three inches in height and tipping the scales at just under 15 stone, he still found it a punishing experience.

Wheeler was a midfielder by trade and new to the full-forward position, and when you're up against the likes of Michael Maher, flanked by John Doyle and Kieran Carey, the learning curve is a steep one.

"I found it the very same as putting a man into a pram – I was just not built for it," says Wheeler wryly.

"I simply didn't have the natural game to be a full-forward. I had a few good games alright, but in the '62 All-Ireland Final I should have played much smarter.

"I should have roamed out the field that day but, instead, I sat on Mick Maher's chest and, in doing so, played right into his hands. If I had moved out the field and dragged him with with me I'd have left more space for 'Hopper' McGrath and Tim Flood inside and we might have won the game, but that's all in the past now.

"John D Hickey called that full-back line Hell's Kitchen and, in fairness to John D, he was on the ball. The rules of that era allowed full-back lines to be ferociously tough and John Doyle, Michael Maher and Kieran Carey were certainly that.

"They've modified the rules since obviously, so defenders can't get away now with what they could get away with back then.

"Many of the great forwards of the current game would have found it a lot more difficult were they hurling back then because it was a much more physical game.

"The forwards of that era had to be very robust themselves to cope. Take Christy Ring, for example. He was built like a tank, and so was someone like Nicky Rackard. They were hard, brawny, tough men, but they had to be to counteract the likes of John Doyle and the rest."

Hell's Kitchen were feared with good reason, but there's no doubt either that the passing of time has embellished their reputation considerably too.

Tom 'Blondie' Walsh certainly thinks so anyway. The star of the Kilkenny attack from '63 until '67, he came against Hell's Kitchen on numerous occasions and doesn't believe they were any more fearsome than other full-back lines of the era.

"The folklore about Hell's Kitchen is baloney as far as I'm concerned, but I came into the game late enough – from '63 on," says Walsh. "Certainly there was as much toughness in the Wexford and Dublin full-back lines at the time.

"My first encounter was with Lar Foley, God be good to him, and he was a physically stronger man than someone like Doyle.

"Doyle was tough too, of course, but I would consider him as a superb hurler first and foremost. I really enjoyed testing myself against him and I would never have considered him a dirty hurler.

"He was a strong and physical man, which was par for the course in that era, but he also had a very shrewd hurling brain. His anticipation of the ball was incredible.

"I wouldn't have rated the rest of the Tipperary defence nearly as highly as Doyle. They wouldn't tie his laces really."

Tony Wall doesn't believe either that the popular image of Hell's Kitchen as a line of defence, that cynically scalped opposition forwards for sport, is an accurate one.

Wall hurled in front of the Doyle-Maher-Carey combination at centre-back for the duration of its existence and believes that, while they might have been tough and ferociously strong, they were also fair.

"If you said that to an outsider they'd laugh at you, but I've been preaching that for years," says Wall.

"When Doyle talked about Hell's Kitchen it created an image of that Tipperary team that has since become ingrained.

"By and large, Doyle himself was a very clean hurler. He was a rough diamond, but he played the ball. He took man and ball at times and, if you stood in his way, he'd drive through you. He didn't hit people though. There was no treacherous pulling.

"The real dirt was the fella with the treacherous pull, and I never saw Doyle do that. The only bad stroke I saw Kieran Carey pull was on Christy Ring, but there was history there.

"In a League Final, Christy split Carey across the back of the head, it was terrible. Then, in the Oireachtais Final, Carey hit Christy an awful blow in the jaw. I think he broke it, but Christy played on.

"Kieran told me himself afterwards that he would never do it again because he thought Christy was dead.

"Maher was probably the toughest of them all. He was rock-solid in the middle and never moved off the square. Any forward really had to earn anything he got off him.

"Doyle would talk about Hell's Kitchen as this great thing and that always fed the myth. They were rough and tough certainly, but they traded on their reputation."

After his retirement, Doyle certainly wasn't in the habit of downplaying the sort of heat that Hell's Kitchen had generated, but felt for the most part they were merely meeting fire with fire.

"I'll put it this way, we got as much punishment as we were supposed to have handed out," said Doyle once. "I can assure you of that. I'd have to say about myself I never hit a fella with a hurley in my life. If I had, that would have been the day I'd have had to give up. Oh, I hit them with my body alright. But with a hurley, no. And I stand over that.

"It was a lot more physical then. But nobody hurt anybody. And there was no big need for frees. Fellas didn't lie down for the sake of lying down. They didn't want to give you the pleasure of saying that a fella knocked them down. I never cared about anybody, physically or otherwise, but I would beat them with my strength and my hurling ability."

That was usually enough.

CHAPTER 22

As Mackey McKenna pulled on his gear for the first Tipp training session of the year he shouted across the dressingroom at Doyle.

"Hey, Doyle, I'm going to bate ya in the sprint tonight."

Doyle was bent over tying his boot laces and looked crookedly at McKenna through the long lock of dark hair that hung low from his brow.

"You wouldn't bate eggs 'Kenna."

The last thing the Tipp team did at the end of every training session after their practice match was to sprint from one end of the field to the other, and Doyle was nigh unbeatable.

McKenna was the quickest man on the team over 40 yards and would build up an early lead, but the long-limbed Doyle always strode past him like a big steeplechaser in the final 30 yards or so.

He wasn't the type to celebrate his victories modestly either.

As soon as he crossed the end line he'd turn around with his face split by a triumphant grin and roar: "Where's 'Kennnaaaaa?!"

Mackey had decided enough was enough. For the past few weeks he'd been training hard on his own to get ready for this night and the chance to finally put one over on his tormentor.

"Put your money where your mouth is, Doyle. I'll bet you ten bob I'll bate you in the sprint."

With his boots tied Doyle rose to his feet and threw an amused look Mackey's way.

"Well, I won't mind taking it off you so 'Kenna."

Usually every training match dragged on much longer than it was meant to because neither side wanted to lose and refused to accept the final whistle, but, when word of Doyle and Mackey's wager spread, everyone was anxious to get to the final sprint of the night as quickly as possible.

Mackey took off like a scalded cat as soon as Ossie Bennett's whistle blew and was a good ten yards ahead of Doyle by the halfway line.

Doyle slowly started reeling him in but Mackey wasn't to be denied this time and beat him to the line by a couple of yards.

Wheeling around triumphantly he roared: "Where's the great John Doyle now?!"

Doyle made a poor attempt to laugh along with his team-mates but his forced smile didn't make it as far as his eyes. Being beaten at something was never a laughing matter for such a competitive animal.

"Come on, Doyle, let's get you get you into the dressing room so you can hand over that ten bob," said McKenna to a chorus of cheers.

"You hardly expect me to carry that sort of money around now Mackey, do ya?" replied Doyle as he slowly recovered his sense of humour.

"But if you give me your address I'll send you out a cheque."

••• ● •••

Like a Rubik's Cube puzzle you finally solve after trying many different combinations, the team Paddy Leahy had been patiently building since 1958 suddenly clicked perfectly into place in 1964.

Sometimes it only takes a little seasoning to turn a good dish into a great one, and the arrival of Michael 'Babs' Keating and Mick Roche onto the scene in '64 provided the dash of spice that Tipperary had been missing until then.

Roche in particular solved what had been a long-term problem position for Tipperary in midfield where Theo English had been campaigning for many years without a top-class and regular partner.

The Carrick-On-Suir man didn't just play with a maturity that belied his 21 years, he was blessed with a skill-set that would, in time, earn him an undisputed reputation as the finest midfielder the county had ever produced.

The great players can read the play a half second quicker than the rest, and Roche had an almost unnatural ability to glide onto breaking ball and be in the right place at the right time.

He possessed the sweet stroke of a born sticksman so his deliveries into the forwards were usually perfectly weighted and angled, and he also acted as a hugely effective screen in front of his defence because he could read the play so well and had perfected the art of the block-down.

Babs Keating brought bulk, boldness and his own unique flair to the Tipperary attack. He had a swashbuckling style of play that the Tipperary supporters immediately warmed to, and any opponent who thought his nickname or boyish looks meant he was a soft touch was quickly put right.

Keating was a talented Gaelic footballer, too, and had been playing senior club football since he was 16 so, by the age of 21, he was already a serious physical specimen.

Playing football hadn't just given him a squat, powerful physique, it had also taught him how to make the most of it. Before the year was out, plenty of opposition defenders would have cause to curse Keating's ability to shiver a man to his very bones with the judicious use of his hips and shoulders.

Babs also drew on his football background to develop what was, at the time, a novel attacking ploy – catching the ball in the air rather than just trying to double on it.

Wexford had been the first team to introduce high-fielding to hurling in the 1950s, but it was an art almost exclusively practised by their defenders, whereas Keating would successfully use it as an attacking weapon.

Roche and Keating weren't the only newcomers in '64. Goalkeeper Donal O'Brien had emigrated to the USA after the '62 All-Ireland win and, two years later, Tipp finally found a man good enough to adequately fill his boots in the shape of John O'Donoghue.

A tall, elegant hurler, O'Donoghue was an agile shot-stopper, rock-solid under a high ball, possessed great balance and positional awareness and his accurate puck-outs would become another weapon in Tipperary's formidable arsenal.

The three newcomers supplemented a couple of other new recruits who had come on board the previous year – abrasive centre-forward Larry Kiely and intelligent wing-back Michael Murphy.

Kiely was an army officer who, as well as being a fine hurler, was also a champion show-jumper who would represent Ireland in the '68 Olympics.

He was a lightly-built man but punched considerably above his own weight and brought a new dimension to the Tipperary attack with his murderous overhead and ground-pulling at centre-forward.

Kiely was a nightmare for opposition centre-backs because he was a bundle of energy who didn't give them a moment's respite from first whistle till last, and was so tough there was little point trying to intimidate him.

If anything, it was he who intimidated centre-backs with his ferocious doubling and pulling on the ball and, by the end of a match, both their hearts and a few hurleys too were likely to be broken.

There was now no weak line in the Tipperary team. O'Donoghue was an utterly dependable goalkeeper and was fronted by the incomparable Hell's Kitchen full-back line.

In the half-back line you had Tony Wall, the greatest centre-back in the game, flanked by the neat and tidy Mick Burns on one side, and the rock-solid Michael Murphy on the other.

The midfield partnership of Theo English and Mick Roche was the perfect balance of athleticism and natural skill, and the combination in the forward line was just as pitch-perfect.

Kiely's abrasive style either kept the ball moving quickly to inside forwards or else broke the ball into space for his lethal wing-forwards Jimmy Doyle and Babs Keating to run on to.

In the full-forward line you had the perfect target-man in Sean McLoughlin and speed and opportunism in the shape of Donie Nealon and Mackey McKenna. And if there was ever a day when any component of that attack misfired, the mercurial Liam Devaney was capable of coming in and playing anywhere across the forward line.

Tipperary didn't just boast great hurlers; they were also the consummate team and had developed a very definite style of play and a number of tactical ploys that were revolutionary for their time.

It was an era of hurling when formations were considered to be utterly rigid – you were picked in your position and you stuck to that patch – but the Tipperary players took it upon themselves to break that mould.

Paddy Leahy picked the team and had his own ideas how best to play the opposition, but it was more so the players themselves who actively hot-housed a style of play that was way ahead of its time.

Tony Wall did more than anyone else to encourage this culture of self-analysis and tactical planning in the team. He published his own instructional book on hurling in 1965, but long before then he was sharing his theories with his team-mates.

He had a receptive audience. After every training session the main topic of conversation over dinner in the Glenmorgan for most of the players was hurling tactics and how best to expose the weaknesses and neutralise the strengths of their upcoming opponents.

The forwards, in particular, were keen to share ideas about how they might best trouble opposition defences, and the result was a free-wheeling attack unlike anything the game had ever seen before.

Corner-forward Sean McLoughlin was the pivot that every other member of the attack rotated around. He'd always lurk around the edge of the small square, but the other five forwards were constantly roaming and switching positions to keep the opposition defence off-balance.

It was an era when the big full-forward on the edge of the square was a staple of most teams, but the pocket-rocket, Mackey McKenna, reinvented the position by drifting out the field and dragging the full-back with him, which both left him more susceptible to McKenna's pace and also created additional space inside for McLoughlin and Donie Nealon to exploit.

The primary job for the half-forwards was not to score themselves but to create opportunities for the full-forward line, and with Kiely's ability to keep the ball moving, and the vision of players like Jimmy Doyle, Babs Keating and Liam Devaney, the inside forwards were spoiled with the service they received.

Whenever it wasn't to their liking, or a half-forward took on a score from a difficult angle rather than pass to a team-mate in a better position, the general of the attack – McLoughlin – would loudly berate them so they'd know better next time.

The forwards also benefited from the intelligence of the Tipp midfield and half-back line, who only cleared a ball aimlessly if under extreme pressure.

As soon as a Tipp half-forward saw either Tony Wall or Mick Burns win the ball in open space, they immediately ran out the field to either collect a low-angled delivery themselves or leave more space in front of the full-forward line for the half-backs to target.

Goalkeeper John O'Donoghue also played a vital role in the game-plan. Unlike most goalkeepers of the time who simply tried to puck the ball out as far as they could, O'Donoghue preferred to pick out a team-mate with an accurate pass, even if that meant shortening his delivery.

Every outfield player would know where the puck-out was going, thanks to a pre-arranged signal that had been agreed on before the game, and there was a set plan for every variation.

If the puck-out was to be directed to Babs Keating on the wing, then Theo English would vacate the space in front of him and Larry Kiely would drag the centre-back to the other side of the field if possible.

And, if it was to be directed straight down Kiely's throat, then Babs would run from the left wing in behind Kiely, anticipating the break to go that way, and Jimmy Doyle would race across from the right wing and in front of Kiely to collect the ball if it was blocked down.

That way, if Keating won it he'd already be on his stronger right side and bearing down on goal and, if Jimmy won it, he was hitting off his stronger left side and had the power to shoot a long-distance point.

Their opponents were always studied in forensic detail to the extent that the Tipperary players would travel in groups together to watch their rivals and, afterwards, the strengths and weaknesses of every player would be dissected minutely.

Every time Tipperary went out to play a championship match they had a good idea of what they were up against and how best to beat them, but, more importantly, they knew how to get the best from themselves.

The entire team was a well-oiled machine and the Hell's Kitchen full-back line was a hugely important component part even if Doyle, in particular, wouldn't have shared the same zeal as many of his team-mates for discussing tactics and systems.

Now 34, he belonged to the old school where you simply concentrated on beating your man and getting the ball away and, as a corner-back, that was still a perfectly acceptable ethos.

And though he mightn't have been as considered a thinker on the game as some of his team-mates, he and the rest of his full-back colleagues had a deep understanding of full-back line play that had been accrued over years of hard experience.

The primary rule was to move the ball from the danger-zone to a safer place by any means necessary. Attempting to rise the ball around the small square was a shooting offence – instead you coursed it out towards the sideline where, even if an opponent won it, they'd have a hard job doing anything too constructive with it.

Once it was out of the red-zone, both Carey and Maher preferred to clip it to one of their half-backs and let them take care of it from there, but Doyle had the hurling to take responsibility of the situation himself and get the ball into his hand, drive out with it, and make the clearance.

In a team that had distilled the game down to a fine science he was the greatest maverick, but that only endeared him to the Tipperary fans all the more. Much of what Tipperary did now was controlled and precise, but Doyle remained brash, exuberant, occasionally reckless and always spectacular.

In 1964 they'd sweep all before them by producing a brand of hurling that redefined the game, but their most unreconstructed player would end the campaign crowned as the greatest hurler in the country.

••• • •••

Wexford were the first team to feel the full force of Tipperary's super-charged team when they clashed in the '64 League Final.

It was billed as a contest between equals, but it was anything but. Tipperary stormed to a 5-12 to 1-2 victory as Jimmy Doyle, Sean McLoughlin, Babs Keating, Mackey McKenna and Donie Nealon all hit the back of the net.

The facile nature of the victory underlined the quantum leap forward the Tipperary team had made. Two years previously they'd laboured to get the better of Wexford in the All-Ireland Final, now they could beat them at their ease.

The victory earned them another trip to the United States – Doyle's fourth – for the 'Away' League Final against New York but, before then, they travelled to London to face Kilkenny in the Monaghan Cup Final.

For the three previous years running Tipp had won the tournament which, since 1958, had been held in the home of English football – Wembley

Stadium – and attracted crowds of over 40,000 Irish ex-pats living in England, Scotland and Wales.

These were tense occasions for a number of reasons. The soccer pitch was only 120 metres long so the play was really congested and the physical collisions came thick and fast, which meant flashpoints were all too frequent.

The soccer nets were too loosely woven to catch a flying sliotar, so rows about disputed goals were regular occurrences too.

The '64 Monaghan Cup Final between Tipp and Kilkenny was probably the most abrasive hurling match the soccer stadium ever hosted, but the tight confines off the pitch weren't solely to blame for that.

There has always been a mutual antipathy between the hurling tribes of Tipperary and Kilkenny, which predates the founding of the GAA.

Folk history has it that, after a Tipperary team lost a cross-county hurling match against a Kilkenny side in the early 1800s, they resorted to throwing stones at their opponents and ever since the nick-name, 'Tipperary Stone Throwers', has stuck.

A slightly more modern, recent reference point for the source of the rivalry was an exchange between rival captains, Johnny Leahy, Paddy's brother, and Sim Walton after Tipp had beaten Kilkenny in the 1916 All-Ireland Final.

Walton is reputed to have said to Leahy: "Ye won, but we were the better hurlers," to which Leahy replied: "Aye, but we were the better men."

The iron-clad belief in Tipperary that they produced hardier hurlers than their neighbours was a huge source of annoyance in Kilkenny, as was the fact that they hadn't beaten Tipp in a match of real consequence since the 1922 All-Ireland Final.

They had only met in three All-Ireland Finals and three League Finals since then but, as far as Tipperary fans were concerned, that was an inconsequential point.

Relations between supporters on either side of the long and winding border the two counties shared were bitterly poisonous, and that usually seeped onto the field of play when their teams clashed.

It happened again in the '64 Monaghan Cup Final when an already simmering contest boiled over entirely as Sean McLoughlin and his marker Cha Whelan were both sent off for using their hurleys on one another like scythes.

Tipp won the match easily in the end but the bad blood from that incident still hadn't been washed away a couple of weeks later when the two teams were reluctantly thrown together again and had to share the same jet-plane to New York.

As reigning All-Ireland Champions, Kilkenny had also been invited to the USA by the lease-holder of Gaelic Park, John 'Kerry' O'Donnell, to take on Tipperary in a 'World Cup' contest after Tipp had played New York in the League Final.

Not a word was exchanged between both sets of players on the long journey and the atmosphere in the plane crackled with tension.

It was only the beginning of an ugly relationship. Before they were done with one another, Tipperary and Kilkenny's mutual dislike would sour into outright hatred.

●●●●●●●

Doyle and Kieran Carey laughed and joked as they walked through Manhattan, oblivious to the fact that they'd turned the wrong way after leaving the pub they'd been drinking in.

Instead of strolling back towards their hotel, which had been the plan, they were now walking further and further away from it and heading instead towards the notorious Harlem district of New York.

The two men were full of the joys of life and not taking too much notice of their surroundings so they marched on into the night, oblivious of their mistake.

It was only when the buildings grew increasingly more run-down and the street-lighting dimmer that they began to realise they had no clue where they were.

"I think we're gone astray, John," said Carey, "I don't remember walking this way before anyway."

The frown on Doyle's brow suggested he was no surer of their bearings, but taking a backward step wasn't something he was ever in the habit of doing.

"I think we have to come out by the park eventually if we stay going this way, and then we'll know where we are."

By a couple of blocks later though, even Doyle had to admit they were hopelessly lost and very much out of their comfort zone.

Their passage through one of Harlem's black ghettos was quickly drawing the attention of the locals who weren't in the habit of seeing two white men dressed smartly in suits stroll around their neighbourhood at night.

The duo were greeted with wolf-whistles and shouts from the darkened stoops and porches of the crumbling town houses and, before long, a loose knot of local youths began shadowing them down the broken pavement.

Doyle looked worriedly over his shoulder, nudged Carey in the side and spoke quietly out the corner of his mouth.

"When I count to three, run for your life."

Doyle had only made it as far as two when Carey tore off down the road like he'd been stung with a cattle prod.

His friend had never beaten him once in a sprint in Thurles Sportsfield, but now Doyle had it all to do to keep up with the super-charged Roscrea man as block after breathless block flashed by in a blur and the frantic slap of leather on concrete echoed loudly off the tall buildings.

Eventually salvation arrived on the scene in the shape of a yellow taxi-cab stopped at a traffic light and Carey nearly ripped one of its door of its hinges before diving headlong into the back-seat with Doyle in close pursuit.

"Where to guys?" asked the driver in a laconic tone that was totally at odds with the panic of his two customers.

"Anywhere!" came the chorused reply.

• • • ● • • •

The 1964 visit to New York was Doyle's fourth trip there with Tipperary and by now he was a very different person to the wide-eyed, 20-year-old who'd first experienced the Big Apple in 1950.

None of the Tipp team were heavy drinkers but, whereas before Doyle didn't touch a drop, now he wasn't averse to having the occasional tipple with team-mates like Kieran Carey, Sean McLoughlin, Mick Burns and Larry Kiely.

And, for young men who were keen to sample the nightlife of New York, there was no shortage of opportunity.

The famous showband singer, Larry Cunningham, had been on the same

1.

2.

3.

4.

5.

6.

TIPPERARY, 1961 ALL-IRELAND HURLING CHAMPIONS

7.

8.

9.

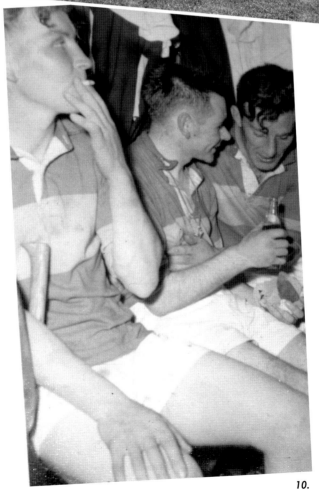

10.

11.

12.

13.

14.

15.

16.

17.

18.

19.

20.

21.

22.

23.

Clann Tiobraid Arann

The Tipperary Association

DINNER

In honour of the Tipperary Senior Hurling Team, on the occasion of the All-Ireland Final, 1965 at Croke Park.

Crofton Airport Hotel,

— WHITEHALL —

5th. *September* 1965

TOASTS

IRELAND

THE TIPPERARY HURLING TEAM

THE G. A. A.

OUR GUESTS

♣ MENU ♣

Arravale & Marlfield Cocktai

♣

Consomme Borrisoleigh
Cream of Holycross

♣

Stuffed Roast Thurles Chicken
Baked Carrick-on-Suir Ham

♣

Borrisokane Peas—Glengoole Cauliflowers
Cashel Sprouts
Roscrea and Ki ruane Potatoes

♣

Nenagh Apple Pie
Burgess Melba

♣

Grange and Toomevara Coffee

27.

28.

29.

30.

31.

flight as the Tipperary team over to New York and all the players were invited as guests of honour to his gigs in the Red Mill and City Center Ballrooms in Manhattan, where he played to audiences of thousands.

The Irish community in the city was also keen to entertain and host the Tipperary players, and no one received more invitations or attention than Doyle.

They liked to call him 'Mickey Mantle' after the New York Yankees baseball player who was the biggest sports star in America at the time. Being favoured with Doyle's company was regarded as a singular honour for any Tipperary ex-pat in the city.

The Tipp players were bankrolled to the tune of $70 a week by the Tipperary County Board, which wasn't a huge amount, but the trips to New York were still regarded as a money-making expedition by the players because you never had to put your hand in your pocket.

The exiled Tipperary natives were only too happy to invite the players into their homes and feed them, buy every drink for them on a night out and even shower them with gifts and, occasionally, cash.

When Liam Devaney lost a $50 bill one day, an impromptu whiparound at Gaelic Park more than reimbursed him for his losses.

The arrival of the Tipperary hurlers was still big news in the city to the extent that New York Congressman James C Healy stood up in the House of Representatives to formally welcome them to the country and then proceeded to give a lengthy and florid speech about the good work of the GAA in New York.

The players themselves weren't the least bit shy about taking advantage of the warm welcome their hosts provided and, if one hurler was invited to dinner by a family, he'd always bring a couple of team-mates with him so they'd return the favour when the offer of a free meal came their way.

With bed, board and entertainment fully paid for, any disposable cash was usually spent buying luxury goods not available in Ireland or other presents to bring home to family or loved ones.

No one was more organised on this front than army man Tony Wall. On their first morning in the New York his room-mate, Mick Roche, awoke to find Wall reading a book entitled, *How to See New York on $5 a Day*.

By the end of their stay there was little of the city that Roche didn't get to see as he traipsed after Wall on his many shopping expeditions that one day even included the purchase of a set of curtains.

Others stocked up on humbler goods, such as shaving foam, which wasn't available back in Ireland where most men still had to make do with shaving sticks.

Foam from an aerosol can was regarded as such a novelty that Babs Keating couldn't help but squirt a huge blob of it onto his hand when he first spotted it in a store.

The problem of what then to do with the foam was solved when a woman walked past him in the shop and he managed to wipe it onto her backside without her noticing.

The Tipp players knew how to enjoy themselves, but neither did they lose sight of the fact that they were in the States to win an important match of hurling.

The New York hurling team at the time was the match of any back in Ireland, and they proved it again in the 'Away' League Final by running Tipperary to four points on a scoreline of 4-16 to 6-6.

With the League won the Tipperary players were let off the leash for the following week, but one team wasn't taking things so easy.

After coming over on the same plane as the Tipp hurlers, the Kilkenny team had immediately caught a connecting flight to Chicago where they'd stayed for a week, played an exhibition match and trained intensively for their 'World Cup' showdown with Tipp.

By the time they arrived back in New York they were fit, sharp and keen to avenge their defeat in the Monaghan Cup Final.

•••●•••

Eddie Keher and Seanie Buckley were up bright and early, the thought of seeing New York in daylight for the first time filling them with a giddy excitement.

As the two Kilkenny team-mates waited for the hotel elevator they debated what sight they'd see first that day, the Empire State Building or Central Park.

The 'ping' that heralded the elevator's arrival at their hotel floor was quickly followed by a sight that made the blood of the Kilkenny hurlers run cold.

Standing in the elevator were John Doyle, Babs Keating, Kieran Carey and Theo English, who looked just as horrified to see them.

"Hello lads," managed Keher half-heartedly, but all he received in reply were a couple of reluctant grunts.

As Keher stepped into the elevator and faced away from Doyle his whole body tensed as if he'd just turned his back on a dangerous animal.

There was utter silence and a painfully strained atmosphere in the elevator as it descended far too slowly for its occupants' liking.

When it stopped on the next floor the American couple that got in immediately sensed the suffocating tension and animosity in the elevator and almost tripped over one another in their haste to get out when it finally reached the ground floor.

The Tipperary and Kilkenny men were no less relieved to escape one another's company, and not a single word of farewell was exchanged as they parted ways in the hotel lobby.

● ● ● ● ● ● ●

The 'World Cup Final' did little to improve relations between the two teams. In the tight and dusty confines of Gaelic Park the rivals tore into one another with a raw abandon and there was some ridiculously reckless pulling on both sides.

Doyle was on the receiving end of a good deal of it from Kilkenny's notoriously tough corner-forward, Billy Dwyer, who was inclined to pull before, during and after the ball was in his vicinity.

One particularly wild swing split Doyle's forehead open. The wound required eight stitches after the match but didn't prevent him from finishing it.

Doyle was bloodied but the collective ego of the Tipp team wasn't all that bruised by their 4-16 to 3-13 defeat to Kilkenny.

They knew the only relevant test would come in the furnace of championship battle against their great rivals, not in the heat of New York, and that showdown wouldn't be long in coming.

When they returned home Tipperary proved their demolition of Wexford in the National League Final was no fluke by hammering both Clare and

Cork in the Munster Championship.

Doyle was named Man of the Match as Clare were beaten by 6-13 to 2-5 and then produced another sterling display in the equally one-sided Munster Final against the Rebels.

The sun had long set on the era of ferociously even contests between Tipperary and Cork and, though they rarely had to extend themselves, Tipperary underlined the gulf that now existed between the teams by crushing their old rivals 3-13 to 1-5.

The fire might have gone out of that rivalry, but a few more coals were about to be thrown on another because Kilkenny awaited in the All-Ireland Final.

Motivation was easy to source for both teams, and not just because of the mutual antipathy that existed between the counties.

A victory for Tipperary would move them ahead of Cork at the top of the All-Ireland roll of honour and salve the still painful memory of the disastrous '63 Munster Final defeat against Waterford.

Kilkenny were desperate to bury their so-called Tipperary hoodoo and prove that, even if Tipp had beaten Waterford in '63, they wouldn't have been good enough to get the better of Kilkenny in the Final.

The stakes couldn't have been any higher and Paddy Leahy left nothing to chance to ensure his players had the best possible preparation for the match.

He insisted that the location of their team hotel be kept a secret, so, rather than stay in Dublin city centre, they billeted themselves in the Lucan Spa Hotel the night before the match.

And, to make doubly sure that word of their base wouldn't be leaked to the public, they decided to assume the identity of an American tourist group rather than book in as the Tipperary team.

The only person in the hotel who knew who they were was the manageress herself. The ploy worked a treat because the team were able to prepare for the game in a completely relaxed environment and even played a couple of holes of golf on the morning of the match.

They arrived at Croke Park a refreshed, relaxed and confident bunch of players – the perfect state of mind to produce one of the greatest displays ever seen in an All-Ireland Hurling Final.

● ● ● ● ● ● ●

CHAPTER TWENTY-TWO

September 5, 1964, Croke Park.
All-Ireland Senior Hurling Final v Kilkenny.

Doctor Pat O'Callaghan walked down the dark corridor into the bowels of the Cusack Stand that led to the Croke Park dressing rooms, and gently felt for the syringe in his coat pocket to make sure it was still there.

When he knocked on the Tipperary dressing room door it was opened by Ossie Bennett, whose eyes opened wide when he recognised it was the double Olympic Gold medal winner standing in front of him.

"Ossie, could you send Babs Keating out to me please," said O'Callaghan.

"Of course, Dr Pat, right away," replied Bennett without hesitation.

A couple of seconds later Keating emerged from the dressing room – he'd been expecting O'Callaghan.

A week earlier he'd fallen and broken a bone in his hand, but rather than tell Paddy Leahy and risk being dropped from the team for the fit-again Liam Devaney, he'd decided to keep the injury secret.

He visited O'Callaghan in his surgery in Clonmel where he knew he'd get a sympathetic hearing from a fellow sportsman, and the pair agreed an arrangement whereby the doctor would administer a pain-killing injection on the day of the match.

The 21-year-old's adrenaline was pumping so much he didn't even feel O'Callaghan stick the needle in his hand after the pair had retreated to a quiet spot at the end of the corridor where the doctor could go about his work without being interrupted.

With his hand numbed, Keating slipped back into the dressing room where his brief absence had gone unnoticed.

As the Tipp team began to leave the dressing room and make their way to the pitch Leahy caught Keating by the shoulder and, for a second, Babs thought his ruse had been uncovered.

"Young Keatin', do you see that big arse of yours?"

Babs nodded in reply.

"Well you're to use that big arse today, do you hear me?

"I do not want Seamus Cleere to hit any ball today, and between your arse and your hurling you have all the credentials to do that job. I don't care if you hit no ball yourself as long as you stop Cleere."

Leahy had good cause for wanting to neutralise Cleere's influence. The year previously the classy wing-back had won the Caltex Hurler of the Year award and was a key cog in the Kilkenny machine.

He was one of the few half-backs around who could drive the heavy sliotar of the day over the bar from inside his own half, and his ability to angle long deliveries into his inside forwards was the springboard of many scores.

The match was only seconds old when Cleere decorated it with a typical piece of brilliance. Kilkenny midfielder Pat Moran won the ball from the throw-in and passed it out to Cleere who, from over 70 yards out, lanced it straight over the bar.

The Kilkenny supporters rose to acclaim the perfect start to the match, but it would be the only time their team would lead and it was the last significant contribution Cleere would make because Babs was about to carry Leahy's instructions to the letter.

As the two of them raced for the same ball from converging angles, Babs met Cleere with an almighty blow into the side with his formidable arse and the impact was so devastating that the crowed gave an involuntary 'ooooh' as Cleere crashed to the turf.

The Kilkenny wing-back's impact on the game was minimal thereafter, whereas Babs went from strength to strength, the worry about his injured hand having totally robbed him of any big-match nerves.

None of his team-mates seemed troubled by that affliction either, and, at half-time, they weren't the least bit flattered by a 1-8 to 0-6 lead.

When John Teehan goaled for the Kilkenny shortly after the break it briefly looked like the match was back in the melting pot, but having their tail pulled only made Tipp bare their claws and, by the end of the match, Kilkenny goalkeeper Ollie Walsh had suffered the death of a thousand cuts.

Walsh was the best shot-stopper in the game and a born showman who loved nothing more than to bob and weave through a ruck of players and send an almighty clearance scudding down the field.

For all his brilliance, though, the Tipperary forwards always felt he was mentally brittle and prone to errors if they could dent his confidence early by pressurising him under a high ball, or flattening him with a shoulder-charge.

Sean McLoughlin was the battering-ram who was always charged with this responsibility, and it was his pressure that distracted Walsh when he let a harmless enough shot from Mackey McKenna in the first half slip through his hand and into the back of the net for Tipperary's first goal.

Walsh never recovered his composure, and dropped another high ball from Donie Nealon straight into the net in the second half as the Tipperary forwards converged on him again.

It was a rare off-day for Kilkenny's celebrated 'keeper, who ended up conceding five goals, three of them to the stick of Donie Nealon, but even had he been at his best Tipperary would have won, such was their total dominance in the second half.

The Kilkenny defence couldn't cope with the movement and clinical finishing of the Tipperary attack, and any time they did manage to clear their lines the ball was returned with interest because the Tipperary back-men were totally dominant.

The Kilkenny game-plan had been to expose the Hell's Kitchen full-back line by fielding their 'three Toms' full-forward line – Tom Walsh, Tom Forrestal and Tom Murphy – who were all small and extremely quick.

They were under orders to drag Hell's Kitchen out the field and then turn them and beat them for pace, but the three Toms found out the hard way that Tipperary's veteran defenders were no slouches.

And when the quality of ball coming into the three Toms progressively deteriorated, they were eaten without salt by the far more physically robust Tipperary defenders.

Doyle, in particular, had a storming match, his never-say-die defiance summed up by one iconic charge from defence when he lost his hurley but still someone managed to dribble the ball all the way as far as midfield by shouldering all-comers out of his path.

Along the way he was lined up for some meaty shoulder charges by Kilkenny men, but as every successive challenger was sent bouncing out of his way the roars from the crowd grew louder and louder until they reached a deafening pitch.

Doyle's cameo summed up the attitude that ran right through the Tipperary team, and, in the end, Kilkenny were burnt to cinders by the fiery physicality of their opponents and beaten by double scores – 5-13 to 2-8.

They were technically outclassed on the day too, something that Kilkenny teams weren't at all used to, but there was no disgrace being bested by a Tipperary team that had just announced themselves as possibly the greatest ever to grace Croke Park.

They were the perfect combination of physicality, skill, experience and ruthlessness, and played a brand of organised and clinical hurling the likes of which had never been witnessed before.

And, at the heart of it all was Doyle who, at the age of 34 and after his 16th Championship campaign, had his status as a living legend of the game franked when he was honoured as the Caltex Hurler of the Year for 1964.

• • • ● • • •

Kilkenny's misery at losing to their great rivals yet again in a major final was compounded when they were forced to spend the Monday morning after the match in the company of their conquerors.

The 'Player's' cigarette company had paid the GAA a sum of money to oblige both teams to tour their Dublin factory together which, understandably enough, wasn't a prospect that filled the Kilkenny hurlers with much joy.

There was a marked contrast between the smiling Tipperary men and stoney-faced Kilkenny hurlers in the publicity shots published in the Tuesday newspapers. Even the gift of as many cartons of cigarettes as the players could carry home with themselves wasn't enough to lift the spirits of the Kilkenny players.

Their suffering at the hands of Tipperary wasn't over either. Two weeks later, the two teams contested the Oireachtas Final and Kilkenny seemed set for some satisfying vengeance when they led by 3-5 to 1-2 after 25 minutes of the match.

It wasn't to be. Tipperary suddenly roused themselves to score 3-4 with just a single point in reply, and though Kilkenny rallied again they still fell to a 5-7 to 4-8 defeat.

It was yet another defeat to their most bitter rivals in a major final, but it only made the Kilkenny players even more grimly determined that they would eventually have their day.

CHAPTER 23

Kieran Carey grabbed Mackey McKenna firmly by one arm and Michael Murphy held him by the other as they half-led, half-ragged him across the runway to the aeroplane.

McKenna had never travelled to the USA or England with the Tipperary team before because he suffered from claustrophobia and couldn't bear the idea of being cooped up in a thin metal tube a few thousand feet above the ground.

Leahy had insisted he travel to England for the '65 Wembley tournament, though, because Kilkenny were the opponents and, by now, every match against them was a grudge affair.

McKenna had refused point-blank initially, but when Leahy persuaded Mackey's father to intercede on his behalf he finally got his way, like he usually did.

His team-mates had poured a few whiskeys into him at the airport bar and, for a while, the warming effect of the liquor chased away any worries he had about the impending flight.

But, as he drew closer to the 'plane, Mackey was having second and third thoughts with every passing step, and when he reached the bottom of the metal stairs that led up to the fuselage he panicked entirely and tried to break free from two escorts.

It was a futile struggle against a pair of men like Carey and Murphy. They simply gripped him by his belt and shoulders and forced him up the stairs like they were leading a prize bull into a crush.

Carey and Murphy sat at either side of him once inside the plane in case their reluctant co-passenger tried to make a run for it and, as the engine fired into life, Mackey put his head between his knees with Rosary beads wrapped tightly around one hand and a baby Jameson gripped in the other.

After 15 minutes or so of desperate prayer, Mackey slowly started to straighten up and was coming around to the idea that maybe air-travel wasn't so bad when the plane suddenly hit a pocket of turbulence and dropped like a stone.

The blood drained from Mackey's face and, when he looked panic-eyed over at Kieran Carey for reassurance, there was little coming.

"Mackey, we're done for," said Carey grimly.

"Ah, Jaysus Kieran, are we? Are we?"

"We are, Mackey. We have a feckin' puncture."

• • • ● • • •

Even with Mackey in their ranks, Tipperary lost that Wembley match to Kilkenny, but it wasn't all that sore a defeat because, a couple of weeks earlier, they'd beaten them in a much more important game – the '65 League Final.

That was a controversial contest pock-marked by ugly off-the-ball clashes and bouts of viciously wild pulling that only served to further sour the rivalry between the two teams.

Doyle, in particular, earned the ire of the Kilkenny fans for a shuddering third-man tackle on the comparatively slight Tom Blondie Walsh, and a chorus of boos greeted his every contribution thereafter.

As the match wore on though it became apparent that, in a test of raw physicality, Kilkenny still couldn't match Tipperary.

They'd given as good as they'd received on that score in the first half but the effort seemed to drain them and, in the second half, it was the Tipp men who were coming out the better in the physical collisions.

The Kilkenny inside forwards simply couldn't cope with the heat that Hell's Kitchen was generating and the climate around the Tipperary half-back line was no more temperate.

In fact, the pick of the Tipperary defenders on the day was their new wing-back, Len Gaynor, who had earned his opportunity because of an injury to Mick Murphy and hurled so forcefully that he'd be a fixture in the Tipperary defence for the next ten years.

With the sting drawn from the Kilkenny challenge, the Tipp forwards once again proved that the reigning League and All-Ireland champions had the technical craft to complement their brute strength.

In the end Kilkenny had no answer to the overwhelming power of Tipperary's total hurling, and their 3-14 to 2-8 defeat was even more crushing than the previous year's All-Ireland Final defeat because they really felt going into the match that they finally had Tipp's number.

They'd blitzed them by 7-10 to 5-7 six weeks previously in a League match in Thurles but the Tipperary defence, and Doyle in particular, were in far more bullish mood now than they had been then.

Tom Blondie Walsh had taken Doyle for three goals in that encounter, but Kilkenny's most dangerous forward found him much less charitable second time around and ended the afternoon with just a single point to his credit.

Once again, when a major national title was on the line, they fell short against their bitter rivals and talk of a Tipperary hoodoo was given more currency.

No one was more crestfallen by the defeat than Kilkenny's coach, Fr Tommy Maher who was, by now, consumed by the challenge of lowering Tipperary's colours.

Fr Maher's own inter-county hurling career had been prematurely ended by the calling of the cloth but, for him, hurling remained as much a vocation as the priesthood.

A teacher of maths and science at St Kieran's College, in Kilkenny, he brought the sort of forensic and structured thinking required to master those two subjects to bear on hurling.

He was a visionary thinker who broke the game down into its many component parts, identified all the individual skills and devised drills that might best enable a hurler to master them all.

Nothing was left to chance. In his study in St Kieran's he even analysed the tools of the trade to the enth degree. Hurleys were balanced and sliotars weighed until he was satisfied how the former could best manipulate the latter.

As a mathematician, Fr Maher believed that every problem had a solution, but this Tipperary team were proving a particularly difficult equation to solve.

He had always been of the mind that pure skill could conquer size and strength, and this conviction was validated in his first year in charge of Kilkenny when they came from nowhere to win the 1957 All-Ireland title.

They were given little hope against Wexford in the Leinster Final that year, and with good reason. Wexford had bossed the province for most of the decade and had won the previous two All-Ireland titles, whereas Kilkenny hadn't claimed a championship for ten years.

Against all expectations, though, Kilkenny's craft, speed and supreme organisation cut Wexford's team of physical giants down to size, but now Tipperary were proving to be a much less obliging Goliath.

The 1964 All-Ireland Final had proven that Tipperary couldn't be beaten by pure skill alone because they didn't lack for that quality themselves, and complemented it with raw strength and a ferocious will to win.

Fr Maher had been convinced that the much-vaunted Hell's Kitchen full-back line could be dragged out of position and then beaten for pace but, instead, they'd comfortably handled Kilkenny's Three Tom's full-forward line.

He realised that Kilkenny would have to learn to play a more physical game themselves and was sure they had the blend right as the '65 League Final approached, so the scale of the defeat was hard to stomach.

It was now clear that Kilkenny's traditional brand of hurling wasn't equipped to get the better of this Tipperary team. There was only one remaining solution to the problem – they had to learn how to beat Tipperary at their own game.

••• ● •••

Tipperary's victory in the '65 League Final reinforced the sense within the team that they were now untouchable and would win every single match of real consequence they went out to play.

This supreme confidence in their own ability didn't dull their competitive edge, it only made them all the keener to maximise their potential while the team was in its prime.

Clare were disposed of with little fuss in the Munster Semi-Final on a score-line of 5-8 to 3-3, a victory that set up a joust with Cork in the Munster Final.

The stage was perfectly set for one of those elemental Tipp-Cork battles of yore. Talk of a Cork revival had amped up the public's interest to the extent that the Gaelic Grounds couldn't cope with the demand for admission.

With thousands locked out of the ground, the main gate was forced open by a desperate surge of humanity that was only forced back after a lengthy struggle with a large contingent of Gardai.

The enthusiasm of the Cork fans wasn't matched by their hurlers though. They were humiliated on the day by a Tipperary team who took great pleasure from mercilessly driving a stake through the heart of their great rivals once and for all.

Men like John Doyle, Jimmy Doyle, Tony Wall, Theo English and Michael Maher had know some bad days against Cork in the 1950s and they weren't inclined to take it easy on their old tormentors now.

The final score was 4-11 to 0-5 in Tipperary's favour, and they weren't flattered by it. Cork scored just a single point in the entire second half and, right to the final whistle, Tipperary hurled as if the fate of the match was still in the balance.

Everyone presumed that Kilkenny would be Tipp's opponents in the All-Ireland Final again, and maybe the Cats took it for granted themselves because they under-performed in the Leinster Final and went down to a shock single-point defeat to a young Wexford team.

Kilkenny had underestimated the challenge that Wexford posed, but Tipperary wouldn't make the same mistake.

•••●•••

September 5, 1965, Croke Park.
All-Ireland Senior Hurling Final v Wexford.

As the Tipperary players prepared to climb the steps to receive the Liam McCarthy Cup, Doyle was hoisted towards the sky by a knot of his team-mates in recognition of his record-equalling eight All-Ireland medal.

When he was raised shoulder-high the muted cheer that greeted him was hardly worthy of the achievement but in keeping with the mood of the day.

Though 70,000 people had crammed into Croke Park for the match the atmosphere throughout was strangely listless as Tipperary won easily enough – 2-16 to 0-10 – without ever really having to extend themselves.

The result was never in doubt after Sean McLoughlin pilfered two early goals, and five points from play by a turbo-charged Mackey McKenna always kept Wexford at a comfortable distance thereafter.

The Leinster Champions hadn't lacked for enthusiasm, but their young forwards were eaten without salt by Doyle and his comrades in Hell's Kitchen.

The convincing nature of the victory was regarded as par for the course by Tipperary fans who, by now, had become a little bit spoiled by their team's remarkable run of success. Had they known what the future held, they may have celebrated the county's fourth All-Ireland title in five years with greater zeal.

Even the players themselves didn't greet the victory with the same enthusiasm they had previous triumphs, because a cloud had been hanging over the team for a few weeks before the All-Ireland Final.

Paddy Leahy had been diagnosed with cancer and the prognosis was bleak. He'd guided Tipperary to eight All-Ireland titles, but the doctors said the 73-year-old wouldn't make a ninth.

When the Tipperary team flew out to America two weeks after the All-Ireland Final to play New York in the Away League Final they did so without their Chairman of Selectors who, for once, had to put himself before his county.

For the second year in a row New York pushed Tipperary harder than any other team had. The League Final was played over two legs and though Tipperary lost the second match they scraped an aggregate victory of 6-19 to 5-20.

They were only one win away now from winning the Grand Slam of Championship, League and Oireachtas titles for the second consecutive season, but the last piece of silverware was going to be the hardest of all to claim.

Waiting for Tipperary when they returned from America was a Kilkenny team grimly determined to make amends for their defeat in the League Final and premature Championship exit.

●●●●●●●

October 17, 1965, Croke Park.
Oireachtas Final v Kilkenny.

Paddy Leahy hugged his trench-coat closer to himself as he walked slowly down the steps of the Hogan Stand and made his way across the Croke Park pitch. The cold found it much easier to seep into his bones these days.

He knew his days were numbered and the time he was spending in Mount Carmel Hospital was only delaying the inevitable, but accepting his fate without a struggle was never an option for a man who had fought for his country in the War of Independence.

The visit to Croke Park to watch his boys in action against Kilkenny was supposed to lift his spirits, but it had done the opposite.

They'd managed just two points in the entire first 30 minutes to Kilkenny's 1-6 and had hurled like men who had forgotten what it meant to wear the blue and gold.

He knew this might be the last time he'd ever see them in action, and he didn't want his last memory of a group of players who had made him so proud in the past to be a sour one.

When he walked into the dressing room the Tipperary players looked wide-eyed at him and a second later hung their heads in shame. They hadn't even known he was in the stadium.

For a minute Leahy stood in the middle of the room and looked slowly around at his players without saying a word.

Those who managed to occasionally raise their heads to look him in the eye couldn't help but notice how frail-looking he'd become since they'd seen him last only a few short weeks previously.

After what seemed like an eternity he finally spoke.

"Listen to me, lads," began Leahy in a voice that was barely above a dry whisper.

"Ye're after beating Kilkenny in the League Final, Wexford in the All-Ireland Final and New York in the World Final. Are ye really going to let Kilkenny beat ye in the Oireachtas after all that?

"The one match that's left this year? Are ye really going to let Kilkenny walk all over ye and take it away home with them?

"I'm ashamed of ye, lads. My God almighty, a team like ye. To see ye backing away from that Kilkenny team.

"This is my last final lads. Don't let me down like this."

With that, he turned on his heel. His players were too ashamed to even look at each other and the only sound in the dressing-room was the low sobbing of those who were failing to hold back the tears.

The spell was only broken when Kieran Carey eventually strode to the centre of the room and brought his hurley down on the table with a splintering crash.

With his eyes ablaze he turned to his team-mates and roared one question at them with an untethered ferocity.

"Are we going to let that man down?"

One by one the men in blue and gold rose to their feet with their jaws grimly set and their reddened eyes now cold as ice.

At that moment they would have died for Paddy Leahy, but they made do with breaking Kilkenny into kindling by producing the most devastatingly perfect 30 minutes of hurling Croke Park had ever seen.

When the final whistle blew Tipperary had won the match by 2-12 to 2-7, and Paddy Leahy was no longer feeling the cold in the Hogan Stand.

CHAPTER 24

2011

It's a lovely sunny day in the rural idyll of Kilruane in North Tipperary, and Len Gaynor is making the most of it by pucking a sliotar around the garden with his young grandson.

All is going well until the session finishes up with a spot of shooting practise and Gaynor does his grandfatherly duty by letting in a few soft ones. It's not a charade that comes easily to him though.

"Oh, it kills me to let the ball in," he says with an almost embarrassed chuckle afterwards. "Pure kills me!"

The competitive spirit that made him such a formidable hurler in his playing days is clearly still as much a part of his DNA as it ever was, but that's hardly a surprise.

In a way, Gaynor the man is a product of the winning mentality that made Tipperary such a great team between 1961 and 1965.

When he joined up with the panel as an impressionable 20-year-old in 1964, he was moulded in an environment where winning was the Alpha and Omega, and that attitude shaped him as a human being as much as it did a hurler.

"It was a huge eye-opener for me and a huge part of me becoming an adult and growing up," he admits.

"I was only a child really at 20 when I first started hurling with them, but I really grew up amongst those great men. I was very lucky to come in at that late stage and be part of it.

"There was a very strong bond there. I was a newcomer but I was made to feel like an important part of the outfit, and those men definitely made a major impact on me as a person.

"You really got the sense that this was serious business we were on, and you knew you were expected to do your job.

"You really felt it was important to be hurling for Tipperary and that Tipperary had to win. That was in the air all the time. Once you walked into that dressing-room you were in the business of winning, whatever the importance of the match you were about to play."

When Gaynor first walked into the Tipperary dressing-room, no one personified that voracious will to win for the honour of the blue and gold more than John Doyle.

For years he'd viewed him starry-eyed from a distance as the very embodiment of Tipperary hurling, and observing him up close and personal only deepened his respect for the man.

"He just had a pure passion for hurling," says Gaynor. "He wouldn't suit the modern game because he wouldn't be into the drills or anything like that. He just wanted a match in training so he could have a battle with someone.

"The contest was what motivated him. He'd do the gallop around the field with everyone else because that was something else to win but, as far as he was concerned, pucking the ball around was a waste of time.

"He just wanted to test himself and beat all before him all the time. He just loved that and couldn't see any other way.

"I remember one day we were playing a League match against Laois. It was an awful day and the square was full of muck.

"We had them well beaten coming into the last few minutes of the game. They had a 21-yard free and I remember thinking to myself that I hoped he'd put it over the bar and we'd get away handy out of there.

"As yer man was bending to take the free Doyle started roaring at him, 'You sir, you sir. Go for a goal, go for a goal'. He wanted to be challenged all the time even though the match was over as a contest and it was horribly wet and mucky in the square. But that was Doyle for you."

The Tipperary team of the '60s certainly didn't lack for passion or desire, but what made them really special was that the fire was complemented by ice.

They didn't just go out there with the intention of out-hurling their opponents, they deliberated about how best to do so and were always motivated by the challenge of self-improvement.

No one personified this ethos more than centre-back Tony Wall. In 1965 he published an instructional book on the skills of the game, *Hurling*, which remains as relevant today as it did back then.

"I was thinking about the game constantly," says Wall. "I was intrigued by it really. I don't believe that made me particularly special or unique though.

"I once read a great book written by the former Kerry footballer, Dick Fitzgerald. It was about strength and conditioning training, tactics, and how to kick the ball in different ways. It was written in 1913.

"You'd swear strategy was only invented in recent years the way some go on, but people always had a mind for tactics. There was always men like Dick Fitzgerald, Paddy Leahy and myself.

"They weren't all gobshites back then. There was a native cunning about all these things. It wasn't all mayhem. You'd always have rough fellas, but there were plenty of others thinking of how best to get things done."

Wall's shrewdness and hurling intellect were complemented by the natural leadership qualities that would eventually earn him the rank of Adjutant-General of the Irish Army later in life. When Wall spoke, his team-mates listened.

"There was no such thing as managers talking tactics back then so I suppose I began driving the tactical side of things myself," he says.

"The time we discussed things was when we sat down in the Glenmorgan for a meal after every training-session.

"The likes of Jimmy Doyle and Donie Nealon would be involved, and then when Babs came along he would have taken an interest as well. Himself and Mick Roche were the making of that team really in 1964."

Roche and Keating were both richly talented individuals, but they made the impact they did that year because they immediately bought into the team ethos.

Egotism or individualism simply wasn't tolerated in the Tipperary dressing-room, and the reason the team performed with machine-like consistency and effectiveness was because everyone accepted they were simply one gear dedicated to the performance of the whole.

"The main thing that squad had was huge discipline," says Babs Keating.

"I don't mean that in terms of dirty play or anything. I mean that in terms of discipline in how we used the ball and discipline with each other.

"We put a lot of thought into the way we played and there was a message on every ball that was struck.

"Anybody that behaved differently or played for themselves rather than the team was brought over the coals fairly quickly.

"Everything I learned about coaching was from those lads. We were a team effort and individualism had no part to play in it.

"I'll always remember the All-Ireland Final in '64. I mooched back around centre-midfield and picked up a ball in the half-back line.

"Things were going well so I let fly and it went over the bar. It was as good a score as I ever got, but I still got a belt on the arse from Tony Wall who told me to fuck back up the field where I should be. Even though it was a great point, it wasn't part of what Tipperary hurling was all about."

What Tipperary hurling was all about was best personified by Paddy Leahy. Ask any of the veterans of that team what it was that made them such a potent force, and his name is usually the first invoked.

The impression he made on them has been a lasting one. Mackey McKenna is as jovial a man as you could ever meet, but when talk turns to the time an ailing Leahy visited the team at half time in the '65 Oireachtas Final, he's as unable to hold back the tears now as he was all those years ago.

"He was an absolute genius and we all adored and respected him so much," says McKenna. " I'll never forget the way he came into the dressing room like that in '65. We were all crying for a finish but he got the reaction he wanted."

He usually did. It's clear from talking to his former charges that Leahy wasn't just a very shrewd hurling man, he was also an amateur psychologist.

"He was our senior counsellor," says Donie Nealon. "He was nice to everybody and had a great old brain. He'd get the best out of you and everyone was very fond of him. He was a real, old father figure.

"He never said a wrong word to anyone ever. He just coaxed the best from you and had a way of making you really believe in yourself. He had a great natural understanding for how a team should be picked and who should play where.

"He was hugely regarded by the players and, when Paddy spoke, you'd certainly listen to what he had to say to you."

So, just how good was the team that Leahy built? The best qualified to judge are those who hurled against them.

When Tipperary were at their very best in '64 and '65 their keenest competitors were Kilkenny and Eddie Keher, for one, is unequivocal about how highly that Tipp team should be regarded.

"I always said of that Tipp team that it was one of the best teams of all time," says Keher. "I felt that their performance in '64 was the peak of that team. It was absolute perfection.

"We were slight favourites going into it because we were All-Ireland Champions but we were wiped out really.

"They beat us all over the field in every aspect of the play. We just had no answer to them because they didn't have a single weak link.

"They had super forwards like Jimmy Doyle, who was one of the greatest in my mind, as well as Babs, Donie Nealon, Larry Kiely, Liam Devaney and Sean McLoughlin

"They weren't all just great forwards, they complemented one another perfectly because they were a blend of strength, playmakers and natural finishers.

"I'd say they were one of the first teams that started moving during a match, apart from the switches that the selectors would make. They used to move around of their own accord, which was unusual at the time, and confused opposition defences. It certainly confused us in '64.

"Then you had Mick Roche, who was an outstanding hurler in midfield. He had wonderful hands that allowed him to strike well off either side and a great hurling brain that saw him read the play and control the whole midfield area.

"Beside him you had Theo English, who was a very workmanlike hurler who never wasted a ball. Everything he hit had a purpose and was always put on a plate for the forwards.

"Their three half-backs – Burns, Wall and Gaynor – were all fine hurlers, and even if you got past them you had the Hell's Kitchen full-back line who were tough and uncompromising and played the game to the rules of the time. That Tipperary team had it all really."

Imitation is the sincerest form of flattery and, ultimately, Kilkenny decided that the best way to compete with Tipperary would be to beat them at their own game.

"There was an acceptance in Kilkenny that we had to fight fire with fire," agrees Keher. "We trained for that. We had to match physicality with physicality, and that was the way we played.

"And when two stone walls meet like that there's always going to be fireworks, and there were.

"The ironic thing is that, of all the teams we subsequently played and all the players I know from hurling, my best friends are on those Tipp teams. We can look back and laugh now. But it was certainly no laughing matter at the time."

It certainly wasn't. No modern rivalry has since come close to the enmity that existed between the Tipperary and Kilkenny players and supporters in the 1960s.

"It took the good out of it," says Mick Burns. "Cork and Wexford were a great crowd because you fought it out on the field and there was no bitterness, whatever the result.

"There was a great camaraderie there and you'd go to places like the Blackrock and Glen Rovers clubhouses and have a few jars with the Cork players.

"They were great guys and great sportsmen, but it was different with Kilkenny. It was pure bitter. They were out to do us but it didn't work out for them. We were beating them the whole time and they didn't like that."

It's often the nature of high-achieving sportspeople that, despite all they've won, they can't help obsessing about the one that got away.

The veterans of that Tipperary team are no different. Winning four All-Irelands in five years was an incredible achievement, but missing out on an unprecedented five-in-a-row remains a real regret.

The reason it rankles so much is because they fell so short of playing to their potential in the '63 Munster Final against Waterford when they were beaten by 0-11 to 0-8.

Considering they scored a cumulative total of 25-74 in the next six

Championship matches they played, their failure to ignite that day is all the more baffling.

"That's the one match I'd still regret," says 'Mackey' McKenna. "If a team is better than you, they're better than you and you can accept it. But, that day, we were ten points a better team than them but just couldn't get a goal.

"The ball hardly passed into our half of the field in the second half. I saw Larry Kiely come in with one ball and he hit the upright with it. It came out to Donie Nealon and he hit the other upright with it.

"Then Devaney came in and caught it and I said to myself, 'this is going to be it', but he drove it over the bar with the whole goal open.

"Usually, if a couple of us had an off-day, then someone else would play well, but that day every single forward played poorly.

"We were only beaten by three points. I really think we would have won the five-in-a-row if we didn't have such an off-day against Waterford in '63."

The failure to put five All-Irelands back to back is only a minor lament in the greater scheme of things though.

When they look back on their hurling days now, and what they achieved together, to a man they feel blessed. Not just to have won all they did, but to have been part of such a special collective of people who were united by a common cause.

"I adored that team of the '60s because there was a bond there between players that has only been rivalled since by the Kilkenny team that won the four-in-a-row," says Jimmy Doyle

"You hear of a bond of soldiers, well we were a bond of hurlers. We were all great friends and we all bonded together like brothers even though we were from different clubs. There was no jealousy, bitterness or anything like that.

"It's a sad sight now to see them all go out one by one. We've lost Kieran (Carey) and John (Doyle) and I get lonesome when I think of them, but we'll all join up with them again eventually.

"I often sit here and just think and think. It's hurling I'm always thinking about. Hurling, hurling, hurling. They were fabulous men. Really great men. It was a privilege to have hurled with them all."

CHAPTER 25

May 17, 1966

The grey sky wept a steady rain as the mile-long funeral cortege slowly wound its way towards Holycross village.

In life Paddy Leahy had seemed to know everyone worth knowing. In death, they all made a point of being there to wish him well on his way.

An honour guard of members of the Old IRA led the tricolour-draped coffin as it was carried from Holycross church to the old Abbey by Doyle and his Tipperary team-mates.

Right to the end, they served their old mentor well.

There is no other silence like the silence of hundreds of mourners, and, when the 12th Battalion of the Irish Army fired a volley skywards in Leahy's memory, the echo seemed to hang forever in the still air.

The rising, musical swell of the trumpeted Last Post and Reveille finally dissolved it as the coffin was slowly lowered.

It was a fittingly stirring farewell for a man who had dedicated his life to his country and his county and the latter, especially, was the poorer for his passing.

Because, as the first clods of shovelled earth fell with an insolent thud on Paddy Leahy's final resting place, they didn't just echo the finality of a vibrant life extinguished, but also the end of Tipperary hurling's golden era.

● ● ● ● ● ● ●

A week to the day after Paddy Leahy's death, Tipperary were beaten by Kilkenny for the first time in 44 years in a hurling match of real consequence.

The 1966 League Final was a watershed moment for both counties.

Tipperary's air of invincibility was shattered and Kilkenny had finally ended their miserable sequence of defeats against their great rivals in national finals.

It wasn't just a great victory for Kilkenny hurling, it was a triumph, too, for their coach, Fr Tommy Maher. His team had carried out their orders to the letter and, in doing so, had beaten Tipperary at their own game.

The positioning of regular full-back Pa Dillon at full-forward was a statement that they were taking the fight to Tipperary and to Hell's Kitchen in particular.

Dillon was far from a natural forward, but he was the toughest man in the Kilkenny team and had a reputation for pulling first and asking questions later. Fr Maher wanted to see how Hell's Kitchen would like a taste of their own medicine.

As it happened a Tipperary full-back line, minus the considerable presence of Michael Maher, was the most effective component part of their team on the day, but further out the field they lost most of the key battles to Kilkenny.

It wasn't just the new-found tenacity of the Kilkennymen that was posing difficult questions, it was the brand of hurling they were playing.

Tipperary had long been regarded as the greatest exponents of ground-hurling in the game, whereas Kilkenny preferred to get the ball into their hands and adopt a more considered approach; but the '66 League Final marked a new departure for the Cats.

Fr Maher had realised that, any time the ball slowed down and there was a contest of possession against Tipperary, there was a good chance you'd come off second-best, so he drilled his team to keep the ball moving on the ground as quickly as possible.

Not only did this deny the Tipp defence the opportunity to grind down the Kilkenny forwards by engaging with them in strength-sapping tussles, it increased the pace of the game, which tested the legs of an ageing Tipperary team.

At half time Kilkenny led by 0-8 to 0-3 but, when Tipperary tacked on the first three points of the second half with the help of the considerable breeze, it looked like a familiar script was writing itself again.

Kilkennny had had enough though. This time they weren't for flinching. For the remainder of the match their defence hurled with the sort of ruthlessness that had long been the preserve of their opponents, and the Tipperary attack was withered by the heat they generated.

Both teams only managed one more point each in the remaining twenty minutes and when the final whistle blew, Kilkenny had persevered by 0-9 to 0-7.

All had changed, changed utterly.

• • • ● • • •

Tipperary had two weeks to regroup for the first round of the Championship against Limerick, but without Paddy Leahy at the helm the ship was quickly sinking.

Before the League Final the Tipperary training sessions had been sporadic and ill-planned and, as the Limerick match approached, they were no better.

Without Leahy, the selection committee lacked a natural leader who had the total respect of the players and the ability to inspire as well as delegate.

A bad situation was made much worse by the injury, or unavailability, of a number of key players for the Limerick match. Tony Wall was on duty with a UN peacekeeping force in Cyprus, while Mick Roche, Jimmy Doyle and Larry Kiely were ruled out through injury.

Mackey McKenna and Sean McLoughlin were selected to play, but neither was fully-fit after coming back from injury and illness.

Despite all these handicaps, the expectation was still that Tipperary would win handily enough. After all, over the course of the previous two years they'd won their championship matches by an average of 15 points.

Limerick were dismissed as a team that had done nothing of consequence for a long time, which was true, but, unknown to Tipperary, something was stirring beyond their western border.

Limerick had assembled a young, quick and fearless team. Just the sort of qualities needed to expose an ageing and under-strength Tipperary.

• • • ● • • •

June 5, 1966, Cork Athletic Grounds. Munster Senior Hurling Championship First Round v Limerick.

Len Gaynor had been working that morning and only made it to the team hotel in Cork an hour before throw-in.

He looked around the lobby at his team-mates and couldn't help but think to himself that they all looked just as jaded as he felt.

As the team togged out there was little of the keyed-up energy in the dressing-room that was usually a staple of a big championship match. They were walking into an ambush with their eyes closed.

Fifteen minutes into the match, the Cork Athletic Grounds echoed to the sort of frenzied roaring that only a mixture of utter joy and total disbelief can produce.

Limerick led by 2-4 to no-score and the all-conquering Tipperary team were being made look old and pedestrian by their youthful and dashing opponents.

Limerick's ploy of dragging the Tipperary full-back line out the field and using their flying half-forwards to exploit the space left inside was working a treat.

And, when the Hell's Kitchen full-back line were forced to turn and chase them, they just didn't have the legs to get there in time.

Eamon Cregan, the 21-year-old wing-forward, was doing most of the damage. Tipperary simply couldn't cope with his scorching runs from deep, and his finishing was just as impressive as he cracked home three classy goals.

The Tipperary defence lacked direction and control without the great conductor Tony Wall, and the decision to hand his No. 6 jersey to a championship rookie, John Gleeson, was exposed for the folly it was.

Midfield was a wasteland, too, in the absence of the injured Mick Roche, but it was the malaise that afflicted the players who were on the pitch, rather than the absence of a couple who weren't, that was Tipperary's biggest failing.

The relentless physicality that had been the foundation of so many great victories was strangely absent, and the once slick-moving forward division were playing like a bunch of strangers who'd only met that morning.

After Tipp reduced the deficit to just three points 15 minutes from full-time they seemed primed to pull it out of the bag, but when they dug deep for one last big effort they found they had nothing left to give.

Instead, it was Limerick who coasted home, much to the disbelief of their increasingly raucous fans, by scoring seven of the last eight points to win in the end by 4-12 to 2-9.

When the final score was read out that evening on Radio One it was repeated twice over and listeners were assured their ears weren't playing tricks on them.

Hurling's Goliath had just been downed by a stone no one saw coming.

● ● ● ● ● ●

The year 1966 had been a thoroughly miserable year for Doyle. Paddy Leahy, who meant so much to him, was gone, and it looked like the team they'd both devoted a great chunk of their lives to was in terminal decline.

They say bad luck comes in threes and 1966 wasn't done with John Doyle just yet.

For the previous eleven years he'd been just as committed to the Holycross hurling team as he had Tipperary, but without anything like the same reward.

Since their 1954 County Championship triumph, they'd shivered in the long shadow cast by the great Thurles Sarsfields team that had won ten out of 11 Mid-Tipp and County titles.

Beating their greatest club rivals and returning Holycross to the position of prominence in the county it had once held became an obsession for Doyle.

But, no matter how much he and his club-mates plotted and prepared, they always came up short against a Sarsfields team that boasted men like Jimmy Doyle, Tony Wall, Mickey The Rattler Byrne, Sean McLoughlin, Ray Reidy and Mick Murphy.

There was no disgrace playing second fiddle to arguably the greatest club hurling outfit the game has ever seen, but Doyle was never the sort of man for whom second-best was ever acceptable.

So, when Sarsfields were surprisingly beaten by an unfancied Moyne-Templetuohy team in the '66 Mid-Tipp semi-final, the result was celebrated in Holycross almost as much as it was in the parish of the victors.

Holycross had beaten Moycarkey and Thurles Kickhams on the other side of the draw and the prospect of playing Moyne-Templetuohy in the Mid-Final was a much less daunting one than facing the bogeymen of Sarsfields again.

They didn't let the opportunity slip. Doyle produced an immense performance at centre-back that drove his team on to a 4-10 to 3-8 victory and the club's first Mid-Tipperary Championship for 12 years.

Killenaule were trounced in the County Quarter-Final and now only Lorrha stood between Doyle and what would surely be a last chance to play in a county final at the age of 36.

Lorrha scored four goals in the first 15 minutes but, by half-time, Holycross had recovered their composure and led by 4-5 to 4-1. They were still clinging to a single-point lead with time almost up when Lorrha were awarded a 21-yard free in front of the posts.

Lorrha's free-taker Peter Hogan snatched at the shot and Doyle and the rest of the Holycross defenders on the line immediately roared 'wide ball'.

The umpires were unsure whether it was over or not but, after consulting with the referee, they signalled a wide to the fury of the Lorrha players and fans who were convinced it was over the bar.

A minute later the final whistle blew and Holycross seemed set for their first County Final since 1954, but Lorrha weren't done just yet.

They were so convinced their late free had been a point that they requested a replay from Holycross who refused to grant it.

Lorrha then took the nuclear option of objecting to the legality of Holycross forward Roger Ryan because he was a native of Waterford and was living in Thurles so shouldn't be allowed to hurl for Holycross.

Holycross insisted Ryan was a resident at John Doyle's house, but, at the meeting of the Tipperary Appeals committee, Lorrha produced two Thurles men as witnesses who swore that Ryan and his wife lived above Sutton's shop in the town.

Ryan did stay with the Doyles before he was married, but Lorrha had their facts straight.

After he married, Ryan and his wife moved in to a flat above Sutton's shop in Thurles so was no longer strictly eligible to hurl for Holycross.

Their appeal might have been based on solid foundations, but the aggrieved North-Tipp champions didn't have the same pull with the county board that someone like John Doyle did.

Despite the weight of evidence against Holycross, the Appeals Committee voted 6-2 against Lorrha's objection but the affair was far from settled yet.

Once again Lorrha requested a replay from Holycross and said they'd let the Ryan business drop if it was granted, but Holycross stuck to their guns so Lorrha decided to take their appeal to the Munster Council where they were sure they'd get a fairer hearing.

The appeal was to be held in Limerick, and to ensure their delegation carried as much clout as possible, Holycross sent their two most famous sons to represent them at the hearing – John Doyle and Pat Stakelum.

•••●•••

As Doyle looked over at the 12 Munster Council delegates behind their long table the man that worried him most was the Cork County Board Secretary, Con Murphy.

The two had history that went back a long way. For a start, Murphy had been full-back on the Cork team that Doyle's Tipperary had beaten in the classic Munster Championship encounters of '49, '50 and '51.

That wasn't the main bone of contention between the two men though. Murphy was also the only referee to have ever sent Doyle off at inter-county level.

He'd given him his marching orders for a stroke on Waterford's Jim Fives in the 1953 Munster Semi-Final that, according to one match report "appeared accidental to everyone but the referee".

Doyle had a feeling at the time it wasn't just that indiscretion he was being punished for. A few weeks earlier Murphy had refereed a club match in Tipperary involving Holycross and had been under orders not to send off any county players.

Doyle became embroiled in a few incidents and, when Murphy warned him on his conduct, Doyle told him where to go because he knew couldn't be sent off that day. He had no such immunity by the time the match against Waterford came around though.

Murphy was a man who believed implicitly in fair play and, as he listened to the Lorrha and Holycross delegates present their cases, his gut feeling and the weight of evidence told him that the Lorrha version of events rang more true.

After both sides had given their spiel, it was the turn of the Munster Council officers to ask whatever questions they wished.

Murphy looked up from the sheaf of notes in front of him and stared intently across the room at Doyle.

"John, you say that Roger Ryan has been living with you for the past three years and, more recently, both he and his wife have been living in your family home?"

"That's right, Con," replied Doyle confidently. "We have a spare room in the house and it's nice and handy for them."

Murphy pursed his lips, briefly looked back to his notes, and then casually lobbed a grenade across the room towards Doyle.

"And could you tell me what Roger's wife's name is, John?"

Doyle easy self-assuredness drained away suddenly, but not as quickly as the blood from his face.

"Ahh … ahm. God, Con, of course I know it, but for the life of me I can't think this minute."

"You mean to tell me you don't remember the name of a woman who's been living under the same roof as you for a couple of years?" said Murphy, with his eyebrows arched.

"Of course I know her name, it's just slipped my mind, that's all," replied Doyle, a little too defensively.

"I see. I've no more questions to ask," said Murphy, and sat back in his chair with the finality of a man who had made his mind up.

The Munster Council ruled 8-4 in favour of Lorrha and expelled Holycross from the Championship. Doyle's dream of winning one last county title was over.

CHAPTER 26

The cold, night air stung his hot lungs as Doyle jogged heavy-legged around the frozen field with only the watery light of a hand torch to guide his way.

It was pure hardship, but he knew it had to be done if his 37-year-old body was to be up to the rigours of a 19th season of inter-county hurling.

As he slogged up the incline of Maher's field his heart hammered in his chest and the greater effort required sent great clouds of condensed breath billowing skywards.

God, but it was cold. The grass was already crunching under his feet from an early frost and the bitter February wind that whistled through the hedgerows had turned his exposed legs red raw.

For half a second the thought of the warm turf fire at home nearly convinced him to jump the stile after just one lap of the field, but he gritted his teeth and bowled on into the night again.

Whenever he wondered why the hell he was still pushing himself like this the answer arrived quickly on the question's coat-tails: Paddy Leahy.

He had been on the verge of announcing his retirement before the League resumed in '66 when Leahy sent him a letter from his sick-bed in Mount Carmel that ended with a call to arms.

"Hurl again next year and go for the ninth. Don't see any reason why you wouldn't win it."

If it was one of Leahy's dying wishes that he win a ninth All-Ireland medal then, by God, he was going to dedicate every fibre of his being to see it satisfied.

But he knew, too, that he had only so much more left to give. The ninth would have to be won in 1967, or not at all.

●●●●●●●

Doyle was girding himself for one last charge, but he wouldn't be joined in battle again by his old friend, Michael Maher, who had decided the '66 campaign would be his last.

The Hell's Kitchen full-back line was no more and, in every other component part of the once rock-solid Tipperary team, other fissures were appearing too.

By now Tipperary were an old team by any reckoning. Doyle was 37, Theo English 36, Kieran Carey 34, Tony Wall 33, Sean McLoughlin 32, Donie Nealon 32, Liam Devaney 32 and Mick Burns 30.

It wasn't just age that had dulled their edge. Jimmy Doyle was still only 28 but the cumulative effect of his many injuries had left him a shadow of the player he once was.

Tony Wall had always been the most ferociously dedicated player on the panel and a man who led by both deed and example, but the centre-back was no longer as single-minded in his approach to hurling as he once was.

Instead of spending every spare hour he could working on his fitness and conditioning, he was now keenly pursuing a new-found sporting love – golf. He started 1967 with a fifteen handicap and, by the end of the year, had lowered it by nine strokes.

He was far from the only Tipperary player who was no longer as focused as he had once been. Without Paddy Leahy watching on from the sidelines, the team training sessions in Thurles lacked the heat that had previously moulded the team into such a fire-hardened unit.

An 18-point win over Wexford in the first League match papered over the cracks, but they were soon to be exposed for all to see.

Up next in the League were a Kilkenny team who were driven to make amends for losing the 1966 All-Ireland Final to an unheralded Cork side that everyone had expected them to beat easily.

Maybe that's why they so utterly failed to hurl to their potential on the day, but they'd have no such difficulty getting revved up for another joust with their greatest rivals.

• • • ● • • •

March 12, 1967, Nowlan Park.
NHL group match v Kilkenny.

Anne Doyle was on her last nerve and ready to snap.

Every time her husband came out of the Tipperary defence with the ball, the Kilkenny supporter sitting behind her and her young sons, Johnny and Michael, leaned out between them and booed as loudly as he could.

Flashing a few dirty looks had done little to dissuade him and even when nine-year-old Michael turned around and said, "that's my father out there, would you keep quiet," his plea fell on deaf ears.

So, when the red-faced heckler leaned out over them yet again and continued booing her husband undaunted, Anne finally decided enough was enough.

It had been a wet day and she'd brought a golf umbrella with her that was adorned with a fairly impressive metal spike.

Grabbing the brolly firmly she turned on her husband's heckler, pointed the dangerous looking end of it towards him, and issued a threat in a steely tone that stopped him mid-flow.

"If you do that one more time I'll put this umbrella through you."

The look in Anne's eyes, as much as the weapon in her hands, immediately told him this was a woman not to be trifled with, so he promptly left his seat and moved to another part of the ground where his health wasn't in such imminent danger.

It was about the only battle that Tipperary won that afternoon because, down on the pitch, they were being ground to dust by their faster, stronger and much more ruthless opponents.

Kilkenny had once struggled to cope with Tipperary's physicality, but now it was they who were setting the agenda on that front.

No man typified their bristling aggression more than Pa Dillon, who had been relocated to his natural position of full-back, and was doing all he could to make life as unpleasant as possible for the Tipperary forwards.

He was the one Kilkenny player they were genuinely afraid of because they felt he was capable of just about anything. Dillon was a mild-mannered fellow off the field, but when he crossed the white lines he became a different proposition entirely.

A tall, thin lathe of a man, who was made entirely of hard bone and sinewy muscle, he liked to constantly twirl his hurley in his hands, which gave him the look of someone who was itching to use it on the first thing that came near him, be that man or ball.

As Mackey McKenna walked towards him before the throw-in he did so with a heavy heart because he knew from experience that an afternoon in Pa's company was likely to be a sore one.

And he could tell too by the cut of Dillon's gib that he was in an even more combative mood today than usual.

"McKenna, if you step in past that line I'll cut the head clean off ya," said Dillon when Mackey reached where he stood on the 21-yard line.

"Ah, Jaysus, Pa," replied McKenna in mock horror. "I have 14 children. If you kill me you'll have to look after the lot of them."

When his wisecrack didn't even draw a half-smile from the Freshford man, Mackey knew there would be little quarter given today. Confirmation arrived when he received a stinging clatter across the shins when the first ball came between them.

That was all the encouragement he needed to wander out the field where he might pick up a loose ball or two and, more importantly, be out of Dillon's sphere of influence but, when the Kilkenny full-back started clearing ball unimpeded, Sean McLoughlin wasn't long getting on Mackey's case.

"For chrisakes, Mackey would you come in here and mark your man?" roared the corner-forward at his reluctant team-mate.

Mackey cast a jaundiced eye over at Dillon, who was standing on the edge of the square and twirling his hurley in his usual fashion.

"You must be fuckin' joking, Mac," shouted McKenna. "Do you not see your man edging up his billhook inside?!"

McLoughlin's mood wasn't helped a few minutes later when he received a tasty clatter himself from Dillon. Running out to Mackey he shouted: "Your man is after hitting me a right belt in the jaw, what are you going to do about it?"

"I'll tell you what I'll do," replied Mackey coolly. "I won't let him do the same thing to me."

It wasn't just the Tipperary forwards who were struggling to cope with the huge physical intensity their opponents were bringing to bear on the contest, the Tipperary backs were also being actively targeted for special treatment.

Over the years the Hell's Kitchen full-back line had made an art form of flattening incoming forwards with judiciously timed shoulder charges, but now the hunters had become the hunted.

Doyle, in particular, had a big red X on his back. His ability to inspire his team-mates and raise the dander of the Tipperary supporters by charging out of defence with the ball in hand was a weapon that Fr Tommy Murphy was keen to see neutralised.

Wing-forward Eddie Keher was charged with the responsibility of curbing Doyle's influence, and he was well cut out for the job.

Renowned as one of the most technically gifted hurlers the game had ever seen, he was also a serious lump of a man who knew how to make the most of his broad and powerful frame.

Whenever Doyle won the ball and attempted to sally forth with it, Keher would line him up from a distance, charge straight at him, and bury him into the chest with a bone-shuddering shoulder charge.

Doyle wasn't the type to sidestep when he charged from defence and his open style of play more often than not meant Keher could inflict the maximum damage.

He conceded a few frees along the way, but the sight of Tipperary's totemic defender being knocked back and occasionally flattened was a huge source of inspiration for the Kilkenny players and supporters alike.

All over the field Tipperary players were wilting under the heat being applied by their opponents, who could sense a vulnerability in the blue and gold that had never been there before.

Driven on by the scent of blood, Kilkenny forged into a 4-4 to 0-1 lead at half-time and were given a standing ovation as they trotted back to their dressing-rooms by their jubilant supporters.

Tipperary did manage to save some face by out-scoring Kilkenny in the second half to make the final score – 5-7 to 2-7 in Kilkenny's favour – look a bit more respectable, but their long-suffering forwards took a deeper satisfaction from the fate that befell Pa Dillon in the closing minutes.

After a raw pull on Jimmy Doyle he was intercepted on his way back to small square by Babs Keating and the pair became locked in a not-so-loving embrace that was broken up with some difficulty by the referee.

The flashpoint looked like it had passed as Babs bent low to pick his hurley off the ground, but on his way back up he unleashed an almighty upper-cut that sent Dillon crashing to the turf.

That was the cue for all hell to break loose as a knot of Kilkenny fans broke through the wire and attempted to exact retribution while both sets of players jostled and strained against one another around the fallen Dillon.

When order was eventually restored, both Dillon and Keating were sent off and, as Babs walked to the line, a cacophony of booing accompanied him on his way.

He was given a much warmer reception in the dressing-room a few minutes later by his team-mates who were all tickled pink to see the fearsome Dillon finally get his comeuppance.

Mackey McKenna, though, wasn't inclined to join in the general back-slapping.

"Good man, Babs?" he said with his hands on his hips. "Good man Babs me backside! Why didn't he hit him the box in the first five minutes instead of the last five? He'd have saved the rest of us some right belts if he had!"

•••●•••

The defeat to Kilkenny ended Tipperary's involvement in the League, which left them with a 16-week wait before their Championship campaign began.

They busied themselves by playing challenge matches, but draws with Waterford and Wexford and a defeat to Limerick, did little to convince they were capable of recapturing their former glories.

Their Munster Semi-Final opponents, Waterford, had beaten reigning All-Ireland Champions, Cork, in the first round, so Tipperary fans travelled to the match in hope rather than expectancy.

That's why the scale of Tipperary's victory came as such a pleasant surprise. They hammered Waterford by 2-16 to 3-3 and would have beaten them by considerably more had they not eased off the gas when it was clear the win was safe.

Clare provided a much stiffer test in the Munster Final, but Tipperary didn't just pass it, they also proved that there was still a good kick in their ageing legs.

After playing with a strong breeze in the first half they led by just two points at the break and seemed to be in mortal danger when Clare drew level seven minutes into the second half.

In the final twenty minutes, though, Tipperary proved they remained a champion team by producing hurling of sustained brilliance to score 2-6 without reply and run out 4-12 to 2-6 winners.

It was Doyle's 10th Munster Championship – one more than Christy Ring had managed – and the nature of Tipperary's victory suggested they had rediscovered their mojo just in time to propel him to a record ninth All-Ireland title as well.

A familiar foe had other ideas though. Kilkenny awaited in the All-Ireland Final. Three years on from their humiliation in the '64 they finally had the chance they craved to make amends and bury their Tipperary bogey once and for all.

● ● ● ● ● ● ●

It was the last week of August and, if you closed your eyes and inhaled deeply, you could already smell the sweet scent of early autumnal decay.

The ash and sycamore in the hedgerows were still straining towards the sun for all they were worth, but the sheen had gone from their leaves and, in a few short weeks, they'd brown and fall away.

Nothing lasts forever but, as Doyle marched towards him across a field cropped bare of its corn, John D Hickey couldn't help musing that here was a man who looked like he could.

Doyle was 37 now, but seemed no less lean or vigorous than he did when the journalist had first laid eyes on him all those years ago.

In a few days time he'd play his last-ever match for Tipperary, but he looked like a man who had many more left in him. When Hickey said as much after the two men had greeted one another warmly, Doyle shook his head with a sad finality.

"Win or lose on Sunday I will retire, and the only way to do it is to make the clean

break and also give up club hurling."

"Even if you don't win the ninth on Sunday?" wondered Hickey out loud.

"There is no doubt about it, it's now or never, but I think we can do it. I wish there wasn't all this talk about me and that ninth medal though," said Doyle.

"Of course I'd love if Tipperary got the record, but the personal slant is being emphasised far too much.

"What about all the men who have helped me to win my eight medals? How many would John Doyle have, had he been dependent on himself?

"If I am lucky enough to win the ninth, every man I ever played with on the Tipperary team will have a share in it."

Hickey knew Doyle was a man who didn't like to be kept from his work, and, after chatting for a few more minutes, he let him back to his harvesting.

Before he'd gone too far, though, he was halted when Doyle shouted after him.

"Tipperary will win that ninth medal alright."

His days were numbered, but Doyle was still straining towards the sun.

••• ● •••

September 3, 1967, Croke Park.
All-Ireland SH Final v Kilkenny.

The Kilkenny team train had slowed for its approach into Heuston Station but Ollie Walsh hardly noticed.

The goalkeeper was focused solely on the coin in his hand as he carefully felt its weight and eyed the spot where the carriage door met the floor.

Usually the Kilkenny players had a few games of cards when they travelled to a match by train, but no one remembered to bring a pack this time so they were making do with a game of pitch and toss in the corridor of one of the carriages.

Ollie's coin arced gracefully through the air and, when it landed perfectly, he threw his arms out in victory but his moment of triumph was cut painfully short as he drove his right fist through the partition window of the train compartment.

Blood spurted freely from the jagged wound on his wrist and his team-mates called frantically for the team doctor, Dr Kieran Cuddihy.

A towel was quickly wrapped around Walsh's wrist but it did little to staunch the flow and, as he was rushed to a taxi after the train reached the platform, he left a blood-spattered trail in his wake.

At the Mater Hospital the attending doctor who closed the wound with the help of eight stitches told Walsh there was no chance he could go out now and play a hurling match after losing so much blood.

Walsh thanked the doctor for his aid, but there was never an earthly chance he was going to pay any heed to his advice.

The goalkeeper joined up with his team-mates again at their base in the Hollybrook Hotel, in Clontarf, in time for Fr Tommy Maher's pre-match pep talk.

Before every big Championship match, the Kilkenny coach would seat his players in a circle and speak to them individually one by one.

He always seemed to know the right thing to say. If someone was inclined to be nervous he'd settle them down. If someone was too relaxed he'd say something that would focus their mind.

When he reached Pa Dillon, his message was unambiguous.

"Pa Dillon. You're regarded as a sort of an over-robust hurler. You won't be half robust enough today."

• • • ● • • •

Len Gaynor moved down the dressing room bench to make more room for Doyle.

The big man was always tense and nervous before a big championship match, but he'd never seen him this anxious before.

He'd tied his boots a couple of times already and fixed and re-fixed his togs and jersey again and again.

Once or twice he'd shuffled around the room and swung his arms briskly before sitting back down again, looking no less relaxed for having stretched his limbs.

Like every other time they shared a dressing room Gaynor couldn't help but have his gaze drawn by Doyle. He had a way of filling the place with his sheer presence like no one else did.

Gaynor knew this was the last time he'd hurl together with a man he regarded as nothing short of a living legend, and the knowledge of what was at stake had added to the tension in the room.

As he looked around at the men who'd taught him so much about the game, he made a silent vow to himself that he'd give it everything he had to make sure Doyle got that ninth medal and the other veterans, like Theo English, Kieran Carey and Tony Wall, could finish on a high.

The call to arms finally came. Doyle sprang off the bench quicker than anyone else and Gaynor stepped in behind him. Walking out behind Doyle for a match always somehow made him feel bigger himself.

When the dressing-room door was finally opened, Doyle marched out to meet his destiny in his usual fashion – with his shoulders back, his collar up, and his chest out.

● ● ● ● ● ● ●

The first thing both teams noticed when they ran out onto the pitch was the gale that whistled down the field from the Canal End to Hill 16.

The sideline flags strained against their moorings like they had some place better to be, and glorious sunshine darkened to shadow and then burst to life again as the clouds in the sky raced one another northwards. It seemed almost as if the earth itself had been sent spinning more quickly by the tense, frantic energy that coursed through the stadium.

Tipperary captain Mick Roche won the toss and elected to play with the angry elements. He knew Tipperary's best hope was to strike the lead early, put Kilkenny under as much pressure as possible, and then hope their rivals crumpled beneath the weight of history.

Right from the throw-in, though, Kilkenny hurled like men who were inspired rather than inhibited by the 45-year hoodoo their great rivals held over them.

Eddie Keher made it very clear they were going right for Tipperary's jugular when he turned down the simple point on offer from an early 21-yard free.

He lanced the ball low and hard instead but chose his target unwisely. The sliotar flew straight at Doyle who got his hurley to it and pushed it out to the right of the goal.

Martin Brennan pulled it back across the 13-yard line where it was met by the on-rushing Kilkenny full-forward Jim Bennett, but John O'Donoghue somehow got his hurley to the fierce drive.

Kieran Carey collected the rebound and drove it clear, but only as far as Kilkenny midfielder Paddy Moran who returned it with interest. O'Donoghue had just saved a bullet but failed a much less severe examination now as Moran's long-range shot bounced over his hurley and into the net.

The goalkeeper had cause to hang his head again seconds later when his rushed puck-out went straight to Bennett. Kieran Carey had little choice but to pull him back and, this time, Keher popped the close-range free over the bar.

Despite playing with a storm at their backs, it was Tipperary who'd reaped the early whirlwind and now trailed by 1-1 to no-score.

Kilkenny struck another psychological blow a couple of minutes later when Doyle raced onto a low delivery and charged from the Tipperary defence.

Just as he straightened up and was about to open into full stride he was met with a sickening shoulder charge into the chest by Eddie Keher and sent flailing to the ground.

He won a free for his troubles, but the victory was Keher's.

In the '64 All-Ireland Final, Doyle had set the tone for the rest of his team-mates when he coursed the ball from the full-back line all the way to midfield despite losing his hurley along the way. Three years on, Kilkenny weren't inclined to be so obliging.

It was becoming quickly apparent too that, at the other end of the field, Ollie Walsh was also a much different proposition than he'd been three years previously.

Maybe it was because his accident that morning had taken his mind off the match, but whatever the reason, the Kilkenny goalkeeper was displaying none of the nerves that had caused him to unravel in the '64 Final.

He was confidently claiming everything that came his way and wasn't in the slightest bit fazed by the onrushing Tipperary forwards, who were doing their best to rattle him like they had in the past.

One save from a point-blank Donie Nealon shot defied belief. When he then shimmied and skipped his way clear of the crowded goalmouth like a ballerina through a minefield, and drove an almighty clearance down the field, the stadium shook from the roars of Kilkenny supporters.

Tipp were slowly starting to get a grip on the game, though, thanks mainly to the efforts of Mick Roche and Theo English in midfield and the growing dominance of Wall, Burns and Gaynor in the half-back line.

Two points from Roche and a free from Jimmy Doyle, who was playing despite an obvious limp, reduced the deficit to a single point and then, just when it looked like Ollie Walsh would never be beaten, his resistance was broken twice in quick succession by Donie Nealon.

The wing-forward created the first from nothing when he got the better of an aerial clash with Jim Treacy, ran on to the broken ball, and first-timed a zinger to the back of the net.

A couple of minutes later Walsh saved a 21- yard free from Babs Keating, but Nealon followed it up double-quick and lashed the rebound home from close range to put Tipperary 2-3 to 1-1 ahead.

If ever there was a cue for Kilkenny to panic this was it, but they stuck doggedly to their task. Tipp managed only three more pointed frees from Jimmy Doyle in the remaining 15 minutes of the half, and Kilkenny clipped over two points of their own to leave the half time score reading 2-6 to 1-3 in Tipperary's favour.

Would six points be enough of a buffer with a gale-force wind blowing into their faces and the hot breath of the Kilkenny men on their necks?

What seemed a slim chance to begin with became wafer-thin when, four minutes into the second half, Kilkenny scored the sort of goal you usually only get when your name is on the cup.

Tom Blondie Walsh totally fluffed his rise for a 21-yard free but made amends by unleashing a vicious ground-stroke that arrowed towards goal but was stopped on the line by Kieran Carey.

The sliotar glanced off his hurley and arced high up into the air. Carey, Doyle, Wall, Gaynor and O'Donoghue all strained to reach it, but only succeeded in getting in one another's way.

The sliotar pinballed through their thicket of hurleys, flew back across the goalmouth and spun into the net of the left-hand post. Kilkenny were just three points behind now, and Tipp were tottering.

The men in black and amber sensed as much and swarmed forward like bees hungry for honey. Tom Walsh was at the heart of everything good they were doing and was more than justifying Fr Tommy Maher's decision to play him in the unfamiliar role of centre-forward.

Fr Maher knew that Walsh would have an edge in speed on the ageing Tony Wall and, with every passing minute, it was becoming more pronounced as the veteran Tipperary centre-back tired and Kilkenny's blond bombshell made the most of the gaps that were appearing in the Tipp rearguard.

By the 39th minute Kilkenny were level, thanks to points from Walsh, Keher and Claus Dunne and, moments later, they struck what seemed the killer blow when Walsh ripped a ground-stroke to the back of the net and put Kilkenny 3-6 to 2-6 ahead.

Now it seemed only a matter of how much Kilkenny would win by but, when the heavens suddenly opened, the hard-pressed Tipperary defence seemed refreshed by the cooling rain.

The ball was coming back to them with interest whenever they cleared it, but they never wavered. Len Gaynor and Kieran Carey especially were hurling like men possessed and Doyle, too, was raging against the dying of the light.

He rolled back the years with one 30-yard sally from defence that skittled a couple of Kilkenny men sideways and drew a barrage of defiant cheering from the Tipperary fans who allowed themselves to hope again.

As if electrified by the current that ran around the ground after Doyle's charge, the Tipperary forwards finally produced the sort of slick passing move that had come so easily to them just two years previously.

Babs Keating picked the ball up on the left wing and drove a diagonal ball across field to Jimmy Doyle. Jimmy's legs weren't what they were, but his hurling brain was a sharp as ever and he dummied to catch the ball but instead let it fly past him and into the path of Donie Nealon who had run at top speed from a deep position.

Nealon charged forward and made to flick the ball over the advancing Pa Dillon towards Liam Devaney who was in splendid isolation and would surely have buried a goal had the ball made it as far as him.

It didn't. Dillon stretched every inch of his long, sinewy frame to get the very tip of his hurley to the sliotar and prevent history from taking a different path.

Shortly afterwards, Claus Dunne clipped over a free to nudge Kilkenny four points clear, substitute Dick Blanchfield then stretched the lead to five and any danger of a Tipperary revival had passed for good.

As the minutes ticked down and the realisation dawned that their team were about to finally beat Tipperary in an All-Ireland Final for the first time in 45 years, the Kilkenny supporters grew more and more raucous.

Many didn't even see the star of the hour, Tom Blondie Walsh, leave the field injured after what seemed an innocuous challenge by Tony Wall. By the following day though it would be all anyone was talking about.

Just before the end Tipperary summoned a late charge that yielded a point and denied Kilkenny the honour of holding their great rivals scoreless for an entire half of an All-Ireland Final, but it was small consolation.

When the final whistle signalled Kilkenny's 3-8 to 2-7 victory, Doyle shook hands with the man he'd held scoreless, Martin Brennan, and walked over to the Cusack Stand tunnel with his head down while Kilkenny fans, in the throes of elation, invaded the pitch.

When he reached the far sideline every supporter in the front rows of the Cusack Stand, Tipperary and Kilkenny alike, stood up to applaud him as he passed.

Doyle paused briefly as if surprised by the reception. He looked around with a wistful smile on his face, waved in farewell, and then disappeared into the bowels of the Cusack Stand.

An era had ended.

• • • ● • • •

The atmosphere in the Gresham Hotel function room on the Monday after the All-Ireland Final was soured by bad blood.

The Tipperary and Kilkenny teams had been invited to watch a replay of the previous day's match together, and as the images flickered in the darkened room everyone waited for the moment that had taken the good from Kilkenny's victory.

His team-mates didn't find out until after the match, but the injury that had forced Tom Blondie Walsh off the pitch five minutes from the end had been an awful one.

His left eye had been damaged beyond repair, and that morning a surgeon in the Eye and Ear Hospital had removed it. He was just 23, but Kilkenny's brightest young star had played his last game of hurling.

Tony Wall hadn't realised at the time that he'd hurt Walsh, or even that he'd left the field injured. In those final hectic minutes of the match he'd just presumed Walsh had been switched to another position.

When he found out later that night that Walsh had been hospitalised he went to visit him. But when he got to the hospital he was warned not to go in because the Secretary of the Kilkenny County Board, Paddy Grace, was like a roaring lion.

Grace's daughter, Angela, was engaged to be married to Tom Walsh, so the Kilkenny official's fury was understandable.

Wall had never struck a foul blow on the hurling field in his life, though, and the one that had laid Walsh low was a tragic accident.

He could remember deciding to run past Walsh from behind to anticipate the flight of a sideline cut. But at the very moment he moved past the centre-forward, Walsh turned into him because the sideline was going to go beyond them both.

Wall felt the hand of his hurley make contact with Kilkenny man, but he never realised at the time it had caused such terrible damage.

Tony's conscience was clear, but that didn't make him feel any better about what had happened.

He knew too from the way the Kilkenny players had glared at him when they took their seats in the function room that he was guilty in their eyes.

As the moment of truth came closer, and Paddy Moran prepared to take that fateful sideline cut again on celluloid, the room became choked with an expectant tension.

"This is it, this is it," Wall heard a couple of Kilkenny players whisper urgently behind him.

The replay showed the injury had been a tragic accident rather than a premeditated blow, but that did little to lighten the mood.

When the lights came up and the Kilkenny and Tipperary players filed solemnly out of the room, the rivalry that had animated them both for so long now seemed churlish and insignificant.

EPILOGUE

The braying fog signals that split the night-sky brought Doyle back to a time when he saw the world through very different eyes.

Eighteen years previously, those distinctive notes had celebrated the first milestone of a remarkable journey. Now they sounded suitably funereal and final.

As the train slowed into Thurles Station, he allowed his mind to briefly wander and, for a few seconds, he was back in 1949 again.

The platform cloaked in steam and smoke from the old coal-engine; the night-sky licked by glowing bonfires; Pat Stakelum lifted shoulder-high with the Cup in hand; the sea of smiling faces and rising swell of chorused cheering.

All a long time ago now, and the driving wind and slashing rain that whipped his face when the carriage door was opened brought him back to the present with a jolt.

It was a wild and wretched night, but the people of Tipperary braved the elements in their hundreds to pay tribute to the county's favourite son.

Bonfires sizzled defiantly against the sheeting rain all along the Railway Road as the Moycarkey Pipe Band led the team bus on its short journey to the Premier Hall.

The players were congratulated, one by one, on the raised stage by Archbishop Morris, and Doyle was afforded the honour of being presented to the crowd last.

The standing ovation that greeted him only subsided when he was handed a microphone and turned to address the crowd.

"This is the last time myself and some of the others will stand in front of you all as Tipperary players," he began.

"So, I'd just like to thank you all for coming out tonight, and for all the other years you did, too.

"I hope that you have enjoyed watching us as much as we have enjoyed playing for you. Thank you all very much."

And, with that, Doyle walked off into the wings, eighteen years after he first strode onto centre-stage.

The applause that followed him on his way was long and loud.

It had been quite a show.

REFLECTIONS

Anne Doyle

The years flicker by with undue haste and the sands of time have a way of covering over the past until it's all but forgotten.

It's Sunday in Glenbane, Holycross, but the air isn't filled with the sounds of men and boys at play like it once was.

Maher's field lies empty, the gently swaying high grass barely whispering tales of the furious battles that hardened John Doyle into the hurling warrior he became.

On the other side of the road though, little has changed. The Doyle family home looks much as it always has, the white gables giving way to a sudden entrance that's flanked by a pair of Tipperary flags fluttering in the breeze.

Anne Doyle opens the door with her usual warm welcome and points to the newly-framed photograph on the hall-table.

It's her husband, pictured with Christy Ring at the opening of a pitch in Ruane in 1971. Both are drinking cups of tea and Doyle is looking as dashing as ever in a chequered jacket with his thick, dark hair neatly slicked back.

"Oh, he was certainly a handsome man alright," agrees Anne in a wistful tone.

It's hard not to feel like an interloper in his house when the man is no longer around to invite you in, but the ever-chatty Anne has a knack of quickly making you feel at home.

Like her husband she has a strong and forthright personality, and it's easy to believe that John Doyle fell in love with and married her because he saw the same sort of strength of character in her that he possessed himself.

And, as legendarily tough as he was on a hurling field, his wife is clearly made from equally stern stuff. She's beaten cancer three times, once emerged from a car wreck with hardly a scratch and even survived an altercation with a bull that left her with six broken ribs.

If ever you wanted to definitively prove the adage that behind every great man is an equally great woman, Anne Doyle should be your first port of call.

Her husband's physical gifts and ferocious will to win made him the hurler he was, but it's doubtful his career would have been such a lengthy or successful one were it not for the support and hard work of his wife back home on the farm.

"I used to say that to him alright – that he would never have won all those All-Irelands if he didn't have me to do the work for him here on the farm," says Anne with a smile.

"He'd be saying: 'What are you talking about, shur didn't I have three All-Irelands won before you ever came here'. And shur then I'd say that was because you had your father here then!"

She can almost look back and smile at her stubbornness now, but there's a regret, too, that she allowed her life to become one of such hard labour.

Confronted by the shock of what it meant to be a farmer's wife in 1950s' Ireland, she embraced the challenge rather than shirked from it but, along the way, made it even tougher for herself than it possibly had to be.

"I really found it very hard," she admits. "The general feeling around was probably that I wouldn't stick it there for a month, with the result that I went the other way and I wasn't going to give in.

"I had never been in John's house before we were married, and, when I arrived here after the honeymoon, it was a rude awakening I can tell you. They did have the electric light here, but they didn't have running water.

"There was a well down in Tubberadora and you'd go there every day with a tractor and trailer. All the cows and cattle had to get water and drawing the water was a big thing.

"You'd have separate buckets here for the house then. I suppose I got used to that eventually, but it was a massive difference from turning on a tap.

"There was no bathroom or toilet, and I remember when he told me that I got an awful shock. I didn't know a thing before I moved in.

"Mikey Ryan, our neighbour, tells me that the expression that was fixed to my face for the first few days I was living here was priceless.

"Once I got married my parents were very supportive but they didn't like to see me working the way I did. They would have preferred to just see me working inside.

"Sometimes they'd pull into the yard and I'd be coming down with two buckets after feeding calves. They never said anything, but I don't think they were too happy to see me like that.

"They were right, it was too much. I was forever lifting things and, if I saw my girls lifting the things that I did, I'd kill them.

"My mistake was to learn how to do too much, from milking to everything else. And the more I learned, the more I was left with. That's the way life goes."

Her husband had always been a very hard worker himself and he was only too happy to encourage his wife's determination to master the demands of farming. When she did occasionally complain about her new circumstances, she received little indulgence.

"He took it for granted that I should do it. That's the way it was back then. And, if I wanted to go to town, he'd say: 'There's no other woman around here who has to go to town two or three times a week. There's a woman over there in Tubberadora, Mrs Walsh, who only goes to town once a year, and that's at Christmas, and she's as happy as could be staying there at home!'

"The whole going to town thing was a bit of an issue between the two of us. He used to say, 'you're in the country now'.

"That's just the way it was really. Every other girl around here was reared in this sort of environment.

"We'd have had a much quieter life if I hadn't argued with him so often and just gone along with things."

The most divisive issue was the other passion in Doyle's life – hurling. Anne was his most enthusiastic supporter, but the commitment he gave to the sport, and the effect that had on his home life, was also a huge source of dismay.

"He'd be gone every Sunday between League, Championship, tournaments and hurling with Holycross," says Anne. "I remember one particular year that Christmas fell on a Sunday, and that's the only Sunday that year that

John wasn't hurling.

"He used to go training in Holycross every Sunday morning and, when our sons Johnny and Michael were big enough, they'd be gone too and I'd be left here making the Sunday dinner.

"When I was growing up in Thurles we'd always make a point of having our meals together, and that was something I thought was very important. I'd have the dinner ready here at one o'clock for everyone else but they wouldn't come back from the field until half-past two.

"I'd be with saucepans of water trying to keep the dinners hot for them. Needless to say that didn't go down too well with me.

"John was just gone a lot with the hurling, and it was a tough time for me, and a lonely time too. I wouldn't complain to anybody, or even say it to my parents, because their attitude would have been that I made my bed and now I had to sleep in it."

Any attempt to persuade John to rein in his commitment to hurling always ran into the same immovable road-block – Paddy Leahy.

Doyle couldn't have sustained such a lengthy hurling career without the support and sacrifices of his wife, but it's just as unlikely he would have hurled for 19 Championship campaigns were it not for the urgings of Leahy.

And, when it came to a tug-of-war for his loyalty, Anne found out the hard way that Leahy's opinion carried more weight than hers did.

"I used to get annoyed with Paddy because of the GAA, but I had a high regard for him too. You'd always have a regard for someone who was older than you and Paddy was the same generation as my father.

"He was a great character too. He had the hat at an angle on his head and he was always full of fun, but of course we had our run-ins too because of the hurling.

"To the day he died, John would never hear a word said against Paddy Leahy and, in his own way, Paddy was very good to me, but the hurling was non-stop.

"Paddy was a bachelor who never married and he had a man working for him, Jim O'Connor, who did everything for him, both inside the house and out on the farm.

"So, because Paddy always had someone doing so much for him I don't think he understood the consequences of the sort of commitment he was asking from John.

"And, when I'd give out to Paddy about all the time the hurling was taking up he'd tell me off and say there's plenty of other women who were doing as much as I was doing but were complaining much less.

"But, while Paddy might tell me off, he wouldn't stand for anyone else saying anything about me to him. He was always telling other people what a great woman I was. I used to hear back these stories all the time, but he never said it to me.

"Himself and John were just extremely close really and that's why Paddy's opinion meant so much to John. Paddy would have been that father-figure for John after his own father passed away."

Those who knew them both will tell you that Doyle and his father, Tim, were very different characters but, despite that, they had a very good relationship.

Perhaps it was rooted in the guilt of having to give his son away when he was an infant, but Tim was always keen that John would never lack for anything, and he never did.

"John would always say, 'my father was terrible good to me'," says Anne. "I'd say, 'I hope you were good to him back'.

"A few years ago then he said: 'It's a pity my father was dead when you came here, he would have been mad about you.'

"I thought that was a nice thing to hear. I said: 'God, I hope so. Why do you think he would have been mad about me?'

"And John said: 'Because all he wanted to do was to be going some place and you're the same way, always on the go. And you'd have been able to drive him so ye'd have been great together!'

"But he did speak a lot about his father and a few times he'd mention that Tim would go on his bicycle for a pint on a Sunday night and then he'd come back and talk to John about his mother, which was the only time that would be raised."

We can only speculate as to what effect having no mother had on Doyle, but though he never knew her he was always conscious of there being a void left in his life by her premature death.

He may not have experienced the love of a mother, but, according to

Anne, his upbringing didn't lack for care and affection.

"Now and then, when he was feeling sorry for himself, he used to say 'and I not having any mother'. I used to tell him to go away out of that because he was spoiled rotten.

"His neighbours around here completely ruined him. Mrs Maher would have his dinner ready for him down there most days, I think, and I'm sure he was totally spoiled by Tim as well.

"John was certainly in no doubt that his father loved him. He'd always say, 'my father was mad about me, you know.'

"People didn't say 'I love you' very much to your children in those days, but you knew they did.

"He always missed his father a lot. Up to a few months before John died he spoke an awful lot about him, and, when Tim passed away, it definitely hit him hard at the time, even though he would never have been much good at talking about his emotions.

"I didn't go to the funeral because I thought it wasn't the thing to do. Times are so different now. We weren't engaged or anything like that, so that's the way you'd be thinking.

"I met him sometime afterwards and we were parked up in his car. I remember him saying as clearly now as if he said it yesterday, 'I'm all on my own now'."

"I didn't know how to answer. I couldn't say to him, 'haven't you me?', because that wasn't the done thing."

Conversations where emotions were laid bare were few and far between anyway. Doyle wasn't the type to show his soft side all that often and it was only after she left Thurles to work in Shannon Duty Free that Anne began to realise just how strongly he felt about her.

"You'd never be sure of him," she says. "I took it for granted that when I went to Shannon it was the end of the romance. When he started writing I got a land because he wouldn't have been a great man for writing letters or showing his emotions.

"He wrote quite a few letters but didn't like me referring to that afterwards. I probably didn't appreciate, at the time, the effort he was making to drive all the way down and back, because there were no motorways or that sort of thing at all.

"I must say that the fact that he had car was always a bit of an attraction. He was a very good-looking man, too, though I'd never say that to him.

"The girls in Shannon were very impressed when he started coming down. I got to be mad about him really and I started going to all the matches and that."

After they were married she continued going to every match she could. Hurling might have been a divisive issue at times between them but, for as long as Doyle hurled for Tipperary, his wife supported him to the hilt.

It wasn't simply a case of showing loyalty to her husband, either. Tipperary matches were the highlight of the summer social calendar and a great source of honest-to-goodness fun in a way she doesn't think they are now for the younger generation.

"I was talking to Eileen McLoughlin, Sean McLoughlin's wife, recently, and we were just talking about the fun we had going to matches," says Anne.

"It's not like nowadays when the best thing that people say about going to the match is that they made it home in good time from it.

"We were never in that sort of a rush. We'd take our sandwiches and make sure we had enough for after the match as well as before it.

"We had great fun altogether. There weren't tickets or anything so you'd have to be in Limerick at 12 o'clock to get in for the sideline seats.

"You'd be there for three hours before the game but you'd never feel the time going because everybody would be around having great craic and banter.

"You'd be mad to see them win and you'd be fierce disappointed if they didn't. John was great to take a defeat on the chin, though.

"You wouldn't know what to say to him after a match and if you said, 'hard luck', he'd give a bark because he never thought bad luck had anything to do with it. He didn't like being beaten, but by the following day he'd be over it."

Back then wives of successful inter-county players didn't benefit from any of the occasional fringe benefits that the current set do nowadays.

There were few invites to award nights or other social functions, and the only real occasion that wives and girlfriends had a chance to come together as a group with the Tipperary team was in the Glenmorgan on the Monday after an All-Ireland Final triumph.

"They're looked after much better now," says Anne. "We didn't get any hop at all, really. Back then the Irish Nationwide used to present cut glass to the team of the year, and the men would be inside in the room having a meal and the wives would be sitting outside waiting for them to finish. It was only after the dinner they could go in and join them for the dancing.

"That's the way it was until Tony Wall, who was the Tipperary captain at the time, gave a speech at the awards night criticising the fact that the women weren't allowed enjoy the meal as well.

"I remember we all thought that was brilliant but there were plenty others giving out saying he shouldn't have done it. After that, though, the women were let in to the meal, which was a big breakthrough really."

Long after his own career had ended, the invitations to award nights and social functions kept coming thick and fast for Doyle. As the winner of eight All-Ireland medals he was a living legend, and the reception he was always afforded on those nights reflected that.

Considering the level of acclaim that was directed his way for the vast majority of his life, he remained remarkably unaffected by it. He enjoyed the status that was afforded him by his achievements, but he was never the type to clamber up on a pedestal uninvited.

"He was used to everyone clapping him on the back, but he wouldn't be getting a swelled head around here," says Anne with a chuckle.

"If we had a disagreement I'd be saying to him: 'Just because when you get clapped on the back, and told you're a great fella whenever you go into a pub, doesn't mean that you are one.'

"In fairness to him, though, he really and truly didn't have a swelled head. The eight medals were something to be very proud of, but the fact that he had won the eight medals wasn't as important to him as the fact that Tipperary had won eight All-Irelands.

"When they made up that song about him he'd be saying, 'do you hear that? The great John Doyle'. I wouldn't always let on, but of course I was very proud of him."

Like every marriage, there were plenty of times, too, when pride wasn't the primary emotion her husband stirred in her. Doyle was a strong-willed and stubborn character, which didn't always make him the easiest man to live with.

"It's hard to describe his personality, really, but he was definitely a bit rigid in his views," says Anne.

"If he didn't want our children going out with someone he was quite strict with them. If he didn't like someone he didn't like them, and that was it. He wouldn't give them a reason. If you asked him why he didn't like them, he'd just say he didn't like them, and that was it.

"He could be very impatient and set in his ways but he definitely had a good sense of humour. I probably didn't appreciate it half the time, though, because he could also drive you mad with his stubbornness and impatience.

"He was the sort of man that, if his dinner wasn't ready when you said it would be, he'd be banging his knife and fork on the table until it arrived."

Another obvious character trait was a relentless energy that had found a productive outlet for so long in hurling. So, it was hardly a surprise then that, when the hurling was finally over, he initially struggled to cope with the void that had been left in his life.

"You could tell he was missing it a lot as soon as he finished. But then the politics came along very quickly and I think he threw himself into that to fill the vacuum," says Anne.

"He was involved in the club, too, and then the county board and Central Council of the GAA but, despite everything else he did, he always really missed the hurling."

When he hurled for Tipperary, Doyle seemed unbreakable and it was easy to believe that he was. In 19 senior championship campaigns he never missed a match through injury and was never substituted.

None of us are indestructible though, and Doyle discovered that, just as the rest of us will some day too.

He took on a brain tumour and won that battle convincingly, but didn't fare so well when he suffered a couple of strokes in his latter years.

He battled on bravely to the end but, for a man who was defined for so much of his life by his God-given strength, feeling it slip away from him was difficult to cope with.

"It was very hard on him," says Anne. "He didn't accept it. If he could have still been able to drive that would have been easier on him because he would have still had his independence.

"He would say to me, 'it's alright for you, but look at me, I can't go anywhere'. I wouldn't give in to him and I'd say that there's no one stopping you going anywhere and that I would drive him wherever he wanted to go.

"He would say, 'that's not the same', and I know myself it's not. Once you can't drive your independence is gone. He used to get very frustrated and even stopped going to hurling matches for a finish.

"He could have taken his walking aid and gone to them but he didn't want to be seen with it. I was saying to him that he was depriving himself.

"Timmy Floyd, from the County Board, would always ring to see if John wanted to attend a match, but he would have had to go in a wheelchair and there was no way he would do that.

"That was the pride in him. He didn't want to have people saying, 'Isn't it a holy terror that John Doyle is gone like that?'"

Right to the end Doyle could lean heavily on a pillar of strength that has always remained constant – his wife, Anne. And now that he's gone, she misses the reassuring weight.

"It's very difficult to cope with. It's just very different now. A friend of mine said to me that the more someone needs you, and relies on you, the more you miss them when they're gone, and that's definitely true."

$$\bullet\bullet\bullet\,\bullet\,\bullet\bullet\bullet$$

The Doyle Family

Great platters of sandwiches, chicken wings and cocktail sausages are ferried around the table and the air hums with two or three different conversations as voices strain to be heard above one another.

As the stories flow and the laughter grows, it's becoming increasingly clear that growing up in the Doyle household was rarely quiet and never dull.

John and Anne Doyle had seven children – Margaret, Johnny, Michael,

Sandra, Collette, Liz and Ann-Marie in that order – and they're gathered together around the kitchen table now with their mother as they were so many times in their youth.

Just like when any large Irish family comes together, there's no shortage of tales to be told at one another's expense or reminiscences of childhood dramas that seemed serious business at the time, but can be laughed at now in hindsight.

"We had great fun and laughs really growing up as kids, there was never a dull moment in our house," says Liz with a hearty laugh.

It certainly sounds like a life less ordinary as colourful tales of hay-barn infernos, abducted Shetland ponies and Brendan Boyer doing the Hucklebuck in their kitchen are told.

The conversation zips here and there, and explores the occasional cul-de-sac, but before too long it returns to the man that has always loomed large over their lives, their father, John Doyle.

"My earliest memories of him were when his Holycross team-mates would come up to the house and they'd all sit down together to have tea, sandwiches and barmbrack," says Margaret.

"This was around 1962 or '63. They'd always be sitting around talking tactics.

"Men like Pat Stakelum, Michael Maher, Francis Maher, my father and the rest. The smoking that used to go on would be phenomenal. My father smoked an unreal amount even when he was hurling.

"I do remember, too, as a small child going to the Railway Station after Tipp had won an All-Ireland.

"They'd come off the train dressed in their black blazers with the Tipp crest. They were treated like Take That had just arrived in town! There was no crowd control, and how someone wasn't killed I'll never know.

"They were taken from the station on a truck down to the Cathedral where the Bishop would introduce them to everyone and from there to the Glenmorgan, which used to be mobbed because everyone would try to follow them in.

"My father and mam used to be busy talking to people and myself and Johnny and Michael would be able to run around. We'd always get jelly and ice-cream, which was a great treat.

"It was only really myself and Johnny and, maybe, Michael who could remember the glory days of his hurling career.

"Even after he finished hurling, though, he always had tunnel vision when it came to the GAA and I would say that the GAA was definitely the first love in his life. We often came second as his family."

When Doyle finished playing he took an active interest in the hurling endeavours of his sons, Johnny and Michael, who both went on to hurl with distinction for Tipperary at underage and senior level.

Doyle applied the same high standards to his sons that he had set for himself in his playing days and, at times, he could be a tough task master.

"When we were young lads he'd be giving out stink because he'd expect us to win matches on our own," says Michael.

"There were days we could play poorly in matches and he'd eat you afterwards. But when his grandsons started hurling he had a different attitude with them altogether. He was much more forgiving entirely."

When Johnny and Michael did star on the hurling field he wouldn't be the sort of father who'd make a point of patting them on the back, but his pride in their achievements was clear to others.

"Daddy wouldn't give Johnny and Michael praise, but he was obviously so delighted with them," says Ann-Marie. "He wouldn't let on, but we could all see that he was."

He was never more proud than when his two sons helped Holycross to the 1990 County Championship. It was the club's first title since he won the last of his own three medals in 1954, and he took just as much satisfaction from it as he had any those triumphs.

"In the late-'80s and early-'90s when we played in three county finals he'd be hell-bent on them. It was as if he was playing himself," says Johnny.

"He'd be down at training and interested in how this lad and that lad was going. Paddy Kenny was over us at that time and, of course, he was great friends with Paddy, so I'm damn sure there were conversations between the two of them about what was what and who should be playing where.

"In the 1990 County Final we were leading for most of the match but, 10 minutes before the end, Cashel drew level with us.

"He went down to the tearoom underneath the stand in Semple Stadium at that stage and started asking up to others how it was going now. He couldn't bear to stick watching it because he was afraid we were going to be beaten again.

"He was just fierce passionate about Holycross, he loved the place in all aspects, and winning that county title meant an awful lot to him."

On one occasion Johnny and Michael played together on the same hurling team as their father. In the late-'80s Doyle was invited to play in a charity match in Ballycastle in Antrim, and though he was well into his 50s by now he took up the challenge.

His two sons accompanied him for fear their father might need a bit of protection if some galoot attempted to make his name by taking a shot at the great John Doyle, but they were to find out that the years had done little to dull their father's edge.

"When we arrived up there you'd swear Elvis had just landed such was the reception he got," recalls Johnny with a chuckle.

"He was in his late-'50s at this time and we went up to mind him and make sure he wouldn't get a belt, but we needn't have worried.

"He started off corner-back and the Antrim hurler, Dessie Donnelly, was playing full-forward for the other team and going to town on us.

"Himself says to our full-back: 'Hey, young fella, come in out of there and let me in instead'. So in he went and, would you believe, he hurled the lard out of Dessie Donnelly who was in his prime at the time.

"We were driving back down very late on the Sunday night after the match and, as we were coming into Dublin, I knew well what he was thinking

"Sure enough he says: 'Pull over here, I have to go in and see a good friend of mine in the Embankment'. When we arrived the Embankment had been long shut because it was two in the morning at this stage.

"But he gave a knock anyway and didn't Mick McCarthy himself open the door and say, 'how are you John, come right in'.

"We were in there until five in the morning and the only other person that was let in was Ronnie Drew, God rest his soul. It just goes to show the character he was and the charisma he had that Mick McCarthy would just open the door to him like that.

"And I would always say, too, that my father opened a hell of a lot more doors for all us than he ever closed."

Like many Irish fathers though, he wasn't too inclined to open the door too widely when suitors began taking an interest in his five daughters.

When that particular topic is raised, eye-balls roll and heads shake around the kitchen table as the Doyle sisters recall their father's attitude to their prospective boyfriends.

Sandra: "Please don't go there."

Anne-Marie: "He just wasn't into that sort of thing."

Liz: "He'd be summing them up and checking them out!"

Margaret: "If you brought home DJ Carey you were away on a hack. If you brought home a lad who was even thinking about playing for Cork City, you were in trouble. If he had rugby or soccer in his head, forget about it."

Margaret: 'If he didn't play hurling, then he'd tell him to feck off."

Sandra: "It didn't even matter if they played hurling. And no matter where they were from, that place was no good."

Doyle clearly wasn't too shy about laying the law down to his children, who found out the hard way that, if you disagreed with him on an issue, there was little point debating it with him.

But though he was a hard taskmaster at times, they were in no doubt either that he could always be relied upon when they needed him most.

"He was a very opinionated man but, at the end of the day, he was there for everybody too," says Collette.

"He was a hard man, but he was a very big family man. He did have his bad points, but he had his very good points too.

"Michael was right with what he said earlier, that he was different with the grandchildren. They couldn't do any wrong but he would have been harder on us.

"I remember playing camogie years ago. Oh, Mother of God! It was the Tipperary Under-16 team and we beat Limerick by three goals to nil.

"We thought that was brilliant but, in the next match against Waterford, we were beaten by 15 goals. That was the end of the camogie anyway!"

He demanded high standards from his children, and was never the sort of man to sugar-coat his opinions for fear they'd hurt some feelings or cause offence.

"I'd sum him up as a very honest and forthright individual," says Johnny. "He was what you saw. He had his own ideas and wasn't shy about telling them to you. But, as time went on, he was often more right than he was wrong, in fairness to him.

"He'd encourage you a lot and would honestly tell you what he thought whether you'd liked what he had to say or not.

"You had to admire him for that. He was a very strong individual, and a flamboyant character really, and I got on extremely well with him.

"Of course we had our arguments, the way everyone does, and when it came to a debate you'd do well to agree with him, but the bottom line is that we all got a great upbringing from him and my mother."

And, even though they had their occasional disagreements, it's evident that the seven Doyle siblings miss their father terribly now that he's gone.

"He could be extremely stubborn and very unfair in his views so we fought, argued, and rowed plenty," says Margaret.

"But, even though we all had differences of opinion and hugely different personalities, we always had a great time growing up together and we loved our father dearly."

• • • ● • • •

Gerry Chawke – June 2011, Clonmel.

It's a sleepy Thursday afternoon in Clonmel, but walking through the front door of Gerry Chawke's pub catapults you into a different universe entirely.

The place is hopping and most of the noise and laughter is being provided by a large group of Welsh tourists, who are alternately singing beautiful choral hymns and telling filthy jokes. Like many of their countrymen they have a singular talent for both.

It's a strange day you won't find some sort of craic in Gerry Chawke's pub, which is probably what first attracted John Doyle to the premises and then the man himself.

Chawke was Doyle's closest friend for the last 30 years or so of his life, and the sight of the two of them as thick as thieves together was a staple of Tipperary hurling matches for just as long.

They seemed an unlikely partnership to some and, when you ask Gerry Chawke how the friendship was first stuck up, the memory of the day draws a chuckle.

"I'm a proud Limerick man so whenever John Doyle's name came up in conversation in the pub I used to call him the 'hatchet-man'," says Chawke.

"Then one day who walked in the door only Doyle himself, along with Tommy Barrett and Sean Fogarty.

"There was a great character at the bar by the name of Paddy McLeane who, when he saw Doyle, says to me, – 'call that man now what you always call him'."

"I was caught badly but you couldn't give Paddy the satisfaction. So, when I had Doyle's pint poured I said, 'here you are hatchet-man' out of the corner of my mouth so McLeane could hear me but, hopefully, Doyle wouldn't.

"He didn't hear me but just happened to turn around after I said it so it looked like he had. So, of course, I went down to Paddy and said, 'there you go now, McLeane'.

"I had a few pints shortly afterwards with John that day and we just hit it off straight away. We became great friends after that and would go to every sort of a match together, from mid-week minor games to All-Ireland finals."

Gerry did all the driving but Doyle got much more from the relationship than just a willing chauffeur. Chawke is a big, bubbly character with the unmatchable people-skills of a successful pub owner, and was the perfect foil for Doyle who was always at his best when he had someone like that to spark off.

"He was never a man to push himself on others, he was a shy man really," says Chawke. "He'd come in to the bar there and sit down and mind his own business. He'd talk away to anyone that came over to him and he loved a good chat, but he wouldn't push himself on others.

"Some people tended to judge him from a distance. But, when you got to know him, he was a really friendly man altogether. What he loved most was to hear or tell a good story or two or get a sing-song going.

"His own party-piece was 'An Poc Ar Buile' (The Mad Goat). It was only two verses long but it would get him off the hook. He sang it everywhere he went."

And the pair went everywhere together. There were few towns in Munster and beyond with a decent GAA pitch they didn't patronage at some stage, and the banter before and after in a local pub was as much a part of the day as the match itself.

Along the way Chawke got to experience first-hand the sort of status Doyle's achievements on the field had earned him.

"He got a great welcome wherever he went. We'd go up to Dublin for the All-Ireland Hurling Final every year and he had his own room, free of charge for the night, in Barry's Hotel that we called 'The John Doyle Suite'.

"He was good friends with John Deane, the owner, and it was a nice arrangement for both of them because people would love to see Doyle around the place, and he was hugely popular amongst fans of other counties, especially the Cork lads who were absolutely mad about him.

"The night before an All-Ireland Final he wouldn't get to bed until four in the morning because he'd be seeing fellas he hadn't met for the previous 12 months and the craic would be mighty.

"When we were going to matches in Cork we'd stay in the Imperial Hotel and be taken to the ground by Teddy Cronin, who knew every Guard in the City and could drive through all the road-blocks right up to Pairc Ui Chaoimh itself.

"John would knock on the door at the back of the stand and he'd get a great welcome from the Cork County Board officials who'd have two seats right dead-centre of the pitch for us. They were mad about him in Cork alright."

Of all the great days they had on the road together the one that sticks out the most was the 1987 Munster Final Replay between Tipperary and Cork in Killarney.

It was the day John's son, Michael, came off the bench for Tipperary to score two goals in extra time that sealed Tipperary's first Munster Championship triumph in 16 years.

"He was a fierce proud man altogether that day," says Chawke. "We met the whole Doyle family afterwards to celebrate and all the Tipperary players were there too. It was a fierce lively night, but the craic had been mighty even before the match that day.

"We'd had five or six brandies when we came out of Foley's pub and headed to the ground, so we were in good form.

"I was on the footpath and the next thing I looked and wasn't Doyle out onto the middle of the road. 'Come on out here into the road,' he says, 'no one will see you in there!'

"For a finish we got into a jaunting car and the banter all the way to the ground with all the supporters on the road was brilliant. It was a gee-up for everyone to see Doyle waving like he was the Pope, with a big grin on his face.

"He loved all that. Once he had someone with him to draw the bit of craic out of him, and to hop off with the banter, he'd be home and dry. He wouldn't do it on his own though because, at the back of it, he'd be shy enough.

"When he was with me, though, he'd have someone to bounce off and we were known everywhere we went. I'll tell you one thing, they were good sessions."

The pair were usually the life and soul of the party wherever they went, but one night the party turned sour.

"It was after an Under-21 match in Kilmallock, and we were actually back on home turf in a pub in Tipperary when it happened," recalls Chawke with a shake of his head.

"It was myself, Doyle, Tommy Barrett and Sean Fogarty and we were having a grand sing-song, but there was another group of five Tipperary fans in the pub who were absolute messers and kept heckling us.

"I sang 'Limerick you're a Lady' and they heckled that, which didn't bother me that much, but then Doyle sang and they heckled that as well, which I didn't like at all.

"Eventually Barrett and Fogarty headed off home while myself and John stayed on a bit longer. When we eventually decided to hit the road the other crowd said a few smart words to us as we got up to go.

"Doyle says to me, 'we'll keep our backs to the wall when we were passing them', and sure enough didn't they go for us when we were on our way out.

"Doyle was around 55 at this stage, but he was well able to handle himself.

He planted the first fella that came at him and I planted my fella. Doyle caught the third lad that came at us with a beauty of a left hook that drove him over their table and smashed a load of glasses.

"We got out of there without a scratch but it ruined the night because wherever we went we only wanted to have the craic. At the back of it, though, I think Doyle was silently proud that we handled them the way we did."

That was the one and only time anyone was brave enough to take Doyle on face-to-face, but what has always annoyed Chawke far more is the number of people inclined to speak ill of him behind his back.

"A lot of people just didn't get the right impression of him and a lot of his own Tipperary people didn't even talk that well of him, which always baffled and upset me a bit," he admits.

"I got into many arguments with people who should have known a lot better. John Doyle wouldn't do you a bad turn, I can tell you that.

"Anytime he was asked to present medals he did it with a warm heart and never looked for money, or accepted it if it was offered. He did it for the love of the game.

"It's people who didn't know him well who took an opinion against him, but, as far as I'm concerned, it was the wrong opinion.

"The more I looked at it the more I realised it was people who never hurled in their lives who, for some reason, took a dislike to him."

His own tribe have always held Doyle in high regard, both the men he hurled against as well as those he hurled with over the course of his long career.

Waterford might have handed him his worst-ever defeat on the field of play in that 1958 Munster semi-final, and possibly prevented him being part of the only ever team to win five All-Irelands in a row when they beat Tipp in the '63 Munster Final, but, until his death, he remained particularly good friends with many of the Waterford players of that era.

He had an affinity for the county that had its roots in the formative years he'd spent in Dungarvan and, in late-2009, he told Chawke that he'd like to visit the town one last time before he died.

His friend got on the case immediately and organised a trip that included a visit to John's childhood home, which still stands on Thomas Terrace, and ended in a knees-up in O'Connor's pub in Abbeyside, where former Waterford players Johnny and Michael O'Connor, Frankie Walsh, Austin Flynn and Tom Cunningham were waiting to greet him.

"We had a sing-song and the craic was mighty," says Chawke. "I had brought his eight All-Ireland medals in a display case with me and word quickly spread that John Doyle was in town.

"Before long parents were coming in with children dressed in their Waterford colours and Doyle signed jerseys and all sorts of things for them.

"When we eventually left the pub he got a standing ovation and he got fierce emotional and cried. His wife Anne told me afterwards it was all he spoke about for months afterwards and it was the best thing we could have ever done for him."

It was far from the only good turn that Chawke did for Doyle over the years, but he feels himself that he benefited more from their friendship. And now that his old partner in crime is now longer around, things just aren't the same.

The corner of Chawke's pub where Doyle liked to sit will always be a shrine to his achievements and their friendship, but it's a pale substitute for the man himself.

"He always said that I was his best friend, which meant a lot to me. He was certainly a great friend of mine.

"When he died it hit me fair hard for a few days afterwards because we were a long time going around together, and were known everywhere we went. We were fantastic friends and we never had one row, falling-out or disagreement.

"I used to love meeting him, and it was an honour for me to drive him to matches. You knew every time we went somewhere that we'd meet someone or there would be some bit of craic to be had.

"I love every one of his family, too. His wife, Anne, is an absolute lady and all of his children treat me like one of their own.

"I was definitely a better man for knowing John Doyle than he was for knowing me and I miss him an awful lot now that he's gone. That's all there is to say really."

It's enough.

● ● ● ● ● ●

Doyle Remembered – Team-mates and Opponents

The ultimate compliment a hurler can be paid is to earn the total respect of his peers.

Doyle hurled with and against some of the very best who have ever picked up a hurley, and all remember him for what he was – one of the greatest hurlers in the history of the game.

Jimmy Smyth – Clare

"Doyle would have his hair askew, his stockings down, his jersey wouldn't be properly put into his togs. He always looked that little bit wild. That was him, that was his style.

"He was a good man and a very fair hurler. He got a name from people who never understood his type of hurling.

"He was a strong and tough hurler. You could call him rough, but he was a very skilled hurler, as well. He was all the time going for the ball and he'd never strike you with the hurley anywhere in the body.

"But, when you looked at him, you thought he was deadly. He played in every position in the Tipperary defence, and he was just as good in every single one of them.

"He had great confidence in himself. And someone like that is always intimidating. It was very rarely I saw him beaten.

"He could be a rooter. He was always a sucker for a root. You were in trouble then because you'd have arms, elbows, legs and knees to contend with. He'd use every part of his body, but he was after the ball the whole time.

"He had total belief in himself and Tipperary hurling. He was a great hurling man, a great Holycross man and a great Tipperary man.

"He embodied Tipperary hurling really. Tipperary had three great hurlers by the name of Doyle – you had Tommy, Jimmy, John.

"But, if anyone spoke about 'Doyle' they weren't talking about Tommy or Jimmy, they were talking about John. When your name is reduced to either just your first or second name in the popular vernacular, then you're really something.

"There's a Kerry footballer's song written by a fella by the name of Sigerson Clifford and the first verse could have been written about Doyle because it captures him more than anything I know.

Plough and Spade and Seineboat shaped for them the deeds they were to do, street and school and mountain heard their victory cry,

Now their memories arch like rainbows o'er the meadows of the mind, The Alive who live forever, and the Dead who will never die.

"That's true as far as Doyle is concerned. When he was alive he lived forever, and even though he's dead he still lives. He'll always be 'Doyle'. He'll never die and that's his greatness."

Len Gaynor – Tipperary

"John Doyle was a big, powerful man who epitomised everything great about Tipperary hurling. You'd feel bigger yourself going out behind him for a match.

"There was plenty of skill and that as well, but that time the hurling was tough and hard and Doyle epitomised that.

"He took plenty of tough knocks himself, and he dished them out too with his body and shoulders.

"He was a rough and ready sort of character. Before a match he'd say to the county board secretary, Tommy Barrett, 'have you any good hurleys there?', and he'd just pick up a fresh hurley and go out and hurl with that.

"Most lads would be particuliar about their hurleys, but not Doyle. He seemed to pick up a new one in the dressing-room before every game and say, 'Jaysus, that looks alright'. He'd take line-balls and frees and they were perfect every time even though he was using the hurley for the first time.

"He epitomised the will to win in that Tipperary team. He was very serious about his hurling, and extremely keen that everyone would show the same desire that he did.

"He didn't say anything much but he'd pick you up if you weren't doing your job: 'Wake up there young fella,' or something like that.

"Generally he led by example. The incredible thing about him was that he wanted a battle all the time. It was all about the contest for him.

"Even in training. By God, he was serious in training. He was serious in every match he played, too, whether it was a challenge match or a championship. He just gave absolutely everything. The challenge of beating all before him was what motivated him constantly.

"Like the rest of the Hell's Kitchen full-back line he was never afraid to sacrifice himself. He'd put his leg, arm or head in and was never afraid to take a belt if it meant stopping a score.

"Doyle was more than just tough, though. He was a serious hurler and there was none better to bring the ball out of the defence. The ground shook when he came out with it. He just thundered out with it.

"He'd knock all before him and drive it up the field. It was hugely inspirational and he loved doing it. He much preferred to run through a lad rather than around him.

The crowd loved it because it typified Tipperary hurling at the time, and he was their ultimate hero.

"At half time in the '65 Munster Final, I was sitting beside Doyle and a supporter somehow got in and started rubbing down Doyle with my vest. Talk about hero-worship!

"Shur Doyle didn't mind it at all. He was enjoying it. The poor auld cratur was an old guy and he all serious about rubbing down Doyle with my vest. I suppose I should have been proud to have his sweat on it.

"He didn't look for attention but he liked it when it came his way. He'd brush it off, but you could see that he enjoyed it."

Eddie Keher – Kilkenny

"John Doyle was an icon of the game. He's a true legend. He contributed massively to Tipperary from 1949 to 1967 and his stamp was on all of the big games that they won.

"I would say that he was underrated as a hurler because he was a great stickman and had great speed, too. I suppose because he ended up in Hell's Kitchen all the good hurling he did out in the half-back line was forgotten.

"His contribution to hurling in general, not only to Tipp, was massive. I had several encounters with him on the field over the years and he was always a very fair man to hurl against because I never got a dirty belt off him.

"He always went for the ball, got it, burst out and belted it down the field. If there was a man in the way he'd drive straight into him, but that was his look-out for being in the way really.

"He was an enemy of mine when we hurled against each and the rivalry between Kilkenny and Tipperary was at its height, but we became good friends afterwards.

"I saw him in hospital in his final weeks and we had a great time talking about old matches.

"That was a very important moment for me. I felt that I was able to get in touch with his inner self at that time and I felt that our chat really meant something to both him and me.

"I was very fond of John as a person and I feel very lucky to be able to call him a good friend.

"I suppose, because he ended up in Hell's Kitchen, all the good hurling he did out in the half-back line was forgotten."

Donie Nealon – Tipperary

"He never said very much in dressing rooms. He had a quiet role really. You took more inspiration from looking at what he did on the field and his great drives forward.

He led by action rather than by words. He might have a quiet word with one or two, but he wouldn't have been the most vocal.

"He was just so solid and dependable. It was very seldom that he had a poor match.

"I think the most amazing thing about him was that he never missed training, even though he had a big farm and a large, young family. His consistency at training was amazing.

"Even over the wintertime he was always there. The other point I would make is that, even when he retired in '67, he was still hurling very well. There were no flaws in his game even at that stage. He could have definitely tried another year or two."

Sean McLoughlin – Tipperary

"He was seriously competitive and wanted to win every match we played. If it was only marbles he wanted to win it.

"He wouldn't have been the most sociable man on the team. It would be a very small group he'd be part of, Mikey Maher would have be his closest friend.

"As a person he wouldn't go out of his way to endear himself to you. He wasn't that friendly. Still, when it came to a match you always felt that, when you had Doyle in the back-line, you were half-way there.

"He had a great presence about him. He was highly regarded and respected by his team-mates.

"I hear fellas down through the years talking about how dirty Doyle was. The truth is he was as clean a player as you could meet. If anything, he was more in danger of being hit himself because he always left himself wide open.

"I remember one day in Croke Park. He used to come out with the ball and would pass one lad but he would't be happy with that, he'd have to go past someone else, too.

"He was always wide open to be hit and Eddie Keher took advantage of it one day. He drove him from here to the far side of the road with a fair shoulder. He took him off his feet because Doyle left himself wide open.

"Doyle was a hard hurler but he wasn't a bit dirty at all. He was seriously tough though. It's a fair achievement that he never had to go off injured once in all the years he hurled for Tipperary."

Michael 'Babs' Keating – Tipperary

"John Doyle had won six All-Irelands before I came on the scene but never displayed any sort of arrogance because of it.

"He always gave me the impression that, even though I was a young lad, I was welcome as long as he felt I could contribute to the team winning another All-Ireland.

"On the other side of the coin, if he felt you weren't carrying out the strong traditions that him and others had put in place, and if you didn't buy into the belief that the Tipperary jersey always came first, then he wouldn't be long setting you straight.

"He'd say: 'Listen young lad, you're playing with my All-Ireland medal now, and don't ever forget that.'

"What hurts me when people talk about Doyle as being part of Hell's Kitchen is that the skill of the man is often overlooked, ignored, or forgotten.

"He played left half-back in '58 and you don't play there unless you can hurl. He played centre-forward and centre-field for his club and you don't do that either unless you can hurl.

"I only realised how much skill he had when I came up against him in training. He could have played any place he had so much skill. And, when it came to speed, Doyle was one of the fastest lads over 100 yards in that team.

"He was an athlete. He had all those qualities that outsiders didn't always seem to respect in him but those of us who saw him in training had huge respect for his skill level.

"I had to mark him in training a lot and it was never something to be relished. If you hit him a belt you'd want to stay going afterwards.

"It was an awful shame he didn't get the ninth All-Ireland. What killed that great team was the demise of Paddy Leahy. Paddy wasn't a well man through '65 and there was nobody there to instil the discipline that was required to keep the show on the road.

"Nineteen-sixty-six was a disaster. There was no preparation. Limerick beat us and Cork beat Limerick. Before Limerick played in the Munster Final we played them in a tournament game and beat them at our leisure.

"We went down to that first-round match with no preparation whatsoever. We hadn't even been training right because there was no one there with any respect to take you by the hand and counsel you the way young lads need to be counselled."

John 'Mackey' McKenna – Tipperary

"He was a serious man at training and a great example to everyone else. The first time I ever marked him at training he said to me: 'This is the place you'll prove whether you're up to it or not. It doesn't matter what you did in the match before, it's what you do in here that you'll be judged on. You'd want to be going at it hard, because I will.'

"We used to bate the shite out of each other. You had to, because you wanted to keep your place and you were up against the likes of Doyle and Wall and all these great hurlers so you had to give it everything you had.

"Doyle was a seriously tough man. He hurled the exact same way in training as he did in a Munster Final. Just as hard and just as serious about it.

"He'd always be going for the ball though. He wouldn't be hitting you a sly belt or anything like that.

"And even though he took training fierce seriously, you could always knock a good bit of craic out of him too."

John O'Donoghue – Tipperary

"They broke the mould when they made John Doyle. Not only was he an incredibly talented hurler, he was also a unique character.

"He defined Tipperary hurling like no else ever has, and I don't think anyone will ever come close to doing so again because he was such a once-off in every way possible from his personality to his style of hurling.

"He was an incredible physical specimen and he knew how to make the most of it, but he was also a very skilful hurler, so he had it all really.

"Tipperary people adored him and he loved the adulation. He'd never actively seek it out, but he enjoyed it when it came his way.

"He was great company but a complete rogue so you wouldn't know whether or not to believe what came out of his mouth half the time. He was always enjoyable to be around though and I would have travelled to training and to matches with him a lot."

Mick Burns – Tipperary

"What could you say about John Doyle? He was a Trojan man. I saw him play in the 1949 All-Ireland when I was 12 and then I came along and won five All-Irelands with him afterwards.

"When he hit the ball it would go nearly 100 yards every time. After he cleared a ball he'd often turn to me with a grin on his face and say, 'I nearly hit that one out of the island!'

"He was a great man to hurl in front of because he always covered me well and I would do the same for him when it was required.

"He never said a wrong word to me in all the years I was hurling with him. Some fellas might tell you he was bitter, but he wasn't that way at all as far as I'm concerned. We knew what we had to do and we did it.

"We had a great relationship on the right flank of the defence. We'd have good days and bad days because you don't hit it every day, I can tell you, but we never had a cross word because I knew he was doing the best job he could and he knew I was doing the same.

"When he'd get a ball he'd come out with it and I'd go behind him to cover things. He'd always cover me, too, or throw it out to me if I was on the wing and loose.

"He had a great innings and was a great advert for the GAA because whatever he had, he put into it. When he went out on the field he hurled, and there was no codding or messing. It rubbed off on us all.

"Apparently he considered retiring in '57 just when I was coming on the scene. I'm glad he didn't because he would have been an awful thing to miss.

"I didn't go to John's funeral. I couldn't get myself to go. I just felt that man should never die and I always wanted to remember him as the man I knew on the hurling field – big, powerful and indestructible."

Jimmy Finn – Tipperary

"Myself and John came onto the Tipperary team together around the same time and palled around a lot. He used to pick me up in his car and we'd go dancing.

"He had his own little car when nobody would really have one. In he'd pull and off we'd go. They were great times really.

"He was always swinging back the auld hair at the dances. He always had a comb with him and would be sweeping it back.

"As a hurler he was a powerful man. Fierce strong altogether. Fellas would fall off him when he came out with the ball and he loved being the hero.

"He eventually became a real showman on the field but that came later in his career, really. When he started out he would have been a quiet fellow.

"He was strong and a bit rough if you like, but he wasn't dirty. He'd throw fellas out of his way but he wouldn't hit them.

"The real hard man in our period was Sean Kenny. Sean used to say to him: 'Do what you're told now, little boy', and nearly killed poor John in '49 when Borris-Ileigh played Holycross.

"I remember him saying at one stage: 'John, I'd beat you with a table-tennis bat.' Doyle would get a big jaw and that, but Kenny was the real deal. Kenny was a butt of oak.

Mick Roche – Tipperary

"John Doyle didn't do defeat. He just didn't entertain it at all. Whether it was a senior inter-county match or a junior club match. He just didn't do defeat. He was a terribly bad loser.

"He expected you to do your bit and didn't accept it at all if you didn't do your bit, no matter how inexperienced you were.

"He was in the backs and I was midfield when I was starting off. If things weren't going well he'd roar out at you and give you a right tongue-lashing. You'd hear him from a mile off. He could speak fairly roughly when he wanted to!

"He was a lovely individual in his own way, though, once you got to know him. I was lucky enough I got to know him fairly well.

"On a social night out he'd be letting everyone else sing and then, right at the end of the night, he'd sing this song 'as gaeilge' and bring down the whole house.

"He'd let everyone else off and when no one else had anything else to contribute he'd then do his party piece. He always knew when to pick his moment in fairness to him."

Tony Wall – Tipperary

"Doyle was no angel, but he had no treacherous blows or slyness to him. He was rough and tough though, and played with a real aggressiveness.

"I think wing-back suited him better than corner-back. He was a big, rangy fella and he had plenty of legs, plenty of strength, a fine pair of hurling hands and plenty of speed. Over a straight distance he was as fast as anyone.

"Any little fella had to take a big circle to get around him. There was no going through him, and he was so big and rangy that it was a long way around.

"Doyle always played conservatively under the ball. He never went up to contest it, he'd let it drop down and deal with it then. There's nothing wrong with that, it's absolutely solid.

"It was very effective, but it made for very tough hurling because it was always man-to-man under a high ball with Doyle. He'd barge into a man and make sure it was a tussle then by the time the ball arrived.

"Doyle would do the same thing always. Barge into the likes of Christy Ring and the two of them might miss it, then it would fall to the ground and that's where Doyle would have an advantage because he was so strong."

Jimmy Grey – Dublin

"He was a real Matt-the-Thresher hurler. He wasn't the most skilful in the world but he gave great spirit to the team. He was totally committed and there was no holding back.

"He was a hardy fella, too, but he was never a dirty player. The main quality I'll always associate with him was a huge spirit which seemed to inspire the rest of the Tipperary players.

"I always felt he was a better corner-back than a wing-back because small, quick players like Achill Boothman would trouble him out on the wing.

"Away from the game he was great company. You'd have great craic with him when you met him at matches. He had a gas sense of humour and was always very friendly and sociable."

Ned Wheeler – Wexford

"I found John Doyle to be a very tough man on the hurling field. All the defenders of that era were tough though. Men like Mickey 'The Rattler' Byrne, Bobby Rackard, Nick O'Donnell and Kieran Carey were all tough men on the field but, off it, they were gentlemen, and so was John.

"He was much more than just a tough man, he could hurl. He wasn't a mauler at all. He wouldn't have won eight All-Ireland medals if he couldn't hurl, but I suppose he wouldn't have won that many either if he was a softie.

"The hurlers of that era were really playing the Irishness of the game, and John Doyle was a figurehead in that respect. That sort of toughness is gone from hurling now and the sad thing is that we'll never see his like again."

Tom Walsh – Kilkenny

"He was the most outstanding player I ever came up against and it was always a really enjoyable challenge to hurl against him. He possessed qualities that were just remarkable.

"Doyle was by far the best anticipator of the ball I've marked and he'd never give you a good angle to attack it from.

"I would consider Doyle as a superb hurler, first and foremost. He wouldn't have got on the Team of the Century, and the Team of the Millennium, if he wasn't an absolutely brilliant hurler, and I certainly would never have considered him a dirty hurler. He was a strong and physical man, which was par for the course in that era, but he also had a very shrewd hurling brain and his anticipation of the ball was incredible.

"We marked each other a good number of times and, in a league match in Thurles in 1965, I took three goals off him.

"The next day we met was in the 'Home' League Final a few weeks later and I only managed a point and was lucky to get it. When I came home to Thomastown they were saying, 'how could you only get one point off an old man like that?' That's how much they knew.

"The way he hurled in that match was indicative of his capacity to read the game and close you out when the need was highest. I had the height of respect for him as a hurler."

John O'Grady – Tipperary

"He epitomised Tipp in a way. The fighting spirit and resistance. If you weren't going to applaud Doyle coming through four fellas, then you shouldn't have been at the game.

"He was never a man for fancy side-stepping. He would horse them out of his way and then lash it down the field. That was the signal for the Tipperary cheering. He'd toss his head after striking the ball down the field and trot back to his corner, victorious.

"When he retired I wrote a poem in his honour and one little line probably sums him up better than any other: *In memory's backward view, from out the square with tossing hair, he'll still be coming through.*"

Mickey 'The Rattler' Byrne

"You'd never get out in front of Doyle for a ball. He'd be gone like a flash because he was a fantastic athlete and kept himself tremendously fit.

"He was fierce strong for a young fella when he started with Tipp in '49 but he would have been a hard goer on the farm, so he would have been naturally strong. I remember giving him a bit of advice before his first match: 'Whatever you do John, don't tell them you're going to hit them!'

"Himself, myself and Tony Brennan were a strong full-backline. As the fella says, if we didn't get them coming in, we got them going out!"

KING OF THE ASH
(JOHN DOYLE)

John Doyle was the man who carried the can
When Tipp were in doubt or in dread.
He'd face an attack on the flat of his back
With his stick or his head or his leg.
He never was shy and he'd never say die
No matter how tough was the game
This man wouldn't yield but could waltz through a field
And that was the strength of his game.

His courage was pure and his hurling was sure
He sprung from the land as a man
You could never decide as you stood by his side
On a trick or a play or a plan
That would give you a chance as you thought to advance
And side-step your way for a score
He was like a stone wall as he faced the ball
And as strong as a barnyard door.

When he played as a back in the midst of the flack
In the years when the going was rougher.
He kept them at bay and stood in the way
And always that little bit tougher.
This isn't to say that this was his way
He was fair but he rarely was bettered
A giant of the ash with the skill and the dash
Of a freedom that couldn't be fettered.
Yes, life can be rough and life can be tough
A little bit more than a canter
But away from the game John treats it the same
With a smile and a chat and a banter.
But he could inspire and we had to admire
A great heart as he gave it a lash.
The record is there and no one can compare
With John Doyle who was King of the Ash.

By Jimmy Smyth

PHOTOGRAPHS

Section 1

1. John Doyle in Croke Park on All-Ireland Final day.

2. John and Anne's Wedding Day, with Best Man Gerry 'Bowler' Doyle, and Maid of Honour, Peggy McCloskey.

3. John and Anne Doyle with their family and friends at their wedding party.

4. John and Anne Doyle and family: Michael Doyle, Anne Doyle, Sandra Doyle, Margaret Doyle, John Doyle, John Doyle jnr.

5. John and Anne Doyle and family: back row, Sandra Doyle, Anne Doyle, John Doyle; front, John Doyle jnr., Michael Doyle, Margaret Doyle.

6. Anne and John, and their prize bull, 'Charlie'.

7. Another winner at the County Fair: Archbishop Thomas Morris with John and John jnr.

8. Thurles CBS, Croke Cup Champions, 1942. Back row (L to R): P Walsh, L Gleeson, J Gleeson, M Ryan, M Mullally, S Bannon; middle row: P Stakelum, J Doyle, D Foyle, T Tynan, J Kennedy; front row: J Harris, P Kenny, N Egan, F Barrett.

9. Tipperary, Munster Minor Hurling Champions, 1947. Back row (L to R): Sean Ryan (Roscrea), John Doyle (Holycross), John Farrell (Knockavilla), John Cormack (Knockavilla), John Twomey (Tipperary), Patrick McNulty (Roscrea), Tommy O'Meara (Roscrea), Dermot Butler (Thurles); front row: Michael Ryan (Annacarty), Bobby Mockler (Thurles), Con Keane (Thurles), Patrick Crowley (Borrisoleigh), John O'Grady (Moycarkey), Michael Butler (Thurles), Patrick Kenny (Borrisoleigh).

10. Holycross captain, Francis Maher accepts the Dan Breen Cup from North Tipperary Chairman, Fr Ned Murphy after his team's victory in the 1948 County Senior Hurling Final.

11. Tipperary All-Ireland Senior Hurling Champions 1949. Back row (L to R): Phil Purcell, Flor Coffey, Seán Kenny, Tony Reddin, Phil Shanahan, John Doyle, Tim Dwyer, Sonny Maher, Seamus Bannon, Tony Brennan, JJ Callanan, J Doyle; front row: P Leahy, Tommy Ryan, M Ryan, Micky Byrnes, Pat Stakelum (capt), P Caplis (mascot), T Doyle, J Kennedy, Jack Ryan.

12. A familiar scene from a Tipperary Senior Hurling training session at Thurles Sportsfield, in August 1949: (L to R) Mick Blake, Tim Ryan, Tony Reddin, Tom Fanning (Templemore) .

13. Tipperary senior hurling team and supporters following their victory over Cork in the 1949 Munster Senior Hurling final in Killarney.

14. With his sleeves rolled up in business-like fashion, Tipperary captain Seán Kenny (Borrisoleigh) leads his men into battle in Croke Park in 1950. He is followed by Tony Reddin (Lorrha) and Tommy Doyle (Thurles Sarsfields). The mascot is Phil Purcell's son, John.

15. The Tipperary All-Ireland winning team, 1950. Back row (L to R): Phil Purcell, Paddy Leahy, J Ryan, D Ryan, Ph Kenny, S Bannon, J Doyle, P Stakelum, T Brennan, S Maher, P Shanahan, J Kennedy, F Kenny, Fr

Ryan of Borrisoleigh; front row: Jerry Doyle, N Ryan, T Doyle, M Ryan, M Byrne, J Finn, T Reddin, Jim Devaney. Seated – T Ryan, S Kenny, J Everard. Mascot – John Purcell.

16. Tipperary All-Ireland Senior Hurling champions 1950. Back row (L to R): J Ryan (selector), Jimmy Finn, Phil Kenny, John Doyle (Holycross-Ballycahill), Pat Stakelum (Holycross-Ballycahill), JJ Callanan (selector), Phil Purcell (County Secretary); Middle row: D Ryan, Jimmy Kennedy, Seamus Bannon, Tony Brennan, Mick Ryan, Sonny Maher, Paddy Kenny, Johnny Everard, Jack Ryan; Front row: Phil Shanahan, Tommy Ryan, Tommy Doyle, Seán Kenny (capt), Mickey Byrne (Thurles Sarsfields), Ned Ryan, Tony Reddin.

17. Lord Mayor Impellitteri of New York welcomes the Tipperary captain, Seán Kenny, along with other team members and County Board officials on the steps of City Hall, New York, during the visit to the USA of the Tipperary team for the 1950 National Hurling League Final.

18. Tipperary hurlers pictured with Cardinal Spellman in St Patrick's Cathedral, New York, in 1950. Players included are Mick Ryan, Michael Kehoe, John Doyle, Mickey Byrne, Seán Kenny, Tommy Ryan, Jimmy Kennedy, Tomy Doyle, Denis Ryan, Paddy leahy, Seamus Bannon, Jimmy Finn, Jack Dwyer, Phil Shanahan, Phibbie Kenny, Jimmy Kennedy, Tony Brennan, Pat Stakelum and Tony Reddin.

19. Tipperary hurler Phibbie Kenny kissing the ring of Cardinal Spellman in St Patrick's Cathedral in New York in 1950. Also included in the photo are Phil Purcell, Fr Murphy, Pat Stakelum.

20. The Tipperary team and officials pictured aboard the 'Blarney' at Cobh on their return from the United States in 1950.

21. A youthful Pat Stakelum, star of many a Holycross and Tipperary victory.

22. Tipperary players and supporters with the Liam McCarthy Cup at Kingsbridge Station following Tipperary's victory over Wexford in the 1951 All-Ireland Senior Hurling final.

23. Tipperary Senior Hurling panel, 1951. Back row (L to R): Phil Purcell (Moycarkey Borris), Sean Kenny (Borrisoleigh), Jimmy Kennedy (Kildangan), John Walsh, John Hough (Toomevara), T Kevin, Tim Ryan (Borrisoleigh), Dick Blake, Tony Reddin (Lorrha), Sonny Maher (Boherlahan Dualla), Phil Shanahan (Toomevara), Tony Brennan (Clonoulty), Con Keane (Thurles Sarsfields), Rev. John Ryan (Borrisoleigh), John Doyle (Holycross Ballycahill), John Joe Hayes (Moycarkey Borris); middle row: Paddy Leahy (Boherlahan Dualla), Mick Ryan (Roscrea), Tommy Doyle (Thurles Sarsfields), Jimmy Finn (Borrisoleigh), Mickey Byrnes (Thurles Sarsfields), Ned Ryan (Holycross Ballycahill), Seamus Bannon (Drom Inch), P Fleming, Philly Ryan (Borrisoleigh), J Doyle; front row: P Kenny, John Purcell (mascot), Pat Stakelum (Holycross Ballycahill).

24. Action from the 1952 National Hurling League final at Croke Park in which Tipperary defeated New York by 6-14 to 2-5. Tipperary players include John Doyle, Tony Reddin, Tony Brennan and Tommy Doyle.

25. Doyle in action: John Doyle clears the ball against Cork in the 1953 Munster Senior Hurling final. Also in picture is Mickey Byrne (Thurles Sarsfields).

26. Doyle in action: John Doyle and Kieran Carey (Roscrea) at work in defence during the 1959 St Brendan's Cup final between Tipperary and New York in Gaelic Park, New York. Sean O'Meara is the New York player, and Tipperary won by 4-11 to 1-5.

27. Doyle in action: John Doyle comes out of defence against Limerick during the 1962 Munster Senior Hurling Championship in Cork on July 24, a replay which Tipperary won by 5-13 to 2-4. In the drawn game the score was Tipperary 3-12 Limerick 4-9.

28. Doyle in action: John Doyle bravely blocks the ball against Kilkenny during the 1967 All-Ireland Senior Hurling final at Croke Park. This was John's last game for Tipperary and Kilkenny deprived him of his ninth All Ireland medal on a scoreline of 3-8 to 3-7.

29. Doyle in action: John Doyle (right) shows all of his defensive qualities against Galway in Thurles.

30. The great Paddy Leahy: The Tipperary dug-out during the 1960s: (L to R) Martin Kennedy (Kildangan), Philly O' Dwyer (Boherlahan-Dualla), Paddy Leahy (Boherlahan-Dualla) and Tom Fanning (Templemore).

31. The great Paddy Leahy: Tipperary selector Paddy Leahy gives advice to John Doyle and Michael Maher during a game in the 1960s.

32. The great Paddy Leahy: Tipperary dugout during the 1961 All-Ireland Senior Hurling final between Tipperary and Dublin at Croke Park (L to R): John Hough, Roger Mounsey, Seamus Ó Riain, Pat Stakelum, Liam Connolly, Tom Ryan, JJ Maher, Paddy Leahy, Paddy Kenny, Willie O'Meara, Martin Kennedy, Jim Stapleton, Seán Ryan.

33. The great Paddy Leahy: John J Maher (Roscrea) and Paddy Leahy prior to a championship game in Croke Park in the 1960s.

34. John Doyle speaks to a gathering in New York at a Tipperary team reception.

35. Farewell to Erin! Tipperary, National League Champions, 1957, prepare for take-off to the USA.

36. Tipperary senior hurling team pictured during a tour of the USA in 1957. Back row: (L to R) Paddy Leahy (Boherlahan-Dualla), Pat Stakelum (Holycross-Ballycahill), Liam Skelly (Holycross-Ballycahill), John Doyle (Holycross-Ballycahill), Jimmy Finn (Borrisoleigh), Phil Purcell

(Moycarkey-Borris), Billy Hayes (Donasleigh), Phil Shanahan (Toomevara), Tony Reddin (Lorrha), Mick Maher (Holycross-Ballycahill), Fr Michael Russell (Moyne-Templetuohy); middle row: Tony Wall (Thurles Sarsfields), Jimmy Doyle (Thurles Sarsfields), Liam Devanney, Martin Maher (Thurles Sarsfields), John Hough (Toomevara), Mickey Byrne (Thurles Sarsfields), Theo English (Marlfield), Bobby Mockler (Thurles Sarsfields), Seán O' Meara (Lorrha); front row: Mick Ryan (Moyne-Templetuohy), Paddy Kenny (Borrisoleigh), Blackie Keane (Thurles Sarsfields).

Section 2

1. Tipperary, All-Ireland Senior Hurling champions, 1958. Back Row (L to R): Noel Murphy (Thurles Sarsfields), Johnny McGrath, Mick Maher (Holycross-Ballycahill), Kieran Carey (Roscrea), Larry Keane (Thurles Sarsfields), John Haugh (Toomevara), Liam Devanney (Borrisoleigh), John Doyle (Holycross-Ballycahill), Jimmy Finn (Borrisoleigh), Mick Burns (Nenagh), Ray Reidy (Thurles Sarsfields); front Row: Musha Maher (Thurles Sarsfields), Liam Connolly (Fethard), Jimmy Doyle (Thurles Sarsfields), Tom Larkin, Theo English (Marlfield), Tony Wall (Thurles Sarsfields), John O'Grady (Moycarkey-Borris), Mickey Byrne (Thurles Sarsfields), Donie Nealon (Burgess), Terry Moloney (Arravale Rovers).

2. Action from the 1958 All-Ireland Senior Hurling final at Croke Park in which Tipperary defeated Galway by 4-9 to 2-5. (L to R) Michael Maher (Holycross Ballycahill), Mickey Byrne (Thurles Sarsfields), John Hough (Toomevara).

3. Action from the 1960 All-Ireland Senior Hurling final between Tipperary and Wexford. Tipperary players included are Jimmy Doyle (with bandage), Tom Moloughney and Tom Ryan.

4. Archbishop Thomas Morris throwing in the ball in the 1960 Munster

Championship game between Tipperary and Cork which Tipperary won by
two points. Also in the photo are Theo English and Tony Wall (Tipperary).

5. John Doyle celebrates Tipperary's win in the 1959 National Hurling
League Final with team-mates and fans.

6. Munster, Railway Cup Finalists 1960. Back row (L to R): Vince Murphy,
Austin Flynn, John Doyle, Tom McGarry, Jimmy Smith, Seamus Power,
Jimmy Brolan, Larry Guinan, Jim Barry; front row: John Barron, Paddy
Barry, Tom Cheasty, Mick Cashman, Martin Óg Morrissey, Christy Ring,
Frankie Walsh, Jimmy Doyle.

7. The 1961 Tipperary All-Ireland winning team which defeated Dublin
by 0-16 to 1-12: Front row (L to R): S McLoughlin, Jim Doyle, D Nealon,
D O'Brien, M Hassett, W Moloughney, J McKenna, T English, T Ryan,
M Mounsey; Back row: M O'Gara, T Wall, T Moloughney, K carey, L
Devaney, M Maher, John Doyle, M Burns, L Connolly, J Hough, P Ryan.

8. Enjoying post-match celebrations in Barry's Hotel, Dublin following
Tipperary's victory in the National Hurling League final in 1961 over
Waterford by 6-6 to 4-9 at Croke Park. Back row (L to R): John Joe
O' Connor, _____, Jimmy Doyle (Thurles Sarsfields), Theo English
(Marlfield), Liam Connolly (Fethard), Donie Nealon (Burgess), John
Carroll, Jerry Doyle (Thurles Sarsfields), Jim Stapleton, Martin Kennedy
(Kildangan), ____, Mackey McKenna (Borrisokane); front row: Mickey
Byrne (Thurles Sarsfields), Pat Stakelum (Holycross Ballycahill), Matt
Hassett, captain (Toomevara), John Doyle (Holycross Ballycahill), Tom
McLoughney (Kilruane).

9. Tipperary, All-Ireland Senior Hurling Champions 1961. Back row
(L to R): Matt O' Gara (Toomevara), Tony Wall (Thurles Sarsfields),
Tom McLoughney (Kilruane), Kieran Carey (Roscrea), Liam Devanney
(Borrisoleigh), Michael Maher (Holycross Ballycahill), John Doyle
(Holycross Ballycahill), Mick Burns (Nenagh Eire Og), Liam Connolly

(Fethard), John Hough (Toomevara), Pat Ryan (Moycarkey Borris);
front row: Seán McLoughlin (Thurles Sarsfields), Jimmy Doyle (Thurles
Sarsfields), Donie Nealon (Burgess), Donie O'Brien (Knockavilla
Kickhams), Matt Hassett (Toomevara), Billy McLoughney (Kildangan),
John Mackey McKenna (Borrisokane), Theo English (Marlfield), Tom
Ryan (Killenaule), Roger Mounsey (Toomevara).

10. The players relax in the Tipperary dressing-room following their All-
Ireland final victory in 1961, including Tom McLoughney (Kilruane),
Jimmy Doyle (Thurles Sarsfields) and Kieran Carey (Roscrea).

11. Tipperary Senior Hurling Panel 1962. Back row (L to R): Tom Ryan
(Killenaule), Matt O' Gara (Toomevara), Ronnie Slevin (Borrisokane), John
Doyle (Holycross Ballycahill), Tom Mcloughney (Kilruane McDonaghs),
Mick Maher (Holycross Ballycahill), Kieran Carey (Roscrea), Tom Ryan
(Toomevara), Liam Connolly (Fethard), Matt Hassett (Toomevara),
Michael Murphy (Thurles Sarsfields); front row: Mick Burns (Nenagh
Eire Og), Liam Devanney (Borrisoleigh), Donal O' Brien (Knockavilla
Kickhams), John Mackey McKenna (Borrisokane), Theo English
(Marlfield), Donie Nealon (Burgess), Jimmy Doyle, captain (Thurles
Sarsfields), Seán McLoughlin (Thurles Sarsfields), Roger Mounsey
(Toomevara), Chrisy Hartigan (Newport), Tony Wall (Thurles Sarsfields).

12. An injured Jimmy Doyle (Thurles Sarsfields), Tipperary captain,
receives attention following an injury in the 1962 All-Ireland Senior Hurling
final against Wexford in Croke Park.

13. In the Tipperary dressing room following the 1962 All-Ireland victory
over Wexford. Tipperary captain Jimmy Doyle was unable to accept the cup
after the match because of injury, and Tony Wall, who accepted the Liam
McCarthy Cup on Jimmy's behalf hands the cup over to his 'fallen' team-
mate.

14. Munster Railway Cup Hurling Team 1963. Back row (L to R): Jimmy

Brolan, John Doyle, PJ Keane, Tom McGarry, _____, Michael Maher, Jimmy Smith, Tony Wall, Jim Barry; front row: Liam Devanney, Christy Ring, Theo English, Mick Cashman, Jimmy Doyle, Donie Nealon, Mick Quill, Joe Condon.

15. Jimmy Doyle (Thurles Sarsfields) shows his delight following a Tipperary score in 1964.

16. Tipperary Senior Hurling Team 1964. Back row (L to R): Gerry Doyle (Thurles Sarsfields), Tony Wall (Thurles Sarsfields), Liam Devanney (Borrisoleigh), Michael Maher (Holycross-Ballycahill), Mick Roche (Carrick Davins), Kieran Carey (Roscrea), Tom Ryan (Killenaule), John Doyle (Holycross-Ballycahill), Ossie Bennett (Trainer); front row: Mick Burns (Nenagh Eire Og), Peter O' Sullivan (Cashel), Michael Murphy (Thurles Sarsfields), Donie Nealon (Burgess), Seán McLoughlin (Thurles Sarsfields), Theo English (Marlfield), John Mackey McKenna (Borrisokane), Jimmy Doyle (Thurles Sarsfields).

17. The Tipperary team which defeated Cork 3-13 to 1-5 in the 1964 Munster final in Limerick. Back row (L to R): Ossie Bennett (trainer), John O'Donoghue, Tony Wall, Sean McLoughlin, Michael Maher, John Doyle, Kieran Carey, Mick Roche, Gerry Doyle (trainer). Front row: Mick Burns, Jimmy Doyle, Donie Nealon, Theo English, John McKenna, Mick Murphy, Michael Keating, Larry Kiely.

18. Tipperary Senior Hurling team and officials boarding the plane at Shannon to travel for a tour of the USA in 1964. Included are (L to R) – _____, Seamus Ó Riain (Moneygall), Mick Murphy (Thurles Sarsfields), _____, Seán McLoughlin (Thurles Sarsfields), Kieran Carey (Roscrea), Pat Ryan (Moycarkey Borris), Mick Burns (Nenagh Eire Og), Michael Maher (Holycross Ballycahill), Paddy Leahy (Boherlahan Dualla), Liam Devanney (Borrisoleigh), Pat Fanning (Waterford), John Joe Maher (Roscrea), Donie Nealon (Burgess), Peter O' Sullivan (Cashel), Theo English (Marlfield), Mick Roche (Carrick Davins), John Doyle (Holycross

Ballycahill), John O' Donoghue (Arravale Rovers); Back: Tommy Barrett (Thurles Sarsfields), Michael Babs Keating (Ballybacon Grange), Larry Kiely (Gortnahoe Glengoole), Mick McElgunn (Thurles Sarsfields), Tom Ryan (Killenaule), Liam Connolly (Fethard), Jimmy Doyle (Thurles Sarsfields), Tony Wall (Thurles Sarsfields).

19. A group of Tipperary players and officials pictured on Hyde Park, London at Easter 1965. Back row (L to R): Tommy Barrett (Thurles Sarsfields), John Doyle (Holycross Ballycahill), Jody Ryan (Carrick Davins), Donie Nealon (Burgess), Jim Stapleton (Solohead), Liam Devanney (Borrisoleigh); front row: Martin Kennedy (Kildangan), Theo English (Marlfield), Michael Maher (Holycross Ballycahill), John O'Donoghue (Arravale Rovers), Jerry Doyle (Thurles Sarsfields).

20. The ball breaks in the Wexford goalmouth during the 1965 All-Ireland Senior Hurling final. Tipperary forwards Seán McLoughlin (Thurles Sarsfields) and Jimmy Doyle (Thurles Sarsfields) are ready to pounce with Wexford goalkeeper Pat Nolan on the ground.

21. Action from the 1965 All-Ireland Senior Hurling final. Wexford goalie Pat Nolan holds possession despite the attention of Seán McLoughlin (Thurles Sarsfields). Also included are Wexford's Ned Colfer and Willie Murphy, and Tipperary's Jimmy Doyle (Thurles Sarsfields) .

22. Tipperary, All-Ireland Senior Hurling Champions 1965. Back row (L to R): Jerry Doyle (Thurles Sarsfields), John O'Donoghue, Babs Keating, Mick Burns, Michael Maher (Holycross-Ballycahill), Tom Ryan, Seán McLoughlin (Thurles Sarsfields), Kieran Carey, Mick Roche, Tony Wall (Thurles Sarsfields), John Doyle (Holycross-Ballycahill), Ossie Bennett; front row: Liam Devanney, Noel O' Gorman, Len Gaynor, Seamus Mackey (Holycross-Ballycahill), Larry Kiely (Gortnahoe-Glengoole), Donie Nealon, Peter O' Sullivan, Jimmy Doyle (Thurles Sarsfields), Theo English, John Dillon, Paddy Doyle (Thurles Sarsfields), Mackey McKenna.

23. Tipperary Senior Hurling Team 1965. Back row (L to R): Gerry Doyle (Thurles Sarsfields), John O' Donoghue, Liam Devanney, Michael Maher (Holycross-Ballycahill), Seán McLoughlin (Thurles Sarsfields), Mick Roche, Kieran Carey, John Doyle (Holycross-Ballycahill). Front row: Tony Wall (Thurles Sarsfields), Donie Nealon, Mackey McKenna, Len Gaynor, Jimmy Doyle (Thurles Sarsfields), Theo English, Paddy Doyle (Thurles Sarsfields), Mick Burns.

24. John and Anne Doyle at the Caltex Awards Ceremony in 1965 with Jimmy Doyle, Kitty Doyle and Jerry Doyle.

25. Dinner Menu.

26. John Doyle and Christy Ring, with Brendan Boyer at a charity game.

27. Tipperary, All-Ireland Senior Hurling finalists 1967. Back row (L to R): John O'Donoghue (Arravale Rovers), Jimmy Ryan (Carrick Davins), Theo English (Marlfield), Noel O'Gorman (Newport), John Doyle (Holycross-Ballycahill), Kieran Carey (Roscrea), Seán McLoughlin (Thurles Sarsfields), Tony Wall (Thurles Sarsfields), Mickey Lonergan (Moycarkey Borris), Michael Babs Keating (Ballybacon Grange), Pat Arrigan (Carrick Davins); front row: PJ Ryan (Carrick Davins), John Mackey McKenna (Borrisokane), Len Gaynor (Kilruane McDonaghs), John Flanagan (Moycarkey-Borris), Jimmy Doyle (Thurles Sarsfields), Mick Roche (Carrick Davins), Donie Nealon (Burgess), Liam Devanney (Borrisoleigh), Mick Burns (Nenagh Eire Og), Seamus Shinners (Newport), Larry Kiely (Gortnahoe-Glengoole).

28. Three Tipperary hurling greats pictured in Croke Park in 1984.Left to right – John Doyle (All-Ireland Senior Hurling medals 1949, 1950, 1951, 1958, 1961, 1962, 1964, 1965), Tommy Doyle (All-Ireland Senior Hurling medals 1930, 1937, 1945, 1949, 1950, 1951), Jimmy Doyle (All-Ireland Senior Hurling medals 1958, 1961, 1962, 1964, 1965, 1971).

29. John Doyle holds forth in Chawke's public house in Clonmel, in the company of his great friend Gerry Chawke and president of the GAA, Joe McDonagh.

30. John Doyle and former president of the GAA, Paddy Buggy.

31. John Doyle in his later years.

Most of the photos in this book were sourced from the fantastic publication: *Mid-Tipperary GAA 1884-2007, A Photographic History*, compiled by Martin Bourke and Aoife Percy.

The photographs in *Mid-Tipperary GAA 1884-2007, A Photographic History*, were sourced from many GAA clubs and individuals, including Brendan O'Connor, William O'Connor, Michael Boland, Brendan Treacy, Ned O'Shea, Seamus Bourke, John McLoughney, PJ Maxwell, Noel Joyce, Seamus King, Eddie Kinane, Sean Scully, Liam O'Donoghue, John Devane, Mickey Byrne, Jimmy Doyle, Micheal Maher, Paddy Curran, John O'Grady, Jimmy Butler Coffey, John Maher, John Smith, Michael Kelly, Eileen Scully, Thurles Library and the *Tipperary Star*.

••• ● •••